ALTARS OF THE EAST

To Hedda,
in friendship
and affection

[signature] '56

ALTARS
OF THE
EAST

By Lew Ayres

DOUBLEDAY & COMPANY, INC., GARDEN CITY, N.Y., 1956

PREFACE

My recent global tour was taken with the desire that the resulting conclusions might add another small stone to the shaky and precarious structure of world peace. In general, I hoped that by making a film on world religions —by trying to explain why people believe and worship as they do—by revealing and elucidating the most dearly held affections and deepest secrets of the human heart—I might bring the viewing world a little more understanding of its fellow man and more tolerance of what may have once seemed pagan, exotic, or just meaningless mumbo jumbo. This increase of tolerance I thought might cause closer international co-operation (at least perhaps on the personal level) and ultimately help usher in the long-dreamed-of Brotherhood of Man—the World Brotherhood—final acceptance and practice of which would mean world peace.

I must emphasize the term *explaining* religious practices because some of the things in my films may have been seen previously in newsreels and travelogues. Usually, however, such isolated items as festival scenes, holy men, or scraps of ritual ceremony have been only part of a series of haphazard impressions of some exotic land and, lacking explanation, have served only to increase the sense of distance between East and West.

If I was enthusiastic on the subject of world peace before this trip, I am now fanatic. Many months of wandering throughout the underprivileged (a grossly inadequate term) sections of our globe, where human need is at its keenest, where not only lack of nutrition but hunger, even starvation, is commonplace, where lack of shelter, lack of education, lack of inspiration—yes, and in certain areas, even lack of hope for a solution to these problems—gnaw at the vitals of people who are yet further taxed with oppressive burdens of armament—I repeat, wandering through such places has amply driven home in my consciousness the desperate need for world peace *now!*

Let me add that I do not simply think of peace—even world peace—as a wholly desirable end in itself—at least not in the accepted sense of the term. Peace could mean stagnation—there could be peace in chains. Peace may be good; it can also be evil.

The peace with which I am concerned is simply the surcease of international armed conflict at the present time: a period which would allow us the time, energy, and money to tackle and overcome the subhuman environment degrading and demoralizing more than one half of the inhabitants of our shrinking earth.

Just for clarification let me say I'm not advocating any brand of reduction of firm policy on the part of the Western democracies alone. But I do feel that persistent efforts must be made for peace, not only at the diplomatic level, but at every other level—social, sociological, economic, and personal. The last should come from each according to his strength and ability. I felt that my contribution could be a motion picture on religion.

I do not remember when the matter of religion has not given me concern. Aside from the fact that I was raised in the Sunday-school environment of a rather liberal Protestant church I have always seemed to feel an awareness of the power and presence of God in the universe. I think I was blessed at birth with the priceless attribute of faith. This faith, tempered by countless tribulations, doubtings, testings, has enlarged and grown throughout the years.

Because of an inherent love of science and the ways of science, reason, and truth I may have, through unwillingness to be misled, resigned myself to brief periods of agnosticism. But always, circumstance, and at least my personal method of reason—not to speak of a strong, inner-intuitive urging—have led me back, and higher, upon the path of faith.

I have never ceased my inquiry into the possibility of intelligence, purpose, and plan back of the phenomena we know as life. I have tried to investigate every means and channel, within the limits of my intelligence, that would lead me to a closer approximation of the truth—whatever it may be. I feel I have not sought to prove the existence of God without regard to other valid viewpoints.

I think no salient discovery in any branch of science today escapes my earnest scrutiny and humble attempt at evaluation—but my faith has continued to grow, and not in spite of my scientific interest, but because of it.

A word as to why Christianity was not included in the present series: it was just too much for one trip. Originally I had every intention of doing a sequence on it. I went to great lengths getting letters of introduction to church authorities in Europe and the Near East, but after three months out I realized that I had bargained for more than I could handle. Not only was this true from the standpoint of making the photography, but exhibition as well. As things are, I now have material to run three full evenings.

I have a sequence on Hinduism, another on the Jains, the Parsis, and the Sikhs. Those are in India. Then Buddhism, in two different branches, the southern—*Hinayana*—in Siam and Burma, and the northern—*Mahayana* —in China and Japan. I have Confucianism, as found in Hong Kong and Formosa, plus a little on Taoism and the general polytheistic practices of those areas. We'll say that's seven sequences. Then a chapter on Mohammedanism, and another on Judaism, making nine altogether, representing the spiritual ideals of a billion and a half persons.

Moreover in Christianity I would be presenting a religion with which the West is already very familiar. It will have to be shown in entirety, without missing any important denomination or sect. It is a big assignment, the results of which will face severe scrutiny at close range. Actually it should be in a separate category at a special showing by itself. I hope I can make such a film next year.

ALTARS OF THE EAST

CHAPTER ONE

Planning a lengthy round-the-world tour for any reason —even for pleasure—engenders considerable detail. In the case of my project the problem was tediously multiplied. First was the selection of route. I wanted to enter those areas where the major religions were typically represented. I had no intention of showing all variations of religious practice in a particular country. Sometimes I did work on several religions in one country, such as Parsis, Sikhs, Jains, and Hindus in India, but only because they were *there* in their typical major proportions.

There was also the consideration of going at the right time of the year. Naturally I considered that it would be good to show festival and Holy Day material, if only for interest and color, as I well realized the deadly consequences if my material should turn out too dry, too architectural, or too didactic. Years in the cinema have at least taught me that primarily the public wants to be entertained. It will accept a certain amount of documentary information if it's concocted palatably—palatably enough so that one isn't made to feel he's attending a seminar—but be careful when you try to preach or teach on the screen. Just a pinch of overdosage, and in no time at all you can shoot deer in the balcony.

Well, the films have entertaining features—but certainly not because we visited each country at its most colorful season.

It is one thing to have a single mission you want to accomplish. You can familiarize yourself with the subject, pin-point the area and the time you should be there, arrange things, and go. But in this case, to travel so far (I flew 40,000 miles), for so long, and with so many religions to cover, it was practically impossible to be in each area during its most interesting season. Not without long pauses and much skipping back and forth.

Let me add that the phrase "If you had only been here last week—or last month—[or often] even yesterday!" became exasperatingly familiar to me, as it does to hunters or sportsmen the world over.

What I'm saying is that I didn't get many things I would have liked. On the other hand, I got much I didn't expect—phenomena I hadn't even known existed. I would say things just about evened themselves up.

After decisions were made concerning the proper countries to visit for typical areas, there were all the passport applications, foreign visa requirements, and usual travel complications to be cleared. However, ordinary touring, with its accompaniment of snapshots, is one thing (and not so simple at that, sometimes), but believe me, taking several motion-picture cameras, still cameras, thousands of feet of professional-type film, plus a sound recorder and ample tape, is another thing—very much so.

One just doesn't go blithely barging into foreign areas, nowadays so bristling with suspicion, and expect to point lenses in any desired direction. The men there want thorough explanations with proof, in writing. I needed approval and permission. Besides this, I knew I would also need cooperation—from any and all quarters. Checking through my address book, I found very few acquaintances listed among, say, the Sikhs of the Punjab, the Buddhist priesthood of Siam, or the Moslem communities of northern Pakistan and of Africa. In fact, I had no previous acquaintance with anyone in any of the areas I intended visiting, nor actually any Moslems, Sikhs, Hindus, Jains, Zoroastrians, or Buddhists, at all.

Finding channels of introduction into these circles took several months, thousands of phone calls, hundreds of letters. For me this last part was a terrible chore. I've never been a good correspondent.

Yet in the cause of the project I had to write, and I did. First off, to all the foreign embassies on my list, fully outlining plans and particulars. I also got in touch with various public officials and the State Department for reactions and advice.

I was fully aware that public recognition, favorable or otherwise, for my past motion-picture activities would scarcely have extended to the monasteries of the Zen monks near Kyoto or the Taoists on Formosa. I was not wrong; it hasn't. Therefore, I wanted general letters of introduction, character references, and general documentation. For these I made contact with every ecclesiastical and religious organization I could discover. I had many surprises.

Some of the seemingly least likely sources responded to my fully outlined request with great generosity. Several from whom I expected quick recognition were an evasive disappointment.

For my oriental contacts, in many cases, I really had to start from scratch—the yellow pages of the Los Angeles phone book. I got hold of the Japanese Buddhists that way. It took hours of explanation—personal visits, attendance at services—but they finally came through with beautiful letters of introduction to parent temples in Japan. At least they were written in beautiful script. I couldn't actually read them, but I'm grateful to say they really worked. The Japanese are very warm people when you get past that reserve.

While the correspondence was going on, there was the technical side to be considered. What kinds of cameras and film to use, how much film to take along, where and how to have more shipped, a thousand questions about lenses, motors, emulsions, weather and heat resistance, sound speeds, light meters, etc., etc. I had all the countless problems attendant on making a sound motion picture.

Since I have financed the entire project with money from my own unincorporated savings, and since there never was any commercial guarantee whatsoever, it is hardly necessary to point out that I had to be as economical as possible. We all know what movies can cost. They can be astronomical. This venture had to be a shoestring production.

For a time I considered traveling alone, carrying equipment and hiring local technicians when necessary. But it would have been too much. Not only were there technical considerations and ordinary work planning, but people and press to meet, new contacts to be arranged, notes kept, film shipped, travel reservations to make, and atop all—during my spare time—was the necessity of constant and intense research into the doctrines and theological depths of the oriental religions themselves. Many nights I fell asleep with such literature in my hand.

Of course I had familiarized myself with the fundamentals of the various religions since long past. I wouldn't have dared tackle the proposition otherwise. But the details concerning rites and observances—that is an endless something else, which frequently varies from locale to locale and can be learned only in those areas themselves.

Ceremonial observances in all religions differ according to the temperament and background of varying peoples. The most dogmatic of religions must make some allowances for individuality. Think how many ways of observing Christmas there are in different lands.

So I concluded that someone must go with me and I took Bob Duncan to help out on the technical side. I'd say we teamed up very well. We're about the same age, we both love instruments and gadgets, but actually Bob's much the better craftsman—the repair-anything type.

After a time replies began rolling in from my letters to the foreign embassies. In general, they were encouraging; a few were truly cordial. Things were finally taking shape.

The usual yard-long air-flight tickets came into hand. They were the round-the-world type: leave Los Angeles, arrive New York, but no dated reservations. I wanted to stay in each area until I felt I had completed the necessary work there, and this could not be done according to a rigid schedule. Offhand I calculated about a week or two in each of my chosen areas. Mostly we doubled or trebled that time, went fewer places than originally intended, left out one entire religion I had meant to cover, and still felt we could have stayed much longer everywhere.

About all that remained was the final packing. In our case this had to be carefully worked out. Excess weight by air is extremely expensive, especially on hops to places as remote as the Orient.

Of course the equipment was standard and had to go as is. The cuts had to be made in personal belongings. I gave a lot of thought to such things as whether the gray and the blue slacks should go or just the gray. We had different climates to face, too. I wanted very much to have one sequence in snow (the main reason for heading toward Japan in February), so the selection of a wardrobe really took some planning.

It all came out quite well ultimately. We had very little excess, although the cost was not our greatest hardship: it was the strange combinations with which things always had to be packed. Because of size and shape, articles which had unity of purpose could never be assembled. Earphones were in with the tooth paste, socks wrapped around the photofloods, film carefully sandwiched in the bottom of the suit bag. No single, simple act of human necessity such as a change of underclothing could be accomplished without diving into every bag. In ten minutes all was chaos, and it never took less than a full hour to repack. It was completely exasperating and we never solved it; from the day we finally soared out over the Pacific, life was one big snarl.

CHAPTER TWO

Late February in Japan was bleak. Bleak and slightly damp—no snow. I wanted snow. I knew most of the film would be exposed in tropical surroundings and I needed contrast.

Local experts expressed doubts regarding the possibility of additional snow in the Tokyo area for the balance of that season. The first night, before retiring in wonderful Frank Lloyd Wright's old Imperial Hotel, I looked up at the clear, starry night and wondered if I'd get my wish. Next morning we looked out upon six freshly fallen inches. It was just that silently surprising.

Hastily assembling equipment, we dashed out for what I guessed might be a short-lived opportunity, and by noon we had some of the loveliest, frosting-covered architectural shots that could be desired—temples, pines, Buddhas. A few hours later the snow was gone, never to return during the balance of my stay in Japan.

My establishing scenes were in the bag and I felt confident that all my expectations would be fulfilled. I learned later that I was not always to be so lucky.

The principal religion in Japan is Buddhism—brought over by monks from the Chinese mainland some fifteen hundred years ago. It is a part of the northern branch of the faith called *Mahayana* (Greater Vehicle), as distinguished from the southern branch found in Burma, Siam, and Ceylon, and known as *Hinayana* (Little Vehicle) or, more desirably, *Theravada* (Doctrine of the Elders).

Fine distinctions between the two would require more space than is proper to this particular account, but in general it is considered that Mahayana is less concerned with the monastic aspects of Buddhism and more liberally inclined toward providing a message for the average layman. In most sects its priests may marry, and it differs from its southern neighbor in the conception of the Buddha spirit incarnating in a series of saints called Bodhisattvas, or Bosatus, who delay entrance into Nirvana out of love for fellow man, in order to comfort and assist him.

There is also in Mahayana a somewhat different idea of how the human soul passes through a series of heavens and hells before finally attaining a condition of eternal bliss.

Much of what is considered the cultural essence of Japan stems directly from the influence of the Buddhist monks who came as missionaries from China. Architecture, art, music, landscaping, flower arrangements, the charming tea ceremony, the use of characters in writing, and even advancements in agriculture and road building—all have roots extending from the persistent activities of those ancient

1 8

worthy monks. For a thousand years Buddhism and Japanese life have been tightly interwoven.

There are many sects and divisions with differing approaches for varying levels of emotional types. Again exemplifying the liberal attitude, some of them have a juxtaposed relationship not unlike "Catholic" and "Protestant."

Basically the teachings are the same for all branches. To be a Buddhist, one must believe in the Hindu idea of transmigration of the soul—that man's soul lives on through various incarnations—and in the inflexible justice of the laws of Karma—that one's acts determine the conditions under which future lives will be lived. The soul must return again and again, refining and purifying itself, until the final goal is reached by attainment of the state of Nirvana. Descriptions of this last stage receive varying interpretations, from a kind of spiritual nothingness to a celestial sphere where one enjoys heavenly delights.

Much of the Japanese Mahayana school inclines to the latter view—hence its popular appeal—but in the strictest interpretation of Buddhist teaching where the complete aim is directed toward overcoming all earthly desire and material ideas, the final end, Nirvana, must be indescribable in every respect and can never even be discussed. For, after eliminating every aspect of the only consciousness we know, what is left? Most Buddhists, however, are reluctant to use the term "nothingness" when describing Nirvana, since they feel that closing the consciousness to life, as we understand it here, must be accompanied by efforts to open the mind to the so-called true consciousness somewhere within. This is where meditation practices enter in.

Sakya Muni, meaning: "A wise man of the Sakya clan" —called the Buddha or Enlightened One—lived about 500 B.C. and spent his life working out the methods by which man could best speed his progress toward this ultimate state of mysterious bliss. To each it is a personal problem. These precepts are rules of moral and ethical conduct so transcendantly beautiful that those who truly follow them could but evoke the admiration of all civilized peoples, regardless of questions which may arise concerning validity of the theories behind them.

Buddha did not teach about God, though he did not deny Him. The whole question was simply evaded. In the same way the Supreme Patriarch of Siam evaded my question when I asked about his own feelings of proof regarding the theory of reincarnation. He proceeded to relate the incident where Buddha's reply to a query about God was the remark that the sick man would do well to restrict his concern to the remedy and not to technical questions about the physician's methods.

One cannot deny there is something of the modern scientific attitude in this refusal to discuss that which may be beyond the capacity of comprehension, though I have a personal compulsion which insists that I must question everything, and everybody.

In Japanese temples Buddhist services are very irregular occurrences. There are no set periods of worship except certain holidays. Usually in the morning and late afternoon a few priests or monks, called *bonzes*, will gather and chant verses from the Pitakas, or Sutras. A few stragglers may drift in and kneel on the grass-covered floor and then leave after a few minutes.

The temple, with its image of the inscrutable Buddha, is more a place of individual meditation and prayer, just as the prime concern of the religion as a whole is to provide inspiration and power to enable the unaided individual to overcome the lusts and temptations of earthly flesh. Priests, or bonzes, neither baptize nor marry the townsfolk. There are no sacraments. The monks and nuns are strict vegetarians, and they do not touch liquor.

What effect Buddhism exerts on the lives of the Japanese today is hard to ascertain. Surely one could not say it was a dynamic influence. Few mass gatherings were visible (or other demonstrations of vitality), but then such displays as the fervor of a Christian evangelistic prayer meeting would never take place in Buddhism anyway. Evidently the public contributes enough to keep the beautiful wooden temples and environs in a reasonable state of repair. I believe that in general I could see a profound compatibility between these doctrines of stoical acceptance and the patient oriental personality. Yet there are religious movements in Japan which positively radiate exuberance and vitality. These movements are neither Buddhist nor Christian. They come under the category of *Shinto*.

Shinto also is difficult to understand and analyze. The translation of the term Shinto is "Way of the Gods" and originally it applied to religious practices which were found on the primitive Japanese islands before the advent of Buddhism. At present the name is a general classification for all religious movements which do not fall under another known faith such as Christianity, Buddhism, Islam, etc.

Until the end of the war Shinto was separated into two divisions. The first comprised all movements, sects, and native teachings that provided a personal message and method of worship for those persons who chose to select them. The second division was the state religion of the Theocratic Japanese Empire. This strong organization, with its mythical genesis, its own theology and divine genealogy, descending through blood to the person of the Emperor himself, directed and supervised all state ceremonies and provided a powerful means of focusing the loyalty of the Japanese people.

Regardless of what other faith or philosophy you held, if you were Japanese you acknowledged State Shinto and the divinity of the Emperor. The penalty for refusal was the same as for treason. Needless to say, few refused—and survived.

But I met two men who had. Both Christians, among the noblest of those living today, they were Dr. Kagawa and his loyal secretary, Rev. K. Ogawa. Each told me the story of his experience during the war.

It is a published record that throughout the years Dr. Kagawa has endured a tremendous amount of persecution for publicly expressing his dearly held Christian ideals. He has been a powerful factor in developing the force of Christianity as it exists in Japan today.

Both he and Rev. Ogawa, as pacifists opposed to the war effort, were called in for questioning many times and finally imprisoned, for an ordeal of interrogation lasting over two years. The brilliant intellect, utter fearlessness and imperturbability of Dr. Kagawa held his tormentors at bay without difficulty. The jailers ultimately even used the title "Sensi," a term of respect meaning Teacher or Master, when referring to him.

But with Rev. Ogawa—a wonderful, tiny elf of a man about sixty years of age, whose energy and eager, childlike enthusiasm commands love and affection on first sight—it was a different matter. Such charm as his evidently had little effect upon his fanatic militarist inquisitors and as time went on he grew despondent and doubtful. He confessed to me that he had feared a breakdown and had prayed mightily for strength and courage. Then, during one particularly long ordeal, he claims that God's power truly stood at his side when, after turning, parrying, and evading the thrusts of his accusers, he was finally commanded, "Now answer directly: which is the greater, your emperor or Jesus Christ?"

He says he felt himself leap to his feet, in a violent manner, quite unlike any former display of his mild personality, and shout indignantly, *"How dare you*—a supposed loyal soldier to the Crown—how dare you ask such a question? Unless there be doubt in your own mind—unless there be hidden treason in your soul—how could your evil imagination even presume to frame such a question? Why, minds capable of forming monstrous questions such as this would do very well to desist the questioning of others and look deep into the matter of their own loyalty. Yes, far from any further consideration of infamous questions like this, I absolutely demand a full statement of your personal allegiance . . . now! Now!"

All this, hurled with express-train violence into the teeth of his interrogators, caused such electrification that they snapped to rigid attention, saluting and shouting mechanically, *"Tenno haika banzai!"* (May the Emperor live forever.)

23

In the pause which followed there was an uneasy shuffling of feet and under the dominant glare of five-feet-one-inch Ogawa, three confused mental clods turned and left the cell. Interrogation was never resumed.

In due time, after the end of the war, the Japanese Emperor publicly renounced all claims to divinity and State Shinto is now defunct. True, there are occasional rumors and suspicions voiced regarding attempts at revival, but it is doubtful it could ever return as a vital institution. Not after the smashing defeat suffered by the imperial armies.

Since the Emperor now admits and, of course, must have always known, his human mortality, I wonder if it ever gives him a twinge to think of those millions of accusers beyond the grave, those poor misguided souls who died with his spuriously sacred name on their lips. Does he wonder how they must feel as they stand before the bar of judgment, the gates of paradise, with false documents and counterfeit coin in hand? Does he pray that the real Divinity will at least recognize the sincerity of their unthinking faith and mercifully grant them clemency? Does he sometimes wonder if he will ever make solvent his own accountability?

It should not be difficult to envision the spiritual chaos which has descended upon the average Japanese mentality with destruction of what was believed through the ages to be divinely invincible. How can one explain or rationalize an event always thought to be impossible?

I saw the same situation in New Guinea during prisoner interrogation. With little coaxing, newly captured Japanese soldiers consistently told all they knew regarding military strength and position. The reason for this was that they had been told never to surrender, that the act of surrender would, under all circumstances, be considered no less than disgraceful and irreverent. Therefore, unlike American insistence on giving no information beyond that of name, rank, and serial number, the Japanese soldier could hardly be instructed how to conduct himself in case he *did* come in with hands up. So he blithely told all.

To many Japanese, when invincible Japan lost the war and the Emperor withdrew claim to divinity, emotional security crumbled and God was no longer on His throne. It would be a situation comparable to suddenly bringing before the Christian world evidence which indisputably denied the divinity of Jesus. To many it would be a catastrophe totally unbearable.

In Japan loss of the war brought a national spiritual dilemma. Some have turned agnostic, many completely atheistic. Christianity has had somewhat of an upsurge but still remains a very minor factor in the total religious picture. Since Buddhism was so interwoven with all of Japan's past and symbolically shares heavily in emotional attachment to the recent debacle, it cannot be expected to constitute a useful rallying point for national morale today. The tendency for many is to break with all past contacts completely, leaning heavily toward a cynical materialism. This, of course, is excellent breeding ground for communist tumbleweed.

As I mentioned previously, there are a few exceptions to this pessimistic picture: newly formed religious groups falling under the local or "Shinto" heading. These movements, apparently borrowing metaphysical doctrines from a variety of sources, place heavy emphasis on factors such as health and nature healing, joy of living, joy of co-operation, brotherhood, etc. We visited and photographed several such organizations. One of these, called *Tenrikyo*, located outside the ancient capital of Nara, was a fascinating and inspiring sight.

With followers now numbering into the millions, this forty-year-old movement has its central headquarters on grounds surrounding a site mystically revealed by its female founder to be the exact spot where man was created upon the earth. There is a wonderful new temple, a college where the doctrine may be learned, and many fine buildings for housing and offices.

With a capacity for the accommodation of about five thousand members in the general neighborhood this institution has a remarkable program for adapting and indoctrinating a continuously revolving personnel, who stay on an average of one to three months, and then go back to work amid the public at large. It is a seminar. But what a seminar—and what spirit! When we arrived the area bustled with the activity of building another and even larger temple. However, unlike usual scenes of work on such construction, there spread before our eyes the astounding spectacle of no less than three thousand men, women, and children—all ages, all types—lustily engaged in digging and hauling dirt in baskets, while singing, laughing, and rejoicing throughout the whole process. A veritable anthill of man power, rendering service in the name of love and co-operation. No one receives a salary and, additionally, each makes payment for accompanying family members and his own expenses. This period of service by members

26

is donated during leave of absence from their regular vocations.

There are all kinds of chores, around the clock, intermingled, of course, with periods of study and recreation. Bells may ring or drums sound at any hour and work groups of four or five hundred will quickly assemble to tackle some daily task—like scrubbing down the whole temple from top to bottom—with a tempo and energy hitherto unknown. Needless to say, the temple, with surrounding structures and grounds, is immaculate.

In all the Orient one removes shoes before entering a sacred precinct, but, with few exceptions, only in Japan was cleanliness sufficient to make one feel comfortable in doing it. In many cases, like Tenrikyo, it actually would have seemed a sanitary violation and sacrilege not to do so, the floors were so well scrubbed.

One of the unique and specifically emphasized features of Tenrikyo is a graceful and stately religious dance, which we photographed. This dance is shared by all. We also recorded the music, the exotic rhythm of which is quite unlike the dignified turnings, posings, openings and snappings of fans which form the bulk of the Japanese choreography.

When I was first told of their religious dancing, I suspiciously formed a mental image of some libidinous, emotional release. I couldn't have been more wrong. It was serene, graceful, and altogether lovely.

Some features of the religion are more difficult for a Westerner to reconcile, such as the sacred home of the deceased founder, which has been kept in perfect order since her death. Meals are set out and bath drawn every day in repetition of normal routine during her lifetime. In other words, she is presumed to be as alive and present as ever. To some, of course, this procedure is only a devout, commemorative gesture.

We covered the important religious centers in Japan quite thoroughly. We spent a few days at the beautiful mountain shrine at Nikko, artistically the most impressive of all Nipponese architecture. We photographed the great Buddha at Kamakura and there also did a sequence on the meditative practices of mystical Zen Buddhism. At Dr. Kagawa's request the chief abbot of the Zen monastery at Engakuji and his student monks demonstrated the complete routine of monastic discipline. Historically the doctrines and techniques of Zen formed the core and backbone of samurai fearlessness in the past, the practice of mystic stoicism being part of the warrior's daily routine. It is claimed that by persistent concentration one can train the body—specifically the hand which holds the sword—to act in obedience to some higher, invincible impulse. By such training, too, one can eliminate all cowardice and all feeling of pain.

Resistance to pain was amply demonstrated by use of a thick staff in the hands of the chief abbot. He used it to whack the stiffened bodies of his novitiates after they had steeled themselves with a few moments' meditative control. Fearlessness, to the point of reckless suicide, was common in the Japanese Army of World War II. Traditional Zen attitudes made part of that contribution. Of course Shinto, with its promised rewards for dying in the name of the Emperor, also was responsible.

Since way back I knew that Japan was a country with a

large population and a small land area. The statistics are in every geographical textbook. But now, traveling about on the island of Honshu, I finally came to a realization of just what overpopulation meant. As in the whole of the Orient, no matter how remote you think you are, you're never out of sight of other human beings. Not only is Japan overpopulated, and living conditions crowded beyond anything we know in the West, but the demand for food is so pressing that agricultural cultivation is carried to greatest extremes. At least this must be the impression of anyone from wide-open America.

Auto roads generally are not good, but railroads are excellent and, as mile after mile speeds by the window of your coach, you become conscious of the most intense, endless, all-embracing effort at cultivation of all kinds. Up the mountains, into the valleys, no matter where the gaze is cast, there, inevitably, are the symmetrical rows which indicate that man has moved his hand across the face of nature. Everywhere crops, and nowhere an idle plot.

I never saw a dead limb still on a tree. There was only the neatest little scar indicating where one had been. Mountainsides so steep that one thought of ropes and axes for climbing were checkerboarded with crops of some kind. Most of the time planting came so close to the train that there seemed scarcely room enough for the roadbed. In some cases varieties of garden vegetables were actually paralleling the ties, between the rails themselves: an unbelievable economy of arable land.

After a daylong journey through such meticulously manicured territory one can get so that the eye hungers for the sight of some stretch of land in the rough, some instance of relaxed vigilance. Just a dash of profligacy, if only so much as an occasional vacant lot. But it never showed, not once.

The closeness of the planted rows themselves was another novelty to me, as were so many unusual kinds of pruning, irrigating, and cultivating. For certain, the Japanese are absolute masters of the science of maximum yield; and I was beginning to get my first taste of sardine living.

Our period of stay in Japan was definitely during the off season, and yet one pressing concern when nearing any national monument or historical shrine was to allow plenty of time in going and coming because of the crowds of tourists! Public conveyances were nearly always jammed with ardent sight-seers, though not necessarily foreigners.

One also saw these well-regulated Japanese touring parties at all big temples and shrines, lining up in the background for regulation photos to be taken with the sometimes publicly provided geishas, who lend local color by strolling in the forecourts of the shrine premises—the same procedure taken by American tourists and G.I.'s. I'm sure these geishas were the first the little villagers had ever seen, too.

Shinto shrines, like Yasukuni, dedicated to commemoration of the war dead, were especially crowded with a continually revolving audience of these townsfolk. For, as remnants of State Shinto, these particular shrines must receive attention above all. The whole of the Orient has a long-abiding tradition of ancestor worship and, in a sense, the magnitude of Japanese respect for their war heroes might be equivalent to deification. I was told that with the Emperor now out of the religious picture in Shinto desperate efforts were being made by concerned interests to replace him as an object of worship with the war-hero concept. From appearances it could be so.

Other types of Shinto shrines, having no organizational unity, are dedicated to a varying assortment of mythical creatures. One popular cult is that of the "Fox." Another is dedicated to "Hotei"—the laughing god with his bag of riches—quite similar to Santa Claus. There are half a dozen other Japanese deities, each with a different sphere of influence, which still maintain a hold on the loyalty of the simpler people.

Shinto shrines, incidentally, are discernible as such by the bare arch—called a torii—always placed across the walk at the entrance of the sacred premises. Just two tall, upright posts with a curving crossarm, but a graceful symbol with which anyone who has ever seen a picture of Japan is familiar. There must be thousands of them and, while passing through, to catch a glimpse of one now and then in the distance, half hidden by pine trees, is one of the charms of Japan.

Worship at these shrines, and similarly at many Buddhist shrines, is an uncomplicated affair—usually embodying a short, direct, prayerful appeal on the part of individual devotees who arrive at unprescribed times. The petition may be initiated by the brief ringing of a toneless, clanking bell hanging at the front of the temple which houses the image. This, purportedly, is to arouse the deity's attention. A coin may then be tossed into a large, grilled, wooden collection box and, following this, the hands will be clapped smartly together three or four times and finally clasped tightly, while the head is bowed in a short, silent prayer which has the appearance of being an undisguised petition or request.

In the case of a Buddhist temple, according to the sect that is represented, the image may be that of Amida Butsu —a saint who has reached Buddhahood but who, because of his compassion, is believed to have delayed entering heaven, or Nirvana, in order that his spirit may remain behind and assist man. Or it could be the Chinese goddess Kwan-yin, or Kwannon, as called by the Japanese, whose graceful, tender appearance is not too unlike that of the Holy Virgin.

I found it strange to note so few images of Sakya Muni—Gautama Buddha himself. They are seldom present. Ultimately this was made clear: since the founder of Buddhism, who, indeed, had passed from further contact with life by entrance after his death into the state of Nirvana, never spoke of God or gods or advocated worship of any kind, there was really very little in the marblelike austerity of the original Buddhist doctrine to comfort and console the common man. Actually one could say that Buddhism, as first taught, was a philosophy of life and a way of living— no more.

Further, it's a more or less pessimistic philosophy, preaching the futility of all earthly ambition—the hollowness of pleasure and worldly fulfillment of any kind. Moreover, it reveals an exacting discipline, demanding an absolute relinquishment of all desire, and crowned only by the nebulously negative reward of surcease from existence in any imagined form. Thus it is not hard to see that such views would appeal, or be endurable, to few beyond the monastically minded.

Small wonder, then, that as Buddhism made its way over the Khyber Pass and north into China, leaving behind the overcrowded, hopelessly despondent conditions of India and finally entering the fresh, primitive, undeveloped territory of Japan, it would have to undergo changes to accommodate a younger, hardier people who would demand a more optimistic view of life.

Nor are ancestors forgotten in Buddhist temples. Like the Hindu religious custom, out of which it evolved, Buddhist practice also includes disposal of the bodies of the dead by cremation. But the strong influence of Chinese emphasis on ancestor worship is noted in the division of the remaining ashes into three portions. One part is interred in a cemetery and marked with a tombstone. As can be imagined, this kind of burial uses so little space that room for the marker itself is usually sufficient. Hence Japanese graveyards are singular for the intense clustering of stones and markers. Finding an urn could be a four-leaf-clover kind of task, if indeed it could be done.

The second portion of ash remains in an appropriate niche in the family home, while the third goes to the temple. There it is placed with others of that parish, on a shelf in a small room adjoining the area of the altar. Doors between the two rooms are left open in order that the spirit of the beloved relative may receive benefit from the adjacent worship services. Services are often performed at a small altar in the urn room itself.

Sometimes there will be shelves of so-called spirit tablets —little commemorative plaques displaying the name and photograph of the deceased, placed within sight of the worshipers in the temple proper. These somehow lend a warm feeling, as they seem to inject a note of sentimental remembrance into the severe formalism of Buddhist liturgy.

An additional word on the subject of cemeteries concerns the most awesome and unusual one I've ever seen. It was located amid the ancient monasteries of the mysterious and occult Shingon sect, high atop Mount Koya, called Koyasan by the Japanese, about fifty miles from Osaka. The burial ground itself is a confused jumble of elaborately carved stone monuments placed in a narrow band that winds for miles through a dark forest of huge cedars and pines. There one can trace the progress of burials during a period of a thousand years, from the earliest markers gleaming ghostly white through the great wooden giants, with roots that have enmeshed and toppled many of their salient legion, to the latest somber additions, with designs which express trends of the present day.

The town of Koya, with its collection of about thirty temples, stands among eight mountain peaks in a crystalline atmosphere at an altitude of three thousand feet. Some of the temples are quite unusual, and some are very old although they may not appear so, for most Japanese temples, being made of wood, need constant restoration and perpetual upkeep.

At Koya the principal temple is called Kongobuji. It is the headquarters of the Shingon sect and has one chamber called the Willow Room, which commemorates a historic tragedy. This is associated with the untimely end of Hidetsugu, an adopted son of the famous Emperor Hideyoshi. According to legend, Hidetsugu fell into bad grace with his foster father and eventually fled to Koya. The Emperor sent soldiers in pursuit and they apprehended Hidetsugu in the company of the abbot of Kongobuji. After trying vainly to save Hidetsugu the abbot finally counseled him to kill himself. Thus, together with four friends, Hidetsugu committed *hara-kiri* in the now famous Willow Room.

Musing on the tale as I visited Kongobuji, I could not help making note that this illustrates another of the diametrically opposed viewpoints which separate Orient and Occident—the attitude of each society toward suicide. Although many of us can perhaps imagine a set of circumstances being so overwhelmingly hopeless as to make self-extinction a reasonably forgivable act, it is difficult indeed to picture any one of our religious leaders condoning such a course, let alone deliberately advising it.

Oriental grounds for hara-kiri are totally different from what they might be in the Occident. We think of a person in the death throes of some fatal disease as perhaps having a supportable argument for saving himself from further pointless agony. There are even organized movements here trying to promote the legalization of euthanasia. But the Oriental will have no part of this. For him physical misfortune constitutes no possible ground or excuse.

The Asiatic finds suicide permissible seemingly on one premise alone: to escape loss of self-respect. One can think of a number of pertinent situations: an individual's facing certain criminal conviction, for example, or imminent public disclosure that one has morally failed in any way. And here again we have reasons for an act that would in no way seem justifiable to the Occidental. We Westerners are fanatic on the subject of man taking the consequences of his own acts, "facing the music" through to the bitter end when necessary. We deplore the weakness of character in someone unable to "go on" unless, conceivably, it be with the burden of some dreadful incurability. Here, those with suicidal tendencies are classified psychologically as immature, emotional personalities and are treated for neurosis, unless there are signs of mental disease.

Thinking that understanding the reasons for just such opposing viewpoints might help bridge some of the gaps between East and West, I discussed the subject with several Japanese acquaintances. One pointed out that we Westerners had once held similar traditions during Greco-Roman times; Socrates drank the hemlock—although he didn't do it because of wanting to "save face." Evidently Christian ideas of sin were what caused the act to be withdrawn from "respectability," and today the Roman Catholic Church will bury no one who has fallen by his own hand. Further back our tradition stems from general attitudes and Biblical precepts in Old Testament days and presumably must be considered as another contribution to Western society from Judaism.

At one time hara-kiri was obligatory to the Japanese noble who disobeyed the Emperor. He was sent a jeweled dagger, which was returned to the Emperor only when the grisly deed was completed. This practice was legally abolished as late as 1868. Voluntary hara-kiri is still performed after certain private or national misfortunes, but, as my Japanese friends explained, it is condoned only in a moral sense by Japanese society when the act represents a sacrifice greater than would have been legally required for the transgression. In other words, it is an expression of absolute contrition and the supreme gesture of atonement. In oriental eyes, to have voluntarily surrendered that which any man holds most dear, in order to prove the sense of deep regret felt by a transgressor, is a noble deed; it is one which permits descendants and relatives to face society without humiliation. From this viewpoint, I will confess, it sounded better to me.

Hara-kiri is also used as a protest against undesirable national policies in much the same way other peoples will use the threat of self-starvation and hunger strikes, except, of course, that it is a much more direct and violent gesture and not merely an idle threat or bluff. Accordingly, it must be more sincere.

Hara-kiri basically stems from Shinto ideology and, like many other traditional Japanese practices, it is rapidly on the wane. In the light of the magnitude of the recent national disaster suffered by loss of her greatest war, Japan had very few cases of suicide resulting therefrom. Those that did occur, as supreme expressions of apology to the people of Japan, had a far deeper quality of nobility than the cowardly flight from judgment characterizing the suicide of Hermann Göring—a typical example of the ability to dish it out but not to take it. For choice of motive I'll certainly stick with the Japanese.

I have spoken of the Shingon monastery being high atop a mountain called Koya. Before I embarked on this attempt to survey world religions, it never occurred to me that there would be quite so much walking involved— especially up and down hills. For several reasons shrines and holy places of the East are frequently placed on high ground. In some cases, during earlier periods of history, it might have been for protection or, in the case of monasteries, simply a desire for isolation and seclusion. Again, it may have been done so that the structure could be seen as a prominent, distantly visible symbol. Mainly, however, I've found the reason to be that, by going to the great trouble and labor involved in construction work on high, inaccessible places, the builders feel they will have accumulated additional spiritual merit through completion of a more arduous task.

Such merit is also presumed to enrich the record of those living at such inconvenience and, furthermore, even be an asset to persons willing to make the climb as visiting pilgrims or devotees. If this last be true, Bob and I may have somewhat of a substantial credit to our cosmic account. Possibly even a little something additional for the excess weight.

Usually our portable equipment was in the nature of one motion-picture camera, in a carrying case with assorted lenses and a light meter, plus a tripod and several hundred-foot rolls of film. Then the tape recorder on a shoulder strap—spring-wound with batteries for electronics—small but very good quality, considering the circumstances, and one thing we never had trouble with. We carried another bag containing the Rolleiflex still camera, another smaller camera and an assortment of odds and ends like earphones, tools, thermos jug, etc.

Often we carried a second movie camera, this for two reasons. First, the obvious motive of security. (I had one bad experience early on the tour and resolved not to be caught again—especially in these inaccessible areas where you'd be unlikely to return.) The second reason I reveal only because of some gnawing insistence of conscience—actually I'm a little ashamed of it.

Mainly it was to save footage, a consideration of which was always a problem overseas. Our type of film was available only in the United States and could not be processed anywhere else. It had to be shipped out on request and trying to guess the interval of delivery was very perplexing. If it came too soon there was the possibility of deterioration from heat and moisture, not to speak of excess baggage charges. Too late was, of course, fatal. Therefore, we tried to cover the subject thoroughly and yet remain reasonably conservative.

Now then—frankly, it was often difficult to convince people to permit me to photograph their special aspect of religious observance, and there were times when I was bitterly disappointed by refusals. On the other hand, some persons, when finally convinced that our intentions were at least honest, entered into a spirit of co-operation that was boundless. These were wonderful occasions, and periods of most fruitful results. We obtained material never shown before and for which I am deeply grateful. I pray I may be able to justify the confidence they placed in me.

However, sometimes it occurred that the spirit of co-operation grew into an unbelievable zeal and enthusiasm and some persons would feel entitled—perhaps justly—to take over the creative decisions involved. For instance, we would be shown not only sacred rites, objects of veneration, and the inner sanctum, but cornerstones with names of local donors, miles of art works that weren't really art at all, paintings of irrelevant ancestors, movie-struck offspring of influential members, items of purely personal sentiment, and many, many things I felt would be of little interest to the general public—for whom these films were intended.

Furthermore, the value and necessity to all concerned of photographing these suggested items was not only emphasized but insisted upon. It was a very delicate matter and difficult indeed to reject them. To do so might jeopardize the whole local program or, at least, offend the person offering the gift. As things stand, we have a good many reels of footage—nay, yardage—suitable only for a stock library of miscellany.

With such a shortage of film we in desperation resorted to a well-known device sometimes employed by phony talent schools—the empty camera! We used it only a couple of times, but they were at crucial moments in our chain of logistics, and I honestly believe it made everyone happy. Except, of course, it was another piece of equipment to lug up miles of slippery mountain trails.

After three weeks in the Kyoto, Nara section, we returned to Tokyo for a brief windup before leaving Japan. I had previously made arrangements to photograph a service, in the name of world peace, performed by some fifteen Buddhist priests at one of the larger temples, and to interview on tape and film Dr. Nagai, chairman of the Japan Buddhist Council. Also Dr. Kagawa.

The world-peace ceremony we were able to film through the generosity of the United States Army Signal Corps, who lent lights and generator. At least, we have *most* of the ceremony. I was rapidly being initiated into the school of the harsh reality that is the environment of the documentary or newsreel photographer. I was also learning the vast difference in technique of the "rehearsal method" in contrast to the school of "catch as catch can." In this particular instance I considered myself fortunate, for I had the good luck of obtaining full consent from the Buddhists beforehand to witness and record their beautiful service.

But few persons outside the motion-picture industry realize the problems involved in trying to do a professional piece of photography. Often, after a prolonged and suspenseful period of discussion regarding advisability of granting permission for us to do any filming, an affirmative reply might finally ensue—followed immediately, however, by an impatient, "All right, you may take the pictures—well, aren't you ready?"

The wild scramble on our part to set up camera, recorder, and microphone, open boxes of photo floods, find power outlets, etc., was usually needled by additional inquiries regarding readiness. Sometimes the long-awaited performance would blandly and immediately start at the same time they gave word of consent.

The Buddhist peace ritual was a case in point. Generators were being wheeled into place and lights adjusted, when in marched the long, solemn line of colorfully attired priests—a photographer's dream. Thinking that it was a kind of rehearsal or that portions missed by us might be repeated, we took our time: after all, it had been specifically arranged for the benefit of my project.

Ultimately all equipment was in readiness and we methodically proceeded to make a few test long shots—noting, meanwhile, interesting bits of liturgy we had missed. Moments later the climax was reached, a few graceful maneuvers were executed, and the whole assembly of priests and musicians circled and marched out.

We saved the lights, rechecked the equipment, and I

strolled over to express appreciative admiration and inquire regarding next steps—only to find most of the priests had removed their elaborate formal vestments; some had already left the temple and the ritual was definitely at an end.

Only by supersalesmanship was I able to persuade a couple of them to return to the altar for a close-up or two, enabling us to salvage the remnants of a sequence that otherwise might have been a total loss.

We wound up Japan with an interview of Dr. Kagawa and a visit to his pawnshops. This is simply what they are called; they are loan offices, but a great boon to the people in a land where rates of usury are extremely high. Only bare minimum amounts sufficient to meet expenses of handling are charged and it enables the borrower to save tremendously on percentages he'd face from other creditors. It is not a mere shifting of credit and an extension of the burden so cleverly concealed in advertising matter put out by many American credit concerns, but a valid social benefit. Dr. Kagawa, by the way, is an ardent enthusiast of world federation, being vice-president of the "World Movement for World Federal Government," strongly supported in Japan at present.

Japan has become strictly pacifist since the war, for many seemingly good reasons which may or may not be altogether realistic. But at least this new trend has been good for the Japanese as a people, for, by the numerous international assemblies such as the Asian Congress and conferences of non-United Nations members, it has helped and is helping the Nipponese to overcome a basic insularity and national introversion, one of their principal weaknesses and one of the reasons why power-thirsty leaders were able to control them, body, mind, and spirit, through clever devices like State Shinto. Of course, admission to the General Assembly of the U.N. henceforth will further expand their sense of world relationship.

There is no question but that even religion *can* be an evil, perhaps one of the greatest evils. Between the narrowness of those who think their particular religious affiliation is the only path to an infinite God and the excessive indulgence of others who condone any belief under the heading of "religion" lies, in my opinion, a middle course that tolerates all sincere teachings which do not cause their adherents to violate long-established and proven laws of universal ethics.

I would add that no religion or religious practice is, or can be, valid which induces individuals to think that they may blissfully resign all moral decisions, including those of ethical conduct toward fellow man, to the judgment and authority of any other human being, no matter what his accomplishments or station in life.

The test of a true religion is an analysis of its ethical laws. If the doctrinal teachings of the religion are such that its moral commandments may be altered or held in abeyance at the decision of a single leader or any other recognized body of authority, then that religion is spurious and the continuation of its practice should be condemned.

For instance, the Japanese are an educated, highly cultured people, but State Shinto taught them generally to believe that to die for the Emperor was a certain passport to heaven. No matter what their emperor required of them, they would gain celestial merit by blind obedience to his infallible command. Especially was it considered an act of sanctification to have spoken the Emperor's name in the last moment before death. This accounts for the notorious "Banzai" charges by Japanese infantrymen during the last war. The word "Banzai" is a contraction of the phrase "Tenno heika banzai," and indicated that the soldier was dedicating himself utterly to the God-Emperor's command that he should kill.

No authority on earth can justifiably claim such blind allegiance, at least not under the guise of a divinely ordained religion. And theologies that would claim this authority must be unreservedly condemned. Such a theology is undoubtedly integrally woven into Japanese State Shinto. It is, thus, a fiendish evil that must never be allowed to revive.

CHAPTER THREE

Formosa means beautiful. That was the adjective applied
by the Portuguese many years ago when describing a lovely
piece of land in the Pacific islands. Ultimately the adjective
became a noun, the proper name for the well-known island.
Today the Chinese government centered there has restored
the earlier, pre-Portuguese name, Taiwan. I'm not sure
what Taiwan means, but it truly is a beautiful place. "Formosa" fits it.

The mountains are green and lush, for there is a good
deal of rain. Rain enough, on the flatlands, to bring forth
huge crops of rice and sugar and many kinds of fruit. Food
is not scarce on Taiwan.

We went there because I wanted to find out something
about the religions of the Chinese. With my American passport Taiwan and the Hong Kong area were the only Chinese territories accessible to me. Of course they could offer
only a slim idea of the religious currents running throughout the rest of the more than four hundred million people

on the Chinese mainland, but it was the best that could be obtained and it was something.

From my experience on Formosa, including conversations with many of the present refugees from the communist mainland, I have gathered that by and large the Chinese could not be considered a deeply religious people; certainly not in the sense that many other Asiatic nations might be. I tend to think there is something in the general psychological make-up of various races that may cause this to be so. Environment has to do with it also, naturally.

This might be one of the reasons why the Chinese have been contented so long with the worldly philosophy and simple ethical teachings of Confucius. In China no historical figure stands higher than he.

During the last two thousand years many religions have touched or moved through China. Some, like Buddhism, have left a lasting imprint. Others, like Christianity, barely scratched the surface, but none has taken hold in a manner that might be termed the nationally accepted spiritual way. Not as one might speak generally of Western Europe as Christian, or Burma and Siam as Buddhist.

Among the higher-educated, more wordly classes Confucianism is probably the chief source of moral guidance. But this Confucianism should not be considered a religion. True, as I have been told, in certain times and in some parts of old China groups of adherents have venerated Confucian teaching and the teacher himself, to a point that undoubtedly could be termed worship—a commonly repeated historical occurrence with all great teachers and their work. But Confucius himself never advocated such a thing, and even warned against it. Indeed, most Chinese are indignant at the suggestion.

Another set of principles which have molded the thought and character of China are the teachings of a Confucian contemporary, born some twenty-five hundred years ago, named Lao-tzu. In this case, however, the gradual priestly corruptions of his great works ultimately proceeded to such length that the original teachings themselves have been almost forgotten in the emphasis upon a mysterious and magical ritual. The result is a religion, Taoism. Its appeal has been largely to the uneducated masses.

For many centuries the leadership of this religion, centered at a place in Southern China called Tiger and Dragon Mountain, has passed by blood descent from father to son. These descendants have had the position of high priest or pope.

On Taiwan, I sought out the present Pope, Chung-tien Su, who is there now in exile. I found him living at a newly erected temple on the outskirts of the capital city of Taipei. The walled garden surrounding the temple was well kept and nicely planted. The temple itself was very tiny and of typically modern Chinese design—brick with ornate roof— and was very clean. During three visits I never saw a worshiper or another visitor. I do not know the present state of Taoism on the mainland, but the fact that its spiritual leader is in exile does not sound encouraging.

The basic teachings of Lao-tzu are spiritually uplifting and provide a beautiful, reasonable approach to a civilized way of life. They are inferior to no other ethical or moral concepts, but they center around a mystic principle, the true meaning of which is obscure and elusive. Some definitions of Tao have approximated "The Way" and this is considered likely to mean a way to some higher concept of life. But its vagueness has given the prime excuse for fantastic interpretations and clerical exploitation.

There was nothing ceremonious about the little Pope in Taipei. He was plainly attired and unattended. His manner was humble and he answered questions readily. Of course we had to use an interpreter, as was frequently the case throughout Asia, and this was often a grave handicap.

Seldom was I fortunate enough to get an interpreter whose educational background had included the subject matter with which my project was concerned. Much of the time one could only hope we were talking about the same things. Especially, as in this case, when the topic was Tao.

I gathered from the Pope that he hoped soon to get his religious work organized with greater energy now that the new temple was completed; also, that the coming program in the spirit of modern technological Taiwan would be more concerned with the moral teachings of Lao-tzu and be less emphatic on ceremony and magic.

We went inside. On the altar was a little figure of Lao-tzu in a glass case. The Pope casually showed it to me and made no observable sign of respect before it. In the forepart of the temple, however, incense was burning and there were the usual objects found in Chinese temples for determining the answers of the gods.

Chung-tien Su very obligingly consented to don his full ceremonial attire so that we could photograph him. These robes were of gorgeous satin and he carried a little triangular pennant which displayed the insignia and symbol of his powers. There wasn't much to it. We exchanged a few additional words of respectful consideration. The Pope seemed to have very little interest in, or knowledge of, modern religious movements or trends.

We said good-by at the gate to the garden of the little temple. Evidently it is usually kept closed to keep out undesirable local elements. As our car drove away I observed the Pope watching, while the gardener carefully locked the gate.

From textbooks and travelers' diaries I had gathered that Buddhism was the religion of a great number of the Chinese people, but, after my observations in the Taiwan and Hong Kong areas, I doubt that this is so—or, for that matter, that it ever has been in the past. Buddhism, with its rather pessimistic philosophy, negating all that is vital and expressive in earthly life, can only appeal truly to those with a basic or perhaps firmly acquired tendency toward a monastic existence. The moral requirements are such that even far less than strict adherence would mean insistence on a course of personal conduct incompatible with normal secular life.

In the *Hinayana* branch of Buddhism as practiced in Southeastern Asia, the foregoing conclusion is freely admitted and an ultimate monastic existence is the expectancy of every male devotee.

China, however, is considered to be part of the Northern *Mahayana* branch as described in the chapter on Japan. In this there are presumed to be a greater appeal and broader life for the layman. Perhaps so, but the true follower of the Buddha will still be found in the seclusion of the monastery, working for the goal which naught else or no

49

one else can provide, his own spiritual release and salvation. This is also true in Mahayana.

On Taiwan and Hong Kong the Buddhists are in monasteries and convents. There are not many of them, considering the population. Nor do they appear to have an active program among the general public, though there are a few small temples in the cities and at the monasteries where people can drop by, burn a little incense, and say a prayer.

In monasteries and convents monks and nuns dwell in celibate simplicity, supplying their vegetarian needs by light gardening, spending much time intoning the various liturgies or chanting in Sanskrit from the *Pitakas*, and training themselves in the art of meditation.

These devoted adherents represent the merest fraction of the total populace and there is no observable tendency toward a movement of expansion. Sad to say, the foregoing sentence could apply equally to Christians in those areas. There are very few, though numbered among them are Chinese of high character. Chiang Kai-shek is said to be an ardent Methodist. But the most of the twelve to fourteen million Chinese and Taiwanese living in the two areas I visited simply have a respect for an adherence to the various polytheistic cults of each one's particular area, if they follow any religion at all.

Polytheism—many gods—and many there are indeed; many gods for man's many purposes. Each has a separate domain, though numbers of them overlap. Some are gods of the land, and throughout all the farming territories temples are thickly distributed, only a few acres apart.

Most of these temples are simple affairs, built of brick

on Taiwan, some large enough for several persons to enter and light sticks of joss before the crude image; some no bigger than an ordinary-sized doghouse, sufficient in size to enclose the image and nothing else.

Priests preside over the rituals, but none of them lives in the temple. They are not preachers or prophets.

Religious services are of two kinds; those related to the dead, such as funeral ceremonies, and those for the living, which include prayers for prosperity, thanksgiving services for newborn children, expulsion of demons, and prayers for the sick or victims of misfortune.

Besides the priests there are a few other polytheistic professions. These are fortunetellers, sorcerers, and charm composers. Also various "specialists" who select proper days and hours for people to do propitious things.

Actual keepers of the temples do live in them, but they are merely custodians who know nothing more of religion than ordinary believers. Their business is to light the first incense sticks in the morning and the last ones at night, prepare tea for visitors, and keep the temple clean. Of the last chore I never saw much more than a token acknowledgment. Since it is generally the custom not to allow women to sleep in temples, these keepers are often elderly widowers, usually poor.

Scattered throughout the larger towns and villages are quite elaborate temples, some containing altars and images of four or five to as many as several dozen various local deities. These gods have originated from many sources. Some are mythical, others based on actual historical persons. Kings, queens, heroes, and generals have been deified for some particular incidents in their lives or careers. Others were ordinary peasant folk whose lives were in some way touched by a miraculous event and thus became an object of worship.

There are gods of fishermen and gods for the prosperity of tradesmen and craftsmen. The land gods of farmers may have been ancestral owners of the property; their spirits must be appeased to prevent crop failure and ensure the harvest.

In one mid-city temple there is a large section devoted to motherhood; each phase of this state is presided over by a different deity: dozens of images—one for conception, another for birth, one for the child's health, his talents, disposition, obedience, and success. There is a whole clinical staff of gods to call upon.

In fairness it must be said that even the polytheists do have one supreme deity. That is Yu-Hwang-Ta-Ti, the Heavenly Emperor, often called simply "Heaven." He is believed to be the God of Gods, and all other gods are his subordinates who get assignments of work from him and have to make an annual report to him at the end of the year. The date is December 24 and even the venerated Chao Kong, the Stove God, goes with the others to report.

Many households have an image of the Stove God, and at the time of his "departure" a little lump of wet rice will be stuck on his lips to keep him from telling too much about the family.

Like the Japanese, Chinese people of the old regime believed that their emperor was the "Son of Heaven," who reigned in accord with divine will; also that good ethics consisted only in obeying what "Heaven" ordered.

In home worship every morning and evening one member of the family, with incense sticks in his hands, bows to heaven, the household gods, and the ancestral tablets. Dishes of food may also be offered. However, no food offerings are lost, for all edibles are later eaten by worshipers and friends. In general, home worship will be carried out as long as all goes well, but if adversity comes along the various facilities of the temple will be sought.

The oriental inclination toward ancestor worship also gives each individual his own set of spirits to be propitiated. It goes on and on—endlessly.

How seriously all these deities are taken is difficult to determine. It is a matter of individual temperament, of course, but from what I saw I would say that with the majority of the people, particularly the moderns, it was not a devoutly important matter. Most of the worship took the appearance of long-sustained tradition or perhaps the superstitious unwillingness to be neglectful and take a chance on the future.

Polytheism is not organized. It has no sacred literature, no theology, no provision for spiritual comfort or growth. The temples are privately owned and supported by contributions of the local population.

The act of worship is uncomplicated and direct. The worshiper enters, buys a few sticks of incense from the guardian, lights and places the scented sticks before a selected image, bows, and makes a petitionary prayer. He may then determine the god's answer by dropping a couple of crescent-shaped objects for a heads-or-tails-kind of reply, or shake out a numbered sliver of bamboo from a large bunch, taking it to one of the innumerable professional fortunetellers who sit at little concession booths in the forepart of the temple, then paying for an expert analysis. There is little more than this involved.

Traditional festivals and quaint ceremonies are held in celebration or commemoration of personal events, such as marriage, childbirth, birthdays, or happenings of good fortune; while luck, good or bad, is a highly recognized power.

One may ask why this form of worship is the principal religion of the Chinese, why the soul of the average Chinese seems to be content with such primitive concepts when so many other beautiful and profound teachings are available. Or, perhaps, *why* Western missionaries, with such a long record of unselfish zeal in the Orient, have not been more successful in promoting the doctrine of Christianity.

Satisfying answers to these questions would have to come from more scholarly sources, but I will hazard a few personal observations.

One is that in order to understand and enjoy profound or beautiful teachings a certain educational level must be present. The deeper wisdom of Confucius and Lao-tzu, or of Buddhism, is for those with at least the ability to read and write. (There is no more complex written language than Chinese.) These concepts, then, are for the educated few.

It is difficult for an American or European to realize just how low the level of education is throughout the Orient. India and China have a general percentage of illiteracy somewhere between 80 and 90 per cent! Efforts are being made by all Asiatic governments to raise this low standard, but unquestionably overpopulation has advanced to such a degree as to make the task only short of hopeless. I use the term "only short of" because I think those concerned now see a ray of hope, through advances in modern technology, where for centuries there was *absolutely none.*

Other reasons for China's polytheistic religion lie in historical attitudes and qualifications of leadership—and in Asiatic insular tendencies.

In regard to the sometimes puzzling slowness of the development of oriental Christianity a volume should be written. This treatise would take into account the full historical picture of China and the ethnic background of its people. Past mission programs should be scrutinized, as well as the cultural level of missionaries themselves.

In many instances public acceptance of a religion in the past has been induced, promoted, or sustained by strong authoritarian leadership—as in the cases of Constantine, Mohammed, Henry VIII, and Asoka. But Christianity has had no such champion in the Orient and missionaries have been faced with a kind of problem they had not known before. It is now thought by many that the whole approach should be altered, with a new kind of emphasis on "personal" example.

But a truly great stride toward solution of this confusion has been taken, it seems to me, in the recent momentous decision by the American Mission Board. This body has decided that henceforth basic Christian mission strategy will reside in a program of selecting qualified converts in various countries, bringing them to church centers in the West, and *there* training them for an eventual return to mission service in their own lands. A modern solution, indeed—and one wonders if the West has not finally learned some valuable lessons on the subject of indoctrination from those artful masters on the other side of the Iron Curtain.

Most religions seem to need a stirring of emotional enthusiasm to get started—the crusade feeling. I believe this is true with various kinds of Christianity. Many church leaders know well the power of a dynamic evangelism; they court any approach to it. This spirit of religious fervor is the one thing necessary to any large-scale conversion in the Orient. Reasons why it has not been forthcoming would certainly include lack of leadership, though there have been and are many consecrated and talented oriental Christians.

Other reasons must come from an analysis of what the actual needs of the Orient are, and what Christianity has to offer for fulfilling them. There is unquestionably something of a gap here, at least in the types of Christianity commonly offered to the East in much of the past. Christianity offers salvation to mankind, but before a man can be "saved" he must know, or at least be convinced, that he is lost. The centuries of traditional Hindu and Buddhist teaching of reincarnation, with its eternity of "second chances," make it difficult to plant the seed of conviction in the heart of the Oriental that all paths are hopeless except one. He doesn't gravitate toward dogmatism.

Another Christian concept difficult for Asiatics to understand is the doctrine of the Trinity. According to some of the more educated persons I spoke with, this mystery is a real stumbling block. The apparent contradiction of three who are yet one completely baffles them.

In past days Christians were actually persecuted on Formosa because the rulers were perhaps alarmed by the value placed on individualism and by the opposition of the new Christian converts to the traditional religions.

Formal persecution is now past, but it still requires courage for a Taiwanese to identify himself as a Christian, for in so doing, he denies the traditional gods in a land where gods are many and community life is influenced by polytheistic observances. Only Christians give no contributions to temple managers, who call at each house to raise funds for maintenance and repair of their temples.

We didn't stay long on Formosa. It is a small place and I felt a few weeks were sufficient for our purposes. Furthermore, it rained a great deal and I dragged around with a nagging cold, picked up, I guess, on the wild night flight over from Tokyo. It didn't incapacitate me, but I'll admit it added another load to the rigors of mountain climbs to Buddhist monasteries (which were by prearranged appointments and had to be undertaken). In Taipei we stayed for a while at a place called the Friends of China Club, where groups of very Westernized young Chinese men and women came several evenings a week to dance, to my profound surprise, in the latest American style. That is, if my guess is correct and we do still jitterbug and all join in the "Baked Apple" over here.

The members of the Department of Public Relations were very cordial and did their best to show us everything in our line, though it seemed to be quite out of theirs. One fine, small temple, well kept but without a soul around, intrigued me. It was dedicated to Confucius and had a small image of him on the altar.

I was promised an interview with Kung teh Ching—a living descendant of the famous sage, the direct-in-line inheritor of all honors and official duties. He is also considered a fine scholar. At present he lives in southern Formosa,

57

another exile from Red China—a government which has banned all works relating to the venerable sage. Each day his arrival was expected in Taipei, but he failed to come in. I considered going south to meet him, but was afraid we would miss. The day for departure to Hong Kong arrived and I had to embark without seeing him.

CHAPTER FOUR

The mountainous harbor of Hong Kong fascinated me. There is so much life and activity, and withal it is clean and orderly. The narrow channel separating Hong Kong proper, on Victoria Island, from the peninsular mainland, seems to place within reach of the finger tips all the huge vessels that drift silently by the closely touching shores, day and night—and all visible from the hotel-room window. I couldn't keep my eyes away.

Yes, the harbor of Hong Kong is a sparkling beauty, though life itself there is not so beautiful. Not now, at least. Not with the Chinese border, just a few miles back, tightly closed, and both sides glowering, menacing. The situation has put a great strain on Hong Kong—a harbor with enormous facilities but with no one to take or send the mountain of shipping that once passed its portals. Business is off—way off.

Atop this is the refugee situation: several uncounted millions who have fled from the communist mainland, each bringing nothing but another mouth and another heart to be fed. Where they live it is not so clean or orderly.

At this writing the problem has not been solved, nor is it likely to be solved. There is not nearly enough industry in that tiny area to use or support the available man power, or provide the remotest semblance of an acceptable living standard.

The British have not done at all badly in providing emergency welfare, but it doesn't go beyond barest consideration. And where is the future for all these huddled and overcrowded souls? They can't emigrate to an area short of man power, because most such places have a sharply defined color line. Strange to say, some areas with a closer blood relationship bar these refugees because they fear and resent Chinese ingenuity and industriousness. They complain that the Chinese soon take over and own everything.

The refugee situation in Hong Kong is just a sample of the same conditions all over Asia today—or much of the world, for that matter. Formosa is crammed full. Korea is clogged. The Siamese have fugitives from all over Indo-China to provide for. In Burma cities like Rangoon and Mandalay are jammed with families who have fled terrorist elements in the rural areas.

India and Pakistan are burdened with millions of unneeded, unusable human beings, a fearsome product of unnatural displacement.

The Arab-Israel deadlock is another example. In many European areas, too, and even Africa, people huddle and scrounge for crusts, the world's unwanted, the refugees.

In Hong Kong those who suffer most in this packed, unnatural state are not the laboring classes or perhaps even the once-idle rich. It is those of the professional groups—doctors, dentists, attorneys—who have spent so many irreplaceable years in study and training for professions that now find only the most meager outlets. They cannot practice without passing barriers of licenses and examinations in the new territories. To a limited degree the doctors can care for their own kind, but without supplies or the ability to prescribe this becomes a contribution of mere nursing. Besides laboring the attorneys can only perhaps write letters for the illiterate, a shameful waste of talent and a thankless reward for accomplishment.

We began our daily visits to the houses of religion in the Hong Kong area. The monasteries were all very high up—fifteen hundred to two thousand feet in altitude—and very quiet, in many cases almost deserted.

The local temples with their multitudes of gods continue to hold the affections of the Chinese. Especially in these crowded conditions where good luck seems to offer the only hope of escape. Fortunetelling as a profession flourishes here as nowhere else in the world. Literally hundreds of these experts on prognosis fill the temples and all adjacent areas with their little stands and booths.

Entering a temple, one is immediately accosted by the proprietor or caretaker with an insistent demand for a donation. It had better be substantial, too, in accordance with his long-practiced ability to estimate your worth.

After this requirement is met, one is free to wander about the dim, soot-blackened interior among the crudely fashioned, doll-like images. The oily odor of incense hangs heavily in the dank air. Long years of constant burning have supersaturated every corner with this pungency.

Ancient writings about incense tell of its power: "As the curling smoke wafts sinuously aloft from a freshly lighted stick and the first faint whiff strikes the nostrils, a profound symbolism takes effect—even subconsciously. The glowing coal is the spark of life. The smoke signifies the incorporeality and evanescence of spiritual truths, while the fragrance demonstrates the tangible reality and actual penetration of these spiritual truths."

Cautiously used, incense can contribute greatly to a highly satisfying liturgical experience. Excessively used, it simply becomes a revolting, irritating stench. Throughout the Orient incense is used with utter abandon. One's last few coins are spent for it. In many places it has become the custom to use no fewer than three sticks at a time. It is burned profusely, day and night. The temples reek of it. One wonders if there is any significance in the fact that since ages past the temple owners have been the leading incense concessionaires.

If it is asked what possible comfort or spiritual solace is to be taken by any peoples in today's world from a religious concept seemingly so lacking in deeper values, it may require considerable research to arrive at a suitable answer. However, in some respects, not too many elements found in the nobler faiths are lacking.

The Chinese, for instance, have a long-standing tradition of the existence of life after death. This is evident in the many examples of ancestor worship and respect. A code of morals and ethics certainly equal to any other in the world is to be found in the fundamentals of Confucius and

Lao-tzu. At least those necessary to social harmony have long since taken root through influence of leaders and scholars.

The personal relationship of the polytheistic worshiper and his God, or gods, may not have the beauty or subtleties found in the teachings of other religions, but many of these things will gradually unfold in the heart of the believer and seeker. Anyone would agree that it is better if the nobler and more profound aspects of God are taught to us early in life, yet long ago the wisdom of the Orient convinced me there are many truths about God and many approaches to these truths. Regardless of teaching, each believer has his own idea of God down deep inside and it is likely that there are few persons indeed who could not easily find differences of opinion concerning His attributes.

Though I would never approve the "many gods" approach, I have not the slightest doubt that there are numbers of devout, consecrated, high-minded polytheists living presently in Asia, persons whose intentions are good, whose acts are above reproach. I have observed a worship service where the idea of spiritual contact seemed preposterous—where charlatans presided, where the clamor and stridency of the liturgy seemed a mockery. Yet, standing aside, I have seen worshipers whose faces were radiant with a beatific expression of spiritual inspiration turn from the temple in serene exaltation. "Blessed are the pure in heart, for they shall see God."

As the facilities of modern science pave the way for deeper penetration of higher education or even just raise the standard of literacy in these underprivileged areas, primitive concepts of nature will ultimately give way to more spiritual ideas, even though there may be a dangerous period of cynicism between the two. The contact between backward cultures—those of a major portion of the world—and the kind of life potential in the uncovered secrets of our swiftly advancing technology has thrown the whole of mankind into a spiritual upheaval. As has been the case in the past, adjustments must and will be made to bring religious teaching into line with the facts of nature. How long this present state of transition will last is unknowable. Perhaps it would be wise to adopt the attitude of some religions that recommend the expectancy of constant change —a limitlessly expanding spiritual concept to fit the unlimited horizon of this wonderfully expanding life.

The Ching Ming celebrations were under way in Hong Kong, a yearly period of ancestral commemoration among the Chinese, meaning a time to visit and pay respects to the family burial ground. This sounds like the somber tone of a solemn occasion; yet in truth it is quite the reverse. To the local citizenry it means family reunions and a picnic outing.

We embarked on one of the special trains taking over-packed loads of holiday visitors to one of the larger cemeteries some twenty-five miles away. Among the passengers the bulging lunch baskets gave promise of a feast. Good humor and gaiety were predominant.

At the destination, milling around the rail station were throngs of noisy celebrants, while clustered everywhere along the half-mile walk up to the cemetery were innumerable temporary stands and concessions selling the usual souvenirs, toys, and sweetmeats. There was also one line of wares peculiar to the occasion: miniature houses, automobiles, horses, and planes—all kinds of articles, entirely made of paper. These are purchased and burned at the gravesides in the belief that through some kind of mystical transformation they will be useful to the departed spirits. Paper imitation money is also a favorite, and great stacks of high-denomination bills were selling like hot cakes.

Wo-Hop-Shek is a huge cemetery that sprawls over the sides of a rather bare range of hills. The sight, during Ching Ming, of thousands of people clambering about its tombstones amid dozens of little puffs of smoke, all accompanied by constant machine-gun-like reports of firecrackers and drifting strands of music, is like the scene of some fantastic dream.

We climbed up and down with cameras and recorder, nowhere finding anyone sensitive or reluctant to being photographed. The spirit of cordiality is wholeheartedly predominant. One family obligingly displayed the complete traditional graveside routine.

At the start most of the articles of food from the baskets are carefully arranged before the headstones—fruits, viands of all kinds. A glass of wine will be poured out, candles and incense lighted. Then, one by one, each member of the family, starting with the eldest son, will take a turn of obeisance before the offering, kneeling and bowing with abrupt little nods. When all have completed this observance, the foodstuffs will be hastily gathered up and a fire lighted for the consumption of all the miniature paper offerings. As this little conflagration dies away, the eldest of the group places several packages of firecrackers on the embers, and then the whole party turns its back and hastily withdraws while a sharp salvo echoes across the hills. No further filial duty engages the living, and only the pleasant prospect of a family repast in some nearby place of shade remains.

Meanwhile little groups of musicians throughout the cemetery continue to provide background music for the never-ceasing flow of newcomers.

Through every phase of the various rituals for the deceased, from funerals onward, the described attitude of appearing pleasantly undisturbed is typical of Chinese conduct toward death in general. Unlike the wailing and tormented hair-pulling of those from some other religions, with the Chinese it is bad form to give signs of grief in any way, a convention some carry to great extremes. A funeral will never see a wet cheek or any other usual evidence of bereavement.

Part of this custom must be traced to a traditional sense of good manners and oriental face-saving, but surely it speaks volumes as a demonstration of faith in an ancient world-venerated teaching: the doctrine of the immortality of the soul, life after death. And isn't it strange that when so much of the world's religious doctrine revolves around this concept of immortality so few followers really appear to believe it? When they are faced with a situation involving death, the enormity of their doubt is so visibly evident. Of course one could scarcely be heartless enough to deny the sense of misery and desolation wrought by the loss of a loved one, but so many presumably stout Christians are constantly heard bemoaning the misfortune that has befallen someone passed away. Sometimes I've wondered whether this means we are mostly agnostics after all.

66

Chinese consideration for the welfare of the dead goes on to great lengths. Burial of the remains in ordinary cemeteries is seldom considered permanent. It is but temporary interment, until the proper abode for eternal rest has been determined after a family council has rendered a gravely deliberated decision. Primarily a site that will bring the fullest portion of good luck to all concerned must be selected. This decision has often been the source of much high-spirited family controversy, going to the extremes of court cases in some instances.

Since the bones are believed to attract good luck to their immediate vicinity, each descendant will try to find valid reasons why these remains should be buried on or near his particular property; thus the controversy commences, often continuing without a friendly resolution.

Few now living temporarily in the shelter of Hong Kong would be content to be forever buried there, and many thoroughly aged but still well-cared-for corpses are awaiting return to some significant site on the Chinese mainland. The usual procedure is a shallow burial for about five years. Then, during Ching Ming, members of the family dig up the remains, carefully wash and sort the bones, placing them in a suitable receptacle for safekeeping until the site of final reinterment has been determined. These receptacles are usually large urns, kept indefinitely somewhere within convenient reach. Singly, or in groups of threes and fours, uncountable numbers of ancestral urns can be seen dotting the hilly back country around Hong Kong. Each year these bones will be carefully removed from the urn, counted, washed, and returned to place. This is also part of Ching Ming.

A variation of the foregoing, by those with sufficient funds, is to have the body sealed tightly in a casket and then kept in a temporary crypt until the time comes for burial. Crypts in the Hong Kong area are quite large, like huge storehouses. They may contain several hundreds of bodies. All in all, there must be many thousands of corpses held thus in Hong Kong. Some are shipped in from all parts of the world, waiting until they can once again be returned to the now unfriendly mainland of China.

Much of this traditional procedure is traceable to Confucius, for, though he did not originate the concept of ancestor worship, he spoke heavily in favor of maintaining it. Indeed, continued probing on my part uncovered the fact that a large part of what most Chinese do and are, in many respects, echoes loudly the teachings and analects of this noble sage. The longer I stayed, the more I saw that China and Confucius were linked indissolubly. The longer I studied, the more I realized how much I had missed by not having his lineal descendant on my film.

This was to be a stern lesson to me, for I was plagued by the creeping conviction that I had blundered severely by hastening from Formosa without having seen him. I tried to find other ways of answering the problem, seeking out eminent Chinese scholars as substitutes. But none seemed to fill the bill for my purpose so well as Kung Teh Ching, the seventy-seventh grandson of Kung Fu Tsu, which is the true Chinese name for what has been translated into Greek as Confucius.

I hemmed and hawed, rationalized and schemed; but then one day in the quiet serenity of the sole Confucian temple in Hong Kong we had just photographed an ancient portrait of the sage when the very obliging little caretaker drew me aside into a little room and proudly displayed the only object therein. Enshrined on the wall was a childhood photo, taken by the caretaker himself, of the man I had sought on Taiwan—the "living descendant." For some reason that did it. Within an hour we had our reservations for the return to the island.

Several days later we landed at Taipei, in northern Formosa, and sped southward by rail to Tai Chung. A small town, Tai Chung, but in one respect it surpasses many a city of greater size and population: it puts out a fantastic volume of noise. Our hotel stood in the metropolitan center and for sheer racket I have never known the equal.

Without traffic regulations at street corners the helter-skelter scurrying of pedestrians requires that drivers of all vehicles maintain a heavy hand on the horn. This they apparently do with relish. Automobiles are comparatively few, but the innumerable bicycle-drawn rickshas, called "petit cabs," keep up a constant clamor.

Secondly, modern science has at last invaded Tai Chung in the form of the public-address system. It is used for attracting customers to the various shops. There must have been at least a half-dozen speakers emphatically within earshot—each sending forth full-blast an overloaded, beyond-peak-level mixture of entertainment and spiel. On top of this, no one in Tai Chung ever goes to bed at all—well, at least, if that's exaggerated, there is assuredly a certain amply proportioned element that continues to roam the streets, rattle around in little restaurants, play sidewalk games, laugh, argue, and brawl way beyond the usual hour of most cities. And "way beyond" means it absolutely never stopped.

6 9

The Taiwanese are on a crowded little isle. They do not have much. They are poorly housed, but they have enough to eat and they are all friendliness and definitely fun-loving.

Kung Teh Ching was to be found on a quiet little street, quite removed from the stir and din of the civic center, as would be meet and proper. He is a scholar and professor of Chinese literature at a local college. This gives him the air of being older than his actual age of thirty-two years. An authority on the works of his many-times great-grandfather, Kung's official function is to preside at a yearly celebration in honor of the revered teacher, but though he was agreeably cordial and thoroughly Western in appearance, he would not consent to don his official robes for a photograph. His simple explanation was that he would feel ridiculous.

He has been to America but speaks no—or very little— English. Yet, having been advised of my visit, he had arranged for a fellow professor named Thomas Koo, who speaks both languages with such unusual fluency and deftness that one hardly realized a translation was taking place, to be present.

For our filmed interview, held in a rural garden, I advised Kung Teh Ching of my potential questions, but he preferred to wait until the "take" for his answers, to be given through the interpreter.

As usual, I tried to put questions that might have arisen in the minds of a lay audience. For instance, the first query was something like, "What are the chances for continuation and growth of the religion of Confucianism in the world today?"

Kung Teh Ching instantly replied, "Confucianism is not a religion. It is a philosophy."

"But many Western writers refer to it as a religion and, furthermore, you have temples housing the image of Confucius. How about that?"

He answered with a shrug, "They are not so much temples as shrines. In America, you have a shrine to Abraham Lincoln. It is the same."

And so on through the interview, which went smoothly and was very revealing. That evening we sat as guests at a delicious Cantonese dinner, complete with a trio playing rather strident music. Later in the evening Kung Teh Ching himself graced us with several operatic songs in the customary Chinese falsetto style. His multifaceted talent would be hard for a Westerner to evaluate.

Next day before leaving we went around to his modest home once more for farewells. This time a ten-year-old son appeared, a rather slight, sensitive-appearing child, seemingly earmarked, and suitably so, for a lifetime career in following paternal footsteps. He traces his family tree back 4000 years into pre-Confucian days, which is the oldest and longest lineage on Earth. He speaks a few words of English and we conversed a bit. Finally I somehow got across the question regarding present desires for future vocation.

"What do you want to do when you grow up?"

The seventy-eighth descendant of Confucius replied without hesitation, "Play basketball and help Chinese people—like noble ancestor!" I felt then that present descendants were not letting the old sage down.

We took his picture and returned next day to Hong Kong.

Before leaving the Chinese portion of this account I want to tell of a most interesting new organization I encountered in Hong Kong. It is called the Red Swastika Society. Since ancient times, in many parts of the world, the swastika has been used as a symbol of various meanings. In the Orient it is generally associated with Buddhism, where it symbolizes the origin and perpetuity of life.

The present society using the swastika as its mark of identification is wholly religious and was started in Shantung Province around forty years ago by a group including several prominent political and military figures. This last fact instantly made me suspect a possible nazi connection, but investigation proved it to be groundless. Besides it was pointed out that the swastika of the Third Reich was uniquely tilted and turned backward, a sign correctly foreboding grave misfortune, according to most symbolists.

From Canton the organization quickly spread into many parts of the mainland, gathering a considerable membership until the recent communist victory. Lack of communication now leaves the present status of most of these branches unknown. It is possible that the Hong Kong branch is the only one active today.

By telephone I made an appointment with a man considered to be the local leader. We met a few hours later and he escorted me to their temple, a rather plain, three-story structure with a red swastika emblazoned over the door.

On the ground floor were what appeared to be only offices and utility rooms, but on the second floor we encountered a series of small meditation rooms and tiny chapels. Each chapel has an altar enshrining an upright brass plaque bearing the name of one of the great religious figures they venerate. Similarly with other international organizations today the Red Swastika Society considers all profound religious teaching and teachers to be inspired with the spark of divinity, though only five are represented in their temple. These are Confucius, Lao-tzu, Buddha, Jesus, and Mohammed.

In the central, and largest, chapel there is an altar whereon plaques of all these leaders are placed. Hanging behind the altar is a simple, twelve-inch framed photograph with the face of an elderly-appearing, bearded Chinese standing out against a background of clouds. This is claimed to be an actual photograph of God, taken at divine direction some years back by a small party of members during a stormy day on a nearby hilltop. The sworn and attested story is that they were simply instructed to climb the hill at a certain time, point the small camera skyward, and click the shutter. They obeyed, with the result as described.

On the third floor of the temple building there is a room with a device through which it is claimed the aforementioned kinds of spiritual instructions are received. This device is called the Sand Board and Wooden Pen. It is simply a shallow wooden receptacle, about two feet square with a four-inch rim, filled halfway with dry white sand and placed upon a wooden table in the center of the room. Standing nearby is a five-foot rod with an odd, curved wooden appendage about twelve inches long fastened to the center. This rod is held by two men who stand astride the box and use the pointed appendage to write large Chinese characters in the sand. The men are considered to be mediums.

At the end of the room is a carved armchair alleged to be

the seat of honor for the particular spirit invited for questioning by the gathered assembly.

From there I was taken to the roof of the building, where a single, penthouse-like chamber houses another Sand Board similar to the first. This, I was told, is used but once or twice a year, when direct communication with God Himself is desired.

Sacred literature of the society, of course, includes any works attributed to the previously mentioned masters and, besides the spiritualistic side of the religion, there is also a well-outlined course of training in the practice of meditation. This has an objective similar to that of the Hindus, Yogis, and Buddhist monks, namely, "Peace of mind and attunement with the infinite."

I observed several members who had dropped by to spend scheduled time in the meditation chapels. Sitting upright on low stools, they kept eyes riveted on a few candles atop a plain altar at the end of the room, and they appeared undisturbed by comings and goings of others during the prescribed period of their particular session—probably thirty minutes to an hour.

Naturally, after seeing all this, I wanted very much to put it on film and I approached the leaders on the possibility of doing so. Their attitude was quite enthusiastic as I outlined what I thought would be the best way to proceed. But they pointed out that there was no precedent for such an action, nothing concerning them having been photographed before.

"Besides," they went on, "while we are considered the fathers of the organization it is really only a nominal post, for we set no policy or decide anything whatsoever. All direction, all decisions concerning this society come from our leader in the spirit world. We merely execute orders from above."

They then proceeded to say that if I would be content to abide by the decision received via the Sand Board, they would submit my request. Of course I complied.

It was arranged that we would bring our equipment on the following evening at the time of a regular meeting and, if the spirit gave a favorable reply, we could then proceed immediately with photography. I was delighted, for I felt it should be a most interesting sequence.

The next night, promptly on the hour, Bob and I arrived and were greeted most cordially. Some thirty members were assembled and we waited quietly during a general prayer service. At the end of this we were told that the question concerning my request was about to be put to the Sand Board and that if I wished I could observe the procedure. I would have to promise, however, not to make any films unless and until word from the spirits was in the affirmative. I agreed and we were escorted to the same room on the third floor we had visited the day previously.

Lights were on brightly as we entered. The lid had been removed from the Sand Board and the four-man team was preparing to submit the question. No particular act of consecration was noticeable. No effort toward a trancelike state was visible on the part of the two mediums. In fact the attitude of all was much more down-to-earth and businesslike than one usually associates with this type of gathering. There were about ten other observers with us at the end of the room.

Presently the question—or what I gathered to be the question in Chinese—was put to the vacant armchair at the far end of the room, while the two mediums held the pole horizontally between them with the center appendage poised over the smooth sand.

Being unprepared for what to expect, I was mightily surprised at the action of the two upon completion of the question. If I anticipated a rather slow beginning, gradually warming to increased tempo, like the old Ouija-board days of my childhood, I was badly mistaken. Without hesitation the point of the writing nub commenced scratching out large Chinese characters in the sand with such celerity and force that the sand literally flew out of the box.

All responsibility for the guiding impulse was visible in the actions of the number-one medium. He was a wiry man of middle age who, from his expression and slightly squinted eyes, was concentrating intensely on his work. It was obvious that the rod moved solely by his muscular efforts. The arm of the second medium was quite flaccid, acting only as a pivot. In his other hand, the second medium had a small, flattened stick with which he smoothed the sand upon completion of each character.

When I later asked about the obvious muscular force being applied by the number-one medium, the answer came back that this was understood and as it should be; presumably the medium was writing as he was mentally inspired.

The third member of the team stood at one side calling the names of the characters as they appeared, while the fourth member merely acted as a silent stenographer, recording the characters with brush and ink.

The process continued for some time—perhaps twenty minutes—with great gusto. Occasionally the number-one medium would use his free hand to remove a handkerchief from his breast pocket, mop his brow, and then return the cloth without pausing. Sometimes he coughed slightly or glanced around the room.

In an inside pocket I was carrying my little Minox—a miniature camera with precision lens, of the Dick Tracy variety—and it was a great temptation to sneak a couple of shots. It would certainly have been easy in the bright light. I was in the rear of the room and the noise of the sand being scattered from the box, plus the voice of the man calling the characters, would have covered the faint click of shutter. But I'd given my word and I felt certain they'd let us take all the pictures we wanted later.

Eventually the scribe tore off a few sheets and handed them to one of the men I had talked with. The latter summoned me out of the room to hear the verdict.

Back down on the second floor the leaders huddled for some time over the message until they were evidently satisfied, and then one approached me and, translating, read aloud. It was a long, apologetic dissertation on the present state of the world, the conclusion of which was that the world was not ready or sufficiently advanced to be informed on the principles or practices of the Red Swastika Society— at least, not by way of the motion-picture camera.

In typical oriental fashion they were long coming to the point and it was some time before I realized the answer was negative. The spirits had not approved.

Before leaving the description of the religious picture in China I feel impelled to say a few words regarding a religion so far entirely neglected in this book: what is known in our

Western world as Mohammedanism or, throughout the Orient and more correctly, Islam.

Hong Kong has comparatively few Mohammedans, or Moslems; the number is said to be about five thousand Chinese and fifteen hundred others. There are only a couple of mosques and these are not especially interesting, so I didn't see much point in going into detail concerning this faith at the present time; I will take it up in the chapter on Pakistan. However, it is my understanding that in certain parts of China, particularly the western sectors of Sinkiang, Outer Mongolia, etc., Islam is very strong, numbering perhaps over sixty million followers and growing rapidly.

If this is true, it may be that Islam is finally the faith capable of doing what all religions have failed to do, namely, to bring spiritual union to the Chinese common man. I was unable to enter communist China on this tour, so I cannot make a comparison of the practice of the faith there with the expressions of Islam to be found in countries of the Near East. But from the simplicity of the very nature of the faith I would judge the Chinese branch to be similar, if not identical, in all major respects.

It would be interesting to study the working of Islam under communist domination. So much of both concepts is fundamentally opposed. I will hazard the speculation, though, that if Mohammedanism should continue to flourish under the present Red regime and, by some chance, should manage to flare up and spread through China in a burst of evangelistic zeal—as has happened in the past— world-wide consequences would result.

Assuming that the Comintern still held control of the Chinese Government, the living example of a successfully entrenched Islam in its bosom would be an overwhelming argument with which to win all Moslem countries, and possibly the entire Near East, to the philosophy of Karl Marx. Indeed, the alleged serenity of the sixty million Moslems in China today is already a powerful persuasion. It is not even too unlikely that the Reds might try to stimulate a movement of Islamic evangelism just for the tremendous political victory such a maneuver could hold. But it would have to be carefully—so carefully—controlled. It would be a scheme loaded with dynamite, for there could also be the greatest backfire in history and I'm sure the Reds know it.

No matter how cleverly it is glossed over, between a religion which derives its vitality and very existence from an insistent belief in the power and presence of an almighty God and a state which categorically and publicly disavows any such superauthority, the basic differences are such that it seems to me they must inevitably come to bitter conflict.

Besides the reverence for spiritual authority, reiterated dozens of times in the daily prayers of each Moslem and emphasized by the physical postures in his acts of worship, there is his holy book, the Koran, which exerts an influence over Moslem everyday social, political, and economic life far more than the Bible affects the average Christian. The potential explosive power of an Islamic-Kremlin marriage, by comparison, reduces modern hydronuclear processes to the snappings of popcorn.

CHAPTER FIVE

In Siam we encountered Buddhism in fullest expression: the so-called school of *Theravada* ("Doctrine of the Elders"), or *Hinayana* ("Little Vehicle"). It is unquestionably the national religion, almost the only religion. We worked with the Federal Department of Religious Affairs, this being the only way our job could be done, and I like to think we covered the assignment.

Siam (or Thailand, as it's now called, meaning land of the Thai peoples, though older patriots still prefer use of the correct territorial title of "Siam") is largely a flat, delta land laced with canals. Its climate is extremely hot and moist, admirable for rice, sugar, and hemp.

Water buffaloes are ever-present. These stolid, patient creatures are objects of great pride and affectionate consideration by the Siamese farmers. They are enormously strong—capable of pulling tremendous loads—docile, and willing. Their milk is quite palatable. The skin of these beasts lacks glands of moisture, and they are immensely comforted by getting under water. The typical attitude in which the buffalo is found during off-hours is the familiarly depicted submerged position with nothing protruding above the level of a marsh or canal but nostrils, eyes, and horn. There she will remain, for hours patiently chewing her cud. Wherever one goes in Siam this is a most common sight.

One sees the farmer's consideration for his beast's comfort when they are plowing the flooded rice fields during the midday heat. As the driver guides the plow along, he will pause on one foot every few steps and kick a spray of water up over the buffalo's back. This is part of the regular routine.

The Siamese capital of Bangkok is a busy place these days. As with so much of Southeast Asia conversion to Western ways has caused great spiritual upheaval and social turmoil. In the cities automobiles and motor bikes everywhere crowd and jam the too narrow streets, streets designed hundreds of years ago for pedestrian oxcarts and rickshas.

Ultramodern buildings, too, are rising above the creaky, old-time structures of Victorian days, forming the usual hodgepodge of nondescript architecture found throughout the world today. The romance and glamour of the travel-poster Orient is a gross exaggeration! How many times I've stood upon the site of the exact photographic angle of some famous landmark shown by a poster, only to find the landmark practically obliterated by the trash-littered foreground objects the picture had failed to include.

Yet even on this poor earth's surface there are still a few island areas of untouched beauty or simplicity—repositories of culture: a village here, a city section there. Perhaps someday, when the equality of man has been brought into better alignment, these islands will reach out to join hands and spread abroad their treasures.

In the tumultuous city of Bangkok there are islands, too. These are the Buddhist monasteries, called *wats*. These wats architecturally embody the dreams and designs of the Siamese of another age. There are many of them and they are fabulous, fantastic, fairy-tale architecture, sadly isolated but still rising gloriously amid the clamor and clutter of a modern bedlam. There are some twenty thousand temples in Siam.

A wat is a cluster of buildings surrounded by a wall and usually embracing an area equal to an average city block. The primary purpose is to house and instruct the multitude of monks that thrive on the soil of Siam.

First of importance on the grounds of the wat is the main temple, called a *bote*. This highly ornate structure, housing the largest image of the Buddha, is laid out with great care as to traditional symbolism in every facet and dimension.

Second to the bote is another, usually smaller temple, also containing an image, called the *vihara*, used for feasts and general assemblages on lesser occasions. There will also be various living quarters and study halls for the monks.

There are a few shrines and an indefinite number of steeple-like, commemorative structures, similar to a Hindu stupa, called *pra chedi* in Siam. These solid objects, with relics buried at their bases, may rise in a profusion of stalagmites or stand as a single huge monument—like the pra chedi at Patom, which rises 350 feet in the air. In shape they are like an inverted hand bell.

Hinayana Buddhism, as practiced in Burma and Siam,

might be considered somewhat closer to that of the early followers of Gautama than the developments which have subsequently taken place in China and Japan, though, as stated previously, few of the variations found in the northern branch cannot be traced to some statement or inference from the Master's teaching. As is so often the case with all religions, the variation is usually a matter of expedient interpretation, or emphasis upon some particular aspect of a doctrine which enables it to fit better into the local situation.

Basically the Enlightened One, who lived in India and was a follower of Brahmanism, taught that offerings and sacrifices, rites, liturgies, and sacraments do not cleanse the man who cannot abstain from anger, drunkenness, bigotry, deception, envy, self-praise, and other evils. Though Buddhists are nearly all vegetarians (the custom stemming from the doctrine of non-violence), the teachings of Gautama Siddhartha make it clear that abstinence from flesh-eating cannot purify one who is not free from the delusion of the senses.

He advocated a middle course in all things—temperance —with avoidance of extremes in either sensuousness or denial.

These four noble truths were also proclaimed:

1. that suffering is the primary condition of worldly life;

2. the cause of this suffering is desire;

3. the cessation of suffering is the overcoming of desire and the attainment by the soul of Nirvana;

4. the means of attaining this cessation being the Eightfold Path.

The Eightfold Path consists of:
1. right understanding,
2. right resolutions,
3. right speech,
4. right acts,
5. right way of making a living,
6. right efforts,
7. right thoughts,
8. right peace of mind.

The Master did not believe all persons should renounce the world to live as monks, but there was encouragement placed in that direction for those who could stand the rigors of monastic life and who wished to advance more rapidly.

Buddha, it will be remembered, did not preach about God, though he did not deny Him. He constantly stressed transformation of character through obedience to universal moral laws rather than dependence upon ceremonial and sacrificial requirements of the Hindu priesthood in those early days. Even prayer was held to be of little value to anyone enmeshed in the chains of the senses. Each must work out his release through his own efforts. Later developments on this last point have somewhat modified the stern demand for utter self-reliance with the introduction of the compassionate power of the Bodhisattva, or Saintly Spirit. At least the common people now pray for help.

Buddhism is basically a philosophy primarily stressing a pessimistic view of earthly life, with a well-outlined method for overcoming its pains. It was not intended to be considered a religion. Buddha himself was never deified and though he is dealt with as a god, Buddha's teaching was similar to that of Jesus in many ways. For instance, he said:

"Blessings give for curses"; "Let a man overcome anger by love, let him overcome evil with good"; "Practice the truth that thy brother is the same as thou"; "Self is death, truth is life," and many other similar precepts.

Playing down the importance of ritual has resulted almost in an absence of a priesthood in Buddhism. There are ceremonies, and monks who have risen in esteem perform them, but these votaries are not looked upon as intermediaries between man and God, or man and the spiritual world in any sense.

Another important teaching in Buddhism is the doctrine of *ahimsa*, or non-violence. We shall hear a great deal more about this doctrine later on when we discuss India. It can suffice now to say that it advocates non-violence as a virtue in itself, without regard to the reasoning of right or wrong.

In today's Hinayana countries all male Buddhists expect, and are expected, to become *bhikkhus* (monks) at least temporarily, if not for their entire lives. At present in Siam there are about two hundred thousand of these bhikkhus, as renunciation of worldly interests is held in high national esteem.

We worked in a number of monasteries, staying overnight several times to photograph the complete routine of daily life.

To become a monk, one must be at least twenty years of age—novitiates can be entered at the age of seven by parental consent for indefinite periods—and need pass only a few simple requirements. A man needs government approval if he is employed thereby, and he must not be in debt, diseased, be a criminal, or have a criminal record. Thailand is very strict on the last point. Further, if any monk is ever convicted of any infringement of law, he is forever barred from monkhood. Burma, on the other hand, having less organization and control of its monasteries, may not so ably enforce these rulings. Generally speaking, the common people love and support their monks, but they will not be bullied by them or tolerate nonsense from them. Lack of consecration in any form is severely dealt with, and the culprit expelled.

Upon arrival at the monastery the man shaves his head and becomes a novice, or *samanera*. After learning the message of Buddhism and the rules of the order, he may then apply for ordination. Rules of the order include the promise to refrain from injury to any living thing, to refrain from taking that which is not given and from falsehood, to abstain from intoxicating beverage and sexual intercourse. The monk further agrees not to attend stage performances, not to use perfume or to sleep in a luxurious bed (one blanket on the bare floor usually is the rule). Personal belongings consist of no more than seven articles: three pieces of orange-colored cloth (draped and worn as robes), one belt, one razor (head and face must be smoothly shaved), one water strainer (water being strained to prevent the destruction of insect life), one food bowl, and sometimes a needle.

Buddhist monks eat but two meals a day, one at dawn, or shortly thereafter, and the last meal sometime before noon. Thence only water may be taken until the following morning. A monk may not carry money and all food must be obtained by begging, with never more than one day's supply being accumulated at a time.

I had heard about the rule prohibiting the carrying of

money, but frequently saw monks in and around various shops in Bangkok, apparently shopping. When I inquired about it, my informant pointed out that the monk usually was accompanied, or rather trailed, by a small boy who carried his cash, made his purchases, and toted home his forbidden worldly goods. This is a common sight. Also, upon occasions when the monks are given presents for participation at some service in a private home, as is frequently done, the march back to the monastery always includes little boys loaded with loot bringing up the rear.

We managed to get good coverage of two of the aforementioned home ceremonies, by the way. The first was in honor of four little Burmese boys who were becoming novices. As with most of the children in Hinayana countries this was not to be more than a token ceremony for these boys, an event similar in meaning to Christian confirmation but much more of a celebration for all participants.

From early dawn until dusk these seven-year-olds are treated with royal indulgence, dressed in satin robes and bedecked with golden crowns. Attired thus, they are escorted in elaborate parades to and from the temples, often being actually carried. In the home the elaborateness of the daylong festivities will be determined only by the family purse; evidently no lengths are unseemly, with music and feasting for as many as can be accommodated. We have pictures of these boys stuffing themselves with goodies, as at any other kid party in the world.

The climax is reached in late afternoon after an impressive liturgy by perhaps a whole chorus of monks, when the boys' heads are shaved and they are garbed in the customary yellow robes of the order.

Recitation of memorized portions of Buddhist scripture by the novices completes the ceremony, and the following day sees a return to the normal pursuits of secular Burmese childhood.

The other ceremony, similar to the last, was an occasion of ear-piercing for a fifteen-year-old girl. This particular young lady had the attendance of about thirty monks, plus family relations, while the physician made his punctures in her ear lobes. It took place at dawn and was followed, later in the day, by a formal reception and ball for no fewer than five hundred persons. Along with the dedication to Lord Buddha there was something of the coming-out-party feeling associated with the event.

Aside from the period of perhaps an hour succeeding daybreak, in which the day's begging is done, few monks are visible on city streets. During that early period all monks, from highest abbot to lowliest novice, turn to the task, for none is exempt from the command to beg his daily bread or portion of food.

Though the burden of feeding this large body of non-contributing members of Buddhist society falls squarely upon the shoulders of the general lay public, scarcely a murmur is ever heard against the practice. Those who can give do so gladly. They are eligible for spiritual merit by giving. The *bhikkhu* never thanks them.

It is a very colorful sight to see a large city like Bangkok early in the morning with streets still uncluttered by daily vehicular traffic suddenly come alive with thousands of these orange-colored bhikkhus, all walking silently, in groups or alone, each with his dark pottery food bowl under his arm. Begging does not mean that the monk asks for his food. He simply walks the streets looking neither right nor left, until he is stopped by someone with an offering. The food bowl tacitly indicates his need and he must continue walking until his daily requirement is met, or decide to fast that day.

Seldom are the monks seen abroad with their bowls for more than an hour after daybreak, though I have seen some apparently luckless yet determined ones still wandering about, and by that time dodging between vehicles, a considerable while after the commencement of the day's full commercial traffic. There was a kind of embarrassment in the sight.

The food given consists mainly of rice with a few vegetables or fresh fruits piled atop. Occasionally there will be the additional gift of a lotus bud or a few sticks of incense to be used as an offering to the Buddha. Having filled his bowl, the bhikkhu returns to quarters at the *wat*, bathes and cleanses himself, and then eats the first portion of food. Novices have the duty of laying table and preparing the dishes of their superiors before partaking themselves. Breakfast finished, studies commence. These are of great variation, depending upon the stage of individual advancement.

Classes are held in memorization of Buddhist scriptures known as the *Pitakas*, or "baskets." There are three main "baskets": the *Vinayana* (laws of monastic discipline), the *Sutras* (sermons), and the *Abidhamma* (metaphysics). The language is Pali.

From the temples in the wat will be heard large groups of youngsters chanting in unison long passages of the Sutras. The chanting is interspersed with the sound of gongs and

drumbeats, and the droning rhythm creates a hypnotic effect.

About eleven-thirty in the morning a signal is given for
the day's second, and final, meal. All food and utensils are
dispensed with by the stroke of twelve. Thereafter the day
is given to additional classes, lectures, and discussion groups,
private instruction and examinations between master and
disciple, each monk being under the personal supervision
and authority of a superior. Also personal prayers take place
before the altar, and the unceasing oriental practice of meditation is of foremost concern.

The last accomplishment is furthered by a number of
different methods. The purpose of meditation, according to
Eastern theory, being to open the mind to a higher, more
spiritual reality, one must carefully prepare the way.

First, for mental serenity, the cravings and demands of
the body must be subordinated to the will. Ways of
strengthening control of the will over the body vary; there
are schools which assign the student periods in which he
must consciously be aware of every internal organic action,
and those that try to by-pass this long process by teaching a
direct mental attempt in the manner of self-hypnosis.

I have watched and photographed boys of the first school
spending hours slowly walking zombie-fashion about the
grounds of the wat in absolute concentration upon the
minutest fraction of every action connected with each step.
The procedure is also carried into every single physical act
of daily life until, theoretically, the conscious mind under-
stands and can control each physiological function of the
human body. Thence the next step is to sit in silence and,
without sleeping, eliminate all automatic mental images,

bring quiescence to the imagination, and open the way for entrance of the consciousness into a higher plane of existence. A fifty-year-old man, recognized as one of the most advanced masters of this practice, demonstrated his control for me. He used to meditate in a small graveyard adjoining his wat, because he'd be undisturbed there. We dropped in on him several times, in varying kinds of weather. He would be seated, cross-legged and immobile but with eyes open, for hours on end—through the driving rain at midnight or the blistering heat of noonday in Siam. His usual length of stay was two or three hours, which he set for himself by an alarm clock. It took about ten minutes for him to enter his deepest state of coma. At that point flies, ants, and birds could wander over his bare skin without causing the slightest quiver. I saw it happen. It is testified that several times, while sitting thus in this state of *samadhi* in some deep portion of the jungle, this master remained unperturbed by the sniffings of tigers, who ultimately gave up and retired in bewilderment.

Information concerning this higher plane of existence is, and has always been, extremely scanty. Alleged contact with it mostly seems to be an experience somewhat in the nature of an indescribably beautiful dream world. Certainly little that can be shown to be of benefit to anyone beside the practitioner has been forthcoming through the practice of meditation since the enlightenment of Buddha himself.

I have personally spoken to a number of persons who make claim to the attainment of a varying degree of this mystic adventure. None was able to give any description of it, nor was there anything in the content of their conversations which would seem to indicate contact with a higher wisdom which might have benefits for the world at large. An exception might be the example set by the master and his instruction to those desiring to follow his path, or the good to be derived by all from the serenity and poised assurance in the purified character and matured personality which is the usual accompaniment of these mystics. This kind of character development, however, can be promoted by other means, too.

As I have said, it is the aim of all male Buddhists to become monks, some for their lifetimes, some not until later in life after worldly ambitions and involvements have been satisfied.

In many cases the monkhood will be but a symbolic act of short duration, signifying complete acceptance of the Buddha's teaching and implying the intention of a monastic return later in life. In Siam this may be a period of three months, taken usually in late summer and early fall. In Burma, however, the time may be as short as two days, consisting of a primary initiation, complete with head-shaving for the novice on the first day, followed by the final ceremony of initiation into the brotherhood of monks on the second morning. The third day will see a return to normal secular occupation.

When speaking of all Buddhists in these countries, I most assuredly do not mean all Siamese or Burmese. Of course Buddhism is the predominant religion in national consideration in those countries. But for the rest of the population, especially the illiterates, of which there is a high percentage, Buddhism is too complex, too severe, too demanding, and too unsatisfying metaphysically for acceptance as a doctrine in anything but name only. I have seen statistics which make a claim of somewhere in the neighborhood of five hundred million Buddhists in the world, but this most certainly is unrealistic and presumptive. Doubtless such figures incorporate a vast number of Chinese, who I feel sure do not give more than token acknowledgment to the cause. These statisticians must also be lumping total populations in Southeastern Asiatic areas, but from what I could see Buddhism is the nominal religion in that area and little more.

On every side, wherever one glances slightly into the shadow, are unmistakable symptoms and signs of animism and polytheism. Evidence of spirit worship is on every hand. In Siam each home has a small house about the size and shape we put up for wild birds, mounted on a post in a corner of the yard. These are spirit houses, dwelling places provided for various deities of the land. These spirits are considered to be ghosts of former landlords or other persons who somehow have been connected with the territory. Inside the house may be a small image before which incense will be burned and daily offerings made. This practice, moreover, is not confined to the uneducated, but will be found in the gardens of the finest homes. Even a newly erected government building will have a little house for the local spirits. Other examples of polytheism will be found at every turn. At a boxing match, a favorite national sport of Thailand, the Thai boxers in all seriousness invariably go through a lengthy religious rite in the ring before the fight begins. It consists of strange, slow-motion gyrations and posturings which have no connection with either Buddhism or the American television version of wrestling matches.

There is also a good deal of the wearing of little images

and amulets, by those of any rank, as charms. In Bangkok one day I was taken to a small, out-of-the-way temple to visit a man reputedly able to do strange things through the power of these little charms. He claimed to be a Buddhist and his presence and practices were known to local Buddhist authorities. They spoke of him as authentic and seemed respectfully impressed by his ability.

I was introduced to the man, a kind of priest, apparently, and informed by my official escort (perhaps not too seriously) that for a very nominal fee this magician could make me physically immune and impervious to the penetrating power of lethal weapons. The sorcerer had a somewhat sardonic expression, which I didn't understand at the time. I don't believe they actually expected me to take him up, but I did. Later the meaning of his expression became clear.

The priest and I sat cross-legged, facing each other on the floor of the temple, and as a few stragglers gathered around he began a ceremony over me. First he placed a small pointed instrument of some kind atop the crown of my head and, slowly revolving it, commenced a long, mysterious chant. This continued for about five minutes, with increasing pressure, until I began to think the point actually must be breaking through my scalp.

Then followed a welcome pause while I was handed a small clay image of Buddha and told to clasp it tightly in both hands, concentrating meanwhile on the power of the little talisman to protect me. This I did, and the head-boring ceremony was resumed, with even greater fervor than before.

Not knowing what next to anticipate, I began to feel a bit balky and a bit ridiculous. I might even have pulled out of such preposterous goings-on there and then had I not noticed that the little group of bystanders had continued to grow until we had gathered quite a decent audience. As best I recall, I guess I just must have reverted to type. Anyway, there was now sufficient cause to bring out the actor (perhaps I should say "ham") side of my personality, and I became determined to play the role of heroic stolidity for all it was worth. Is it not our deepest tradition that one cannot let his audience down?

At the end of another five minutes the chanted part of the ceremony came to a halt. By now the top of my skull was numb from pressure of the pointed ritual object (the "point" of which I never did altogether comprehend, though allegedly it was thereby that the "spirit power" entered my body), and we went into the second phase of the ordeal. This had to do with knife sharpening.

The priest reached somewhere in back of him and brought forth the neatest set of cutlery imaginable, though use of the term "set" is inappropriate. It was a heterogeneous collection of swords, knives, cleavers, and oriental razor blades, which he proceeded to whet with assiduous care.

First came a long, broad sword. This was hand-rubbed with a stone until by way of demonstration the magician was able to slice a folded newspaper with apparent ease. Meanwhile I had been instructed to continue my clutch on the little idol and maintain a mental attitude of complete confidence in the image's ability to provide my protection. I did my best, bitterly regretting neglect of past opportunities to increase my faulty power of concentration.

And now we were ready for the first test. Grasping my left wrist, palm upward, the priest now lay the cutting edge of the sword across my bared forearm. This done, he gave me a quizzical glance which seemed to ask if I were prepared for him to continue, and for some reason (probably the presence of the audience) I dumbly nodded yes. He then passed the sharp edge of the blade three or four times across my flesh, not without considerable pressure.

It was stifling weather anyway, but the quantity of perspiration which oozed from my skin reminded me of dengue-fever attacks I had had on New Guinea back in 1944. It seemed to me the moisture lubricated the skin somewhat and eased the passing of the blade. There was no blood when he stopped. I did not appear to be cut. I had survived the ordeal—or so I thought, until I discovered it was only Test Number One!

Next the priest took out a curved scimitar-type instrument and, taking hold of the top of my head, pulled me forward, exposing and tightening the skin on the back of my neck. I felt him lay the steel firmly thereon and commence sawing back and forth. It was not a particularly pleasant sensation, but not especially painful. I didn't lose consciousness and when he finished all was the same as ever. I breathed a bit easier now, having passed the second test, and began to glance about at the crowd with what I recall must have been a devil-may-care smirk. They seemed visibly impressed.

Things continued at a fast pace from here on with various knife edges sawing back and forth on different parts of my anatomy. The finale was quite a thriller. A package of regular safety-razor blades was produced and the corner of one blade crisscrossed all over my left arm. And then the cleaver.

It was an ordinary cleaver—the large, rectangular kind

used on meat (I recall wondering how it happened to be in vegetarian country and began to suspect some anti-Buddhist trickery). Anyway, the sorcerer held the cleaver in his right hand, and then, with his left hand underneath my upturned forearm, he waved the cleaver aloft and brought it down with a thud upon the muscle. This time I winced—visibly, I'm sure.

I winced because it startled me and frankly because it hurt. Though it didn't cut, it was a good stout whack on the muscle. I could see a welt rise, but nothing more. The experiment was finished. I was free to leave without loss of face. The crowd was delighted. I had risen to new heights!

The priest and I now congratulated each other profusely, while he assured me of permanent immunity. I'm sure my overexuberant laughter had just the faintest tinge of hysteria. The interpreter asked if I would care to continue with tests using a pistol and live ammunition. For some reason I decided it might be best to leave this part for another day, mumbled some sort of smiling excuse, and changed the subject by rising to shake hands and say good-by. We left rather hurriedly.

Later that day back at the hotel I was telling Bob all about the incident when I noticed him looking at me strangely.

"But it's true, I tell you." I spoke with slight indignation. "Do you think I'd just dream up a yarn like that?"

Bob always takes his time answering. "Sure, sure." He has a slight Oklahoma drawl that can be annoying at times. "Sure, I don't doubt it's true, but how're you going to prove it?"

I reached into my pocket. "Here's my proof," I replied

confidently. "The little clay talisman that saved my life."

Bob looked at the image and just grinned. "There's only one way to prove anything," he informed me. "If it really happened, it can be photographed. Just let me put a lens on it. If it's there, it'll also be on film."

"You mean I should go through the whole fantastic affair again just so you and a few hardheads back home will believe me?" I gasped, shuddering inside. I hadn't mentioned the soreness on my neck and the welts on my arm.

Bob just nodded calmly. "Why not? You said it didn't hurt. Besides, think what a great sequence for the film. It's a natural."

So next day we repeated the performance for the camera with just a few changes. For one thing, I had to use the other arm. The price had gone considerably higher, too, as happens the world over when Hollywood is mentioned.

When the cleaver came down I winced again, harder than the first time, though I was determined not to—and even before it actually hit me. This shows up on the film, too, which is a bit irritating since it destroys the effectiveness of my self-assured manner. However, it's all there now: celluloid proof of my newly acquired indestructibility.

Regarding an explanation of this phenomenon, in all candor I could not ask anyone to take the event too seriously, although I never heard an expression of doubt from any of the Siamese. Like most Orientals, these folk seem to gravitate toward anything that smacks of the supernatural. Their whole background has long prepared them to accept the psychic explanation more quickly than the materialistic doubt.

For myself, I think that the priest pressed and sawed in

some way which prevented the blades from cutting my skin. Actually I was scratched—quite badly. The marks didn't show up until the next day and then gave me a bit of concern as I thought of those ancient, rusty edges. I was liberal with the merthiolate! The welts from the cleaver blossomed into classic bruises.

In the imagination of the East spirits are everywhere. The common people cannot seem to give them up. They house them, feed them, pray to them, fear them, sing and dance to them. To many the local spirits are as real as themselves.

Burma, as another instance, has the *nats*, a term for the spirits of the sky, air, forests, rain, wind, etc. Ghosts of quasi-historical heroes and even certain supernaturals of Buddhism are also nats. All these may be harmful unless they are constantly acknowledged and appeased. There is a little house or shrine for this purpose near Buddhist pagodas and at the end of every village. Attention and consideration for the nats is not overlooked even by most of the Burmese Buddhist monks themselves. There is a specific list in Burma of thirty-seven nats, with an image of each in the Shive-Zi Gon pagoda at Pagan.

With some of the simpler folk there is a strong belief that disease and death are caused by nats; any pain is the bite of a nat; flood nats cause drownings; and one especially terrifying nat drives men mad.

We did extensive photography one afternoon at the home of a cult priestess in Rangoon, where dances of exorcism and propitiation were performed before an altar containing images of all nats. A full ten-piece orchestra of natives beat frenzied accompaniment, and the wide eyes of credulous onlookers peeped through every crack and crevice of the house. It was not arranged for our special benefit and certainly had the appearance of being a regular occurrence. Several of the cultists were dancers of considerable ability, though the gyrations of the priestess herself, always the star of the show, were awkward and lumbering. We stayed something like three hours and finally left just as it seemed to be mounting to full swing. Viewing the film, one finds there is something orgiastic in the whole affair.

Partially this lack of popular acceptance of Buddhism may be caused by the fact that there is little of the type of general instruction and proselytization that characterizes Christianity. There are no Sunday schools, as we know them, and even temple services dwell predominantly on a formalized liturgy. Scriptures may then be read to the congregation, in a highly stylized manner for the most part, and most often spoken in the sacred but dead language of the Buddhist—Pali. Very infrequently are texts of the Pitakas to be found in the script of the native tongue.

At present serious efforts are being made in those southern countries to revitalize the Buddhist faith. There is a Department of Religious Affairs in each government with a minister who is a cabinet officer. Important international Buddhist conventions are now held annually. Burma is especially active in these matters. Elaborate and costly preparations were made for a year previous to the gigantic commemorative convention which opened in June of 1954. This meeting is scheduled to last for three years, during which time all ancient scriptures will be retranslated, reinterpreted, and rearranged in time for the two thousand five hundredth anniversary of the Buddhist religion, to occur in

1957. It is believed by some that this date will usher in the long-predicted period of universal peace.

Further, it is felt that the Burmese, for instance, are trying to invigorate a sense of national pride by associating and promoting Buddhism as their national religion. But it is hard to see how such efforts can hope to meet with significant results. Buddhism is so emphatically monastic, and even though Buddha preached a life exempt from extremes and did not necessarily insist that all men enter a monastery, the fact that the doctrine basically points up the futility of earthly ambition, emphasizing the metaphysical aspect of progressive transmigration and rebirth of the soul, and claims to give its followers the means by which they may overcome the dreadful misfortune of being reborn into another earthly existence, makes for great difficulty in reconciling the religion of Gautama with a spirit of patriotic nationalism of Western character.

Japan is a Buddhist country, but when her leaders wanted to work up a nationalistic fervor they turned completely away from Buddhism and most conveniently toward State Shinto and emperor worship. This religion had the perfect cosmology and ideal metaphysic for militaristic ambition.

Mohammedanism, too, has an element which can be interpreted and used to bolster a determined positivist spirit: the doctrine of the so-called Holy War. At least there is ample excuse for firm, defensive action, justifiable in the actions of Mohammed himself, who took decidedly to attack as a defensive expediency. Today Mohammedans are making great efforts to unite their brotherhood in the cause of social and economic advance, under one banner of Islam. They have a good chance of more than ordinary success.

The Sikhs are followers of another religion with a strong tradition of spiritual and physical unity, giving them ample vitality to withstand aggression.

It's difficult to find justification for worldly ambition, material concern, or even defensive action in the teachings of Jesus. Yet Christian nations, their rulers, and many of the clergy have found excuses and evolved specious interpretations over the centuries which have enabled Western nations to go on the warpath and retain their status of being Christian, their citizens as Christian peoples. One wonders at the reaction of Jesus to the multitude of conflicts and battles fought in His holy name.

But for Buddhism it's a different matter. It's said there has never been a Buddhist war. Never has the holy cause of Buddhism been considered sufficient reason for marching into some neighboring back yard. At least, outside the localized feudings of certain monks in Japan centuries ago, I'm not aware of any important historical episodes that showed Buddhists enlisting force to support their cause. It is truly the philosophy of spiritual withdrawal and emotional restraint.

During our last couple of weeks in Siam we visited every important temple and shrine within a hundred miles of Bangkok. One of the loveliest of these is at the famous site of what is known as the Buddha's footprint, Phra Buddha Bat, about fifty jolting miles north of Ayuthia. There are a number of these alleged footprints, I believe five in all, scattered throughout Southern Asia, in places actually never visited by the Buddha in his lifetime. Another very ancient and famous one, revered for centuries, is in Ceylon. The Siamese print is one of the latest to be found. This discovery took place several hundred years ago, when a certain very devout Buddhist King of Siam was told by monks returning from Ceylon that priests in that area believed that one of the five famous footprints would be found on a hill in Siam. Following this information, the King sent out a command that the hill should be located. Shortly thereafter a report came in that a hunter had had a strange experience in the vicinity of a town named Saraburi.

It seems the hunter had shot an arrow at a deer which, though seriously wounded, had managed to escape into the forest. After a few moments, however, the deer reappeared unhurt. The astonished hunter followed the deer's tracks to a water-filled depression about two feet wide, four feet long and a foot deep, somewhat resembling a huge foot-print, in a stone bed. Thinking that the deer might have drunk some of this water and had its wounds healed, the hunter applied the water to a skin disease of his own and obtained immediate relief.

On hearing this tale the King went immediately to the spot, worshiped the depression as a footprint of Lord Buddha, and had a temple, or *mondop*, erected to house it. This beautiful structure is now a national shrine in Thailand and considered sacred.

Just why or how the Buddha's footprint should be as large as this eight-cubic-foot Gulliver model is not entirely clear. It's not claimed that Sakya Muni himself ever passed in that direction, but the phenomenon has to do with some manifestation of the Lord Buddha concept. This concept is the embodiment of saintlike characteristics which enable Buddhists to pray *to* someone they think can help them.

Incidentally the term "Lord Buddha" used by nearly all followers has at least two meanings. For the lower classes it typifies a worshipful attitude, while to the more advanced Buddhist it simply denotes respect.

I think one of the customs which most differentiate Orient and Occident is the traditional attitude of obeisance and worship that occurs in so many relationships of the Easterner. Especially is this difficult for the independent spirit of the self-assured American to reconcile, and there was always a kind of inconsequential inner problem for me of whether to conform to local customs in the areas being visited or to maintain our customary American aloofness from such things.

One could always fall back on the advice of the ancient axiom that "when in Rome . . ." Since I was making a film on their religions, I certainly had plenty of justification for following suit in whatever manner of worship my guides observed when entering a holy place. Still the decision was hard to make. I was anxious to show the utmost respect for anyone's belief and ideals, if only in the cause of international good will. Too often are we tourists guilty not only of irreverence but of what almost amounts to an unforgivable sacrilege.

There were some observances which did not seem extravagant in any way and which were no problem to follow, except for making certain just exactly *what* they were in each country. For instance, in Japan, hats may be off or on, but shoes must come off. Very well; the temple floors are spotless and usually covered with very clean grass mats. Also, you carry a little pair of soft slippers with you, as I usually did, or they were even provided by the management at times. As far as I could see, nothing more was expected of the foreigner. The same in China.

In Burma not only shoes must be removed but socks too, and often anywhere within the sacred precincts. No slippers, either. This begins to be a bit troublesome. Particularly when your job takes you into nothing but holy places throughout the day. Think of the time taken out for tying and untying, etc. (setting the equipment down in the mud meanwhile). Moreover, temperatures are probably in the neighborhood of 115 degrees and there are lengthy walks to be made over thoroughly heated stone courtyards and steps. Many times Bob and I took off in mad hundred-yard dashes, while the natives must have thought we were bewitched. Nothing bothers *their* feet after those years and years of exposure.

In Siam, however, at the temple entrance upon arrival at the forefront of one of the great Buddhas, our official government guides, after removing shoes, would most often prostrate themselves five full points on the floor—toes, knees, elbows, hands, and forehead—and sometimes even stretch out full length. What does the visitor do then? I wanted to please them by showing any respect or courtesy I felt able to render, but I really did not wish to bow down before foreign gods.

It sounds ridiculous, but the problem arose frequently and we often seemed to be the recipients of reproachful glances from our hosts. Usually the solution resulted in an awkward, halfway, compromise gesture that was a mixture of standing at attention and making a little involuntary bow or nod of some kind. Very clumsy, slightly embarrassing, and never appropriate.

Throughout India one removes shoes and socks in all temples of all faiths. In some cases it is not a pleasant experience. There removal of footgear has no connection with cleanliness, but is purely an expression of respect. Temples, particularly Hindu temples, are often filthy and sloppy from various fluids with which the images have been bathed. It may be water, milk, fruit juices, coconut milk, or the like. Naturally the flies are attracted to it, and souring odors are present. On the stone floor may be scattered bits and parts of crushed flowers, candle wax, and possibly even droppings from animals. Expectoration from the chewing of various herbs, such as betel nut, is a common practice, and is not necessarily confined to a specified receptacle.

Other places of worship are cleaner. Jain temples often have armed guards to keep away those who might defile their elaborate, immaculate interiors. In many the true worshiper bathes and has a complete change of clothing in a special chamber for that purpose before entering the temple proper.

Sikh temples are clean and the marble floors well swept. Before entering each person must remove shoes and bathe his feet in a stone trough placed at the entrance.

In Moslem places of worship, called mosques, preparations for prayer are quite exacting and are as follows:

1. Shoes and socks are removed and handed to a checking attendant, who gets a small tip when they are returned. In some cases shoes may be brought inside if the customary method of carrying them, soles together, is observed. They may be put down this way as long as the bottoms do not touch the floor.

2. Shirts must have long sleeves.

3. Trousers must be full length, but still must *not* touch the ground. (I once made the mistake of trying to enter a mosque in Pakistan during the heat of summer wearing British-style, knee-length shorts and high socks. I was stopped—emphatically.)

4. During prayer the head should be covered, though some Pakistani moderns are not always observant of this.

5. Ablutions, necessary for only those who will pray, consist of squatting before a tank or running stream of fresh water and carefully washing hands, face, ears, eyes, nose, and inside of mouth, using a finger to brush teeth and gums.

A day of visiting religious institutions and shrines in any large city in India is an experience which requires alertness and care. Going from a Jain temple (shoes off but socks on), to a Catholic chapel (hat off and shoes on), to a Moslem prayer service (head covered but shoes and socks always removed) —well, one may be forgiven for forgetting sometimes.

Returning to Siam, for the conclusion of our visit and a summing up, I would like to say that in one respect it left me with the same impression I received from nearly all small countries—particularly in the Orient: they are "closed corporations." There are personal liberties to an extent and certain elements of the democratic process, but because of the high ratio of illiteracy government must necessarily be confined to the decisions of a few. These few, together with relatives and friends, form an influential ruling clique.

To be sure, in areas where overpopulation is not too great, the man with talent and persistence may rise to a higher station in life. He may also have a reasonable amount of freedom of expression, but very little margin for error.

I mean that in a small country a person cannot make a serious mistake and expect to recover. Once he falls out of favor, once he offends, once he fails, he is through. It is unlike America, a big country where you can move away and start over, where you get a second chance.

We saw the situation over and over throughout the Orient, in various government departments—private concerns, too—which were tremendously overstaffed. Man power is the East's chief and cheapest commodity, and there are usually office staffs in excess of triple the number we'd expect in America.

Men were assigned to help and conduct us about in order to facilitate our project. There would always be plenty of personnel available for this task, but none ever dared take one step without consultation with higher authority. Regardless of numerical force a department could never move faster or cover more ground than could the one or two rare, overworked, hard-to-replace chiefs of staff. These few set policy and make every decision, while the rest of the enormous pay roll waits around to carry out only the simplest orders, like an army with a general staff and nothing else but buck privates. Whenever I'd look to America for comparison, I couldn't help thinking proudly of the tremendous power of our great middle class.

There are things I'll recall with affection when I think of Thailand. We met many wonderful people, friendly, warm, eager to accept us of the West. This is by no means true of everyone else in Southeast Asia, or of the Middle East, either. In Siam the people generally seemed happier, better fed, and more carefree than anywhere else we visited. There are reasons for this, one of them being that, unlike

all neighboring states, Thailand has always remained un-
occupied by any European power. It has never lost its sov-
ereignty. It is said that this is not because occupation is
impossible, but because little Thailand sits in a unique hub
position, with Burma and India to the west and Malaya in
the south all in the hands of Great Britain, with French
Indo-China on the east, and the Dutch farther to the south
in the Indies. The great aggressive powers wisely have seen
fit to use Thailand as a buffer state. Therefore, one doesn't
find the slightly bitter, resentful attitude so commonly encountered by European and American travelers throughout
other parts of the East.

The difference is most noticeable when one enters
Burma, the adjoining country to the west, a state similar
to Siam in so many respects. Burma has the same type of
people, same color, same racial characteristics, same religion, and yet, I suppose, because of protracted British occupation, there is a limited but unmistakable atmosphere
of anti-white feeling. Particularly one sees it from the government level, now in the hands of a strongly patriotic, very
independent group of young men.

Looking over the foregoing chapters, I find one aspect
of Buddhism neglected: women. How and where do they
stand in relationship to this religion?

Twenty-five hundred years ago, during the time of the
ministry of the Buddha himself, an order of *bhikkhunis* was
founded. For centuries they lived and worked in nunneries,
as the men in monasteries, although they were always in an
inferior position to the monks. For some reason, however,
the movement declined and at present there are no women

members of the order in the Theravada, or Hinayana, countries of Siam or Burma. Yet there are quite a few women
disciples to be seen around certain unrestricted sections of
various *wats*, being instructed and guided by the senior
monks.

In Japan and China, the Mahayana countries, there are
a considerable number of women actually in the Buddhist
order. Their dress and activities are the same as the monks'
in every way. We visited and photographed one convent in
the mountains outside Taipei. This place had been founded
years ago by a motherly old lady, now in her eighties and
still actively controlling the affairs of her organization.

Like the monks—or *bonzes*—in those areas, the nuns did
not beg their food. Instead, they keep their little domain
reasonably self-sufficient by working vegetable gardens.
During our visit they all treated us cordially, seeming in no
way timid or reticent. They posed quite willingly for the
camera in demonstration of their daily routine, including
the work they performed in the fields. Their garb, as in all
China, was solid gray. Only a few seemed shy about exhibiting their shaved heads and insisted upon wearing large
straw hats. Others, however, didn't seem to mind in the
least. Some of the younger nuns, dashing about bareheaded,
were hard to distinguish from boys.

We encountered quite a few in the Hong Kong area, too,
but most of them there seemed to be elderly women.
Warmhearted and friendly, they were always willing to help
us in any way they could, usually insisting that we at least
take tea and partake of their simple cooking.

CHAPTER SIX

During the month of June the heat in parts of India amounts to volcanic intensity. When I disembarked in Calcutta and walked several hundred yards across the softened asphalt of the airport, the heat danced in waves on every side, with an effect on me like a fever delirium. The sun seems to press down like a giant hand.

There is moisture in the air in Calcutta, too, and although I am used to hot weather in our Western American desert regions, it is dry there and body moisture evaporates with a slightly cooling sensation. The humidity in Calcutta is even worse than that in Washington, D.C. I'm sorry my introduction to India had to be through the Bengal portal —it is pretty much the back entrance.

I knew India had a great deal to offer in the field of my present project. Many of the important metaphysical and doctrinal ideas which have circled the globe through countless centuries seem to have originated here. At least they are traceable on the "subcontinent" way back into the dawn of man's written history.

Much of the tour up till now I felt was a warm-up for the heart of the matter. Buddhism, with which we had spent so much time, had its beginning and first all-embracing acceptance in Northern India and I looked forward to visiting its sacred shrines.

Hinduism, with the largest number of followers, and centered uniquely in this one geographical location, would be primarily considered, but there are other religions too which can be found only here—important, fully accredited religions. Jainism is one, that of the Sikhs is another, and there are the Parsis—small in number but influential and world-renowned.

Aside from the main religions there were the numerous modern sects and offshoots of Hinduism—bewildering in its immensity—filled with overlaps, interminglings, and other confusing aspects.

Just by way of clarification let us examine the difference between religion and sect. As I understand it, a religion as a system of faith and worship is distinct from other religions when it has its own separate founder and leader or teachers, its own sacred literature, and any other features which are uniquely held. Sects may have practices and matters of liturgy and ritual widely separated from each other and yet, because of a common object of veneration and particularly a mutually esteemed literature, they will not be considered separate religions. Thus one sees examples as in Christianity, where interpretations of the identical texts have caused a completely opposite attitude in every phase of liturgy, theology, dogma, or doctrine. The person of

Christ may be thought of as a human mortal teacher or as God Himself, the worship service may be as widely divergent as a papal Mass and a meeting of Quakers, and yet both are generally considered to be in closer contact with each other than with another religion whose practice and attitude may be quite similar and actually nearer in spirit to one or the other of the two sects.

In India there are numerous liturgical similarities between the different religions, some seeming to indicate a common origin, others perhaps from common emotional responses brought about by the solidly massed ranks of overpopulation. All have borrowed or adopted many of the same ethical practices where possible, too. This wisely does much to promote harmony and tolerance. For instance, neither the Sikhs nor the Zoroastrians have scriptural injunctions against eating beef, and yet few if any of either of these groups violate a code which would be so likely to offend their Hindu neighbors.

While the influence of the doctrinal teachings of Hinduism may be felt or seen in other religions and other parts of the world, there are no practicing members of the Hindu faith without Indian blood in their veins. Hinduism has no body of ecclesiastical authority for the determination of dogma, no organization outside of modern minority sects within the faith and, like Shinto in Japan, it is non-proselytizing, non-evangelistic. Although there are certain movements devoted to the spread of portions of Hindu doctrine and no objection to the admittance of foreigners in many cult schools, or *ashrams*, there are still definite limits within which no outsider can enter. These doctrinally circumscribed limitations are determined by one incontrovertible

ALTARS OF THE EAST

factor: birth. One could not become a Hindu any more than one could become a Chinese.

It is difficult for a Westerner to grasp the idea of how this unorganized, uninstituted complexity of ritualistic custom and tradition could have so long endured and molded the thoughts and habits of a whole nation of peoples. I know it was for me. Nearly everything with which we Westerners are familiar requires constant attention and organized nurture for sheer survival. I do not know a successfully maintained practice or custom in our midst which does not have this energetic devotion. But somehow Hinduism, without legal enforcement, without edict, hierarchy or tribunal, without impassioned preachment, plan, or program —seemingly without effort—survived, expanded, and took control of the destinies of hundreds of millions of highly evolved human beings.

Of course by now Hinduism does have one powerful weapon with which to proclaim its might and preserve its domination—social ostracism. The caste system still operates. It is the device which has steadfastly upheld the banner of Hinduism and kept a whole people in a well-delineated circle. Is there a stronger influence on the lives of the majority of us than condemnation or approval of fellow man?

As a Hindu, you are born into one of the four main castes: worker, merchant, warrior, priest. There is no change, ever. There is no intermarriage without ostracism. Lack of educational facilities for the bulk of the populace almost negates opportunities to rise by means of talent to any appreciable degree, except in rarest instances.

There are sects within the Hindu ranks who have abolished caste. They have been getting stronger in recent years; many will continue to grow. Caste is not what it once was and is diminishing, but the change will be slow, with only small gains for a long time. Meanwhile the old system still operates.

Life in India is hard—very hard. There are great shortages of everything. One needs every break he can get to make a go of things, and I don't mean success as we think of it. I mean *just to live*—to eat, sleep, keep free from disease, to have a wedded life of some kind, and procreate.

There is little or no opportunity for the great percentage of the population ever to have an education, even a rudimentary one. The unofficial figures show something in the neighborhood of over 80 per cent illiteracy. Nor is there much hope for rapid improvement of this situation in the foreseeable future, though the new government is said to be making a commendable effort.

Without education a man needs friends. I've never known a place where neighborly good will was more important than in India. We here in America cannot understand what overcrowding does to man. In India not only is he "replaceable"—a common slang expression—but it's very difficult for any of the mass to view himself as other than woefully unnecessary.

There is not only another person available to fill your place in any field—there are thousands. Skills are few. For a working-class Hindu to pull up stakes and hope to get a job in some other section of the land would be a ten-thousand-to-one gamble—not to speak of the lack of social acceptance he would find. Your trade and opportunities stay within a small family circle and if you want to survive you stick with the crowd. You respect the traditions of the crowd, you obey its customs. There are no caste certificates or identification cards to show the social position of a Hindu, but if he did roam to another section of the land, there would be no way of moving himself up a bracket on the scale and getting away with it, let alone getting a job.

Even within the four main caste groups is a vast multiplicity of lesser gradations (said to number between two and three thousand!), each of which is almost insurmountable socially without disapproval and ostracism. Birth alone decides the position each man will hold in life and, although it would be unfair to infer that the caste system was *originated* by religion, the Hindu religion teaches that by the just laws of Karma each will receive in birth the station earned by actions in previous lives. It is a system with all the answers.

The first encounter with Hinduism occurs on the ordinary bus route from Dum Dum Airport into the city of Calcutta, where, for most Occidentals, the continuous sight of unattended cattle has the look of unreality.

Cows are on every sidewalk, on the crosswalks, going with the signals, going against the signals, chewing the cud or sleeping on the very doorstep of leading hotels and places of business. Everyone knows, of course, that the cow is sacred to the Hindu, but just how these creatures are treated as objects of veneration is not generally understood. I learned that the original cause for this phenomenon might be traced to the economic importance of the animal in Indian life. The cow works for man, in India being truly a beast of burden. It also supplies him with much-needed dairy products. Even the dung is a carefully preserved by-product used as fuel. The cow is the Hindu's mainstay of existence, his most valuable asset. Seeing this impoverished country, one clearly discerns how such an unusual doctrine may have evolved.

As to treatment of the animal, I never saw an instance of cruelty, or any singular act of worship, although I know of certain annual and other occasionally practiced rites. But primarily veneration is manifest in the amount of freedom given the animal, who, although a thoroughly harmless creature, certainly makes no small contribution to a general atmosphere of civic dishevelment.

The Hindu does not kill his cows by direct means, but when an animal outgrows utility or productiveness, it is often refused food and turned loose to wander until overtaken by death. It is not uncommon to see aged specimens staggering about like gaunt skeletons, ready to topple at the slightest misstep.

The first day in Calcutta we visited the Kali Temple. It was a jolting experience. Kali is worshiped by the Hindus in one form as Shakti, the Universal Mother, and in another mood as a goddess of destruction and power, also as the destroyer of evil. The Calcutta temple in her honor is probably her most important shrine. It is similar in many respects to most Hindu temples, which usually consist of a group of structures surrounded by high walls and a gatehouse. Inside will be a courtyard and various small individual shrine rooms for the images. Before entering the sacred enclosure one must of course remove his shoes—if he is permitted to go in at all. Few Hindu temples allow any but their own followers this privilege and often there are large multiple-language signs displayed proclaiming the prohibition.

The Kali Temple is on a noisy, cart-clogged street. An especially holy shrine, it is constantly visited by many pilgrims. Brahmin priests, clothed only from the waist down and wearing the sacred shoulder string, stand at the entrances offering their services as guides to tourist and stranger. A large, burly fellow took charge of our party, escorting us boldly about the premises and bluntly silencing protests from worshipers who outspokenly resented our presence. Hinduism has many levels of worship for various stages of spiritual development and understanding. I would not say that Kali Temple is representative of the highest.

Around the entrance and within the courtyard are vendors of flowers and special fruits to be used as offerings. At one side is a sacred tree, heavily festooned with thousands of cheap trinkets, gift offerings from petitioners of sundry requests. Farther along is the goat merchant with his selection of sleek black bleaters, varying in size to fit the pilgrim's purse. After the purchase is made, the animal is escorted to a blood-spattered chopping block where, to the accompaniment of heavy drum beatings and priestly blessings, well-practiced slaughterers make the kill by severing the neck with one clean cleaver cut. The sacrificer then carries the body away to be used as he sees fit, while the head remains in custody of the temple—for what final disposition I never learned.

In the little shrine rooms are different images. Some will be waterworn stones of odd shape, taken from sacred streams, usually painted bright red. Often they are decorated with two imitation eyeballs, which gives them an appearance somewhat like the body of a squid, or a broiled lobster.

Most Hindu images, unlike the giant Buddhas, are small in size. The Goddess Kali, often carved as an idol about twenty inches high, is characteristically shown as a nude, four-armed creature, holding in her hands a sword and the severed head of one of the demons, and standing on the prostrate body of her husband, the God Siva. She wears a garland of skulls, while hands of the demons she has killed, strung together, form her skirt. Her mouth is open, showing teeth bared and an oversized tongue hanging down. Such features are designed to typify her terrifying aspect and without doubt she is a frightening spectacle. It is not difficult to understand how those convinced of Kali's reality would be willing to make many sacrifices and offerings to incur her protection. It is also a little disconcerting to see them prostrating themselves before this ghastly horror.

Worshipers enter the temple rooms, hand their garlands and a coin to the priest in charge, who offers them in turn before the image. For most pilgrims there will be only a short period of bowing and petitioning prayers and the mission will be concluded, though certain types of cult devotees—such as the Shakti—will have more elaborate rites. All images go through a daily schedule of ritual at the hands of the Brahmin. This consists of regular food offerings, bathing with water and other liquids, change of decoration and garlanding. There are routine periods during the day while the image receives worship or "rests." Some of these ceremonies are very emotional and dramatic, accompanied by a frenzied beating of drums and clanging of bells.

Because it is customary to make charitable offerings at time of pilgrimage, most holy places will be well stocked with a contingent of beggars and cripples. These groups plus the vendors of souvenirs and talismans beleaguer the poor Hindu pilgrim from start to finish.

Outside the temple ground is another building, its bare floor used as sleeping and living quarters for pilgrims who have journeyed long distances. It was at this point on the tour that we were abruptly accosted by our Brahmin guide for a fee. Just in passing I make note of the fact that his insistent demands exceeded those of any previous experience. Gratification would amply have secured center orchestra at any Broadway opening night.

During this first visit I had done no photography and we returned a few days later to do so. It was a difficult undertaking, however, and not too fruitful, with resentment by devotees rising to fever pitch at times. We got what we could, which was mostly atmosphere—a lot of commotion with pilgrims being pursued by hangers-on, and so forth—and made no attempt to capture the rites. These would have to be done where circumstances were less charged with tension.

Near the temple on the banks of a small tributary of the Hooghly River is one of the smaller places of Hindu cremation—a so-called burning ghat—where, after a short ceremony during which the bodies are immersed three times in the sacred river, they are placed upon some stacked cuts of rough logs, covered with more branches and, after another short ceremony, ignited. There were no prohibitions against any kind of visitor activity; perhaps because of the cholera epidemic then in progress all officials were too busy to pay attention to anything else. For various reasons it is customary to dispose of the deceased as quickly as possible after death, often within a matter of a few hours. One of the metaphysical reasons for the custom is that it is considered by many that the soul may remain earth-bound until final dissolution of the corpse.

After cremation the ashes are cast into the river. There is seldom any further commemoration or memorializing, as is appropriate to a people whose belief in transmigration and reincarnation of the soul is so deeply ingrained.

During the first week in Calcutta we made efforts to see members of other religions as well as the Hindus, setting up appointments and interviews. Because of newspaper stories of our arrival many religious groups made unsolicited calls on us, too.

In Calcutta came our first encounter with the Parsis. They form about one half of the surviving followers of the ancient Zoroastrian religion. This faith, named for its founder—Zoroaster (sometimes known as Zarathustra) — flourished centuries ago in Persia and other states of the Near and Middle East. The date of Zoroaster's lifetime is a matter of unsettled speculation, usually placed somewhere in the sixth century B.C.

A Zoroastrian friend in the priesthood sets forth an argument which places this date back anywhere from 1500 to 4500 more years. I realize I am not qualified to refute this, but somewhere between 2000 and 5000 B.C. is a very long time ago in the history of man's theological progress, and even a cursory examination of Zoroaster's writing shows spiritual concepts so immeasurably advanced over anything contemporaneous with those remote times as to seem unlikely of attainment even for so monumentally eminent a genius. While I could not think of casting doubt on the good priest's sincerity or the thoroughness of his scholarship, I cannot help noting in passing that often followers of different teachings try to push back historical dates of the origin of their faiths. Perhaps almost subconsciously they feel that age adds weight and substantiation to their particular belief. With many I guess it does.

Anyway we know that Zoroastrianism was a powerful religion in the early centuries before the Christian era. It is even thought that certain advanced ideas found in Judaism were picked up from the Zoroastrians during the Babylonian captivity. Surely much of Zoroaster's thinking, or revelations, was far ahead of most other concepts in his time and place.

From his sacred writings, known as the Zend-Avesta, we find his religion was a kind of dualism. That is, he conceived of two principles or powers in the universe. The good one —personalized as Ahura-Mazda—is arrayed in constant warfare with the forces of evil, headed by a spirit named Angra Mainyu. Man exists midway between these two and can assist in the struggle by virtue of his personal conduct.

Finally Zoroaster taught that at the end of time a saviour would come, the dead would arise, the wicked be punished, hell purified, and the world made good forever. Modern Zoroastrianism places most emphasis upon the single principle of one good God.

Historical details of the religion are vague, but the facts are that from a powerful state institution it gradually lost influence until, in the seventh century after Christ, Islam overwhelmed Persia and Zoroastrianism. There are somewhere around one hundred thousand followers of the faith in Iran today. An equal number, known as the Parsis, are living descendants of Persian Zoroastrians who fled to India from Moslem fanaticism over a thousand years ago. The name Parsi means Persian.

Most of the Parsis live in the Bombay area where they could be considered a very successful group of businessmen, with an influence far in excess of their fractional total of India's vast population. About fifteen hundred Parsis make their homes in Calcutta and leaders of this group did their best to show and inform us of every permissible phase of their religion.

In the main, although there is considerable liturgy, Zoroastrian teachings are clear-cut and simple, containing moral and ethical obligations commensurate with highest modern ideals. These are summed up for convenient reference by the oft-repeated phrase of the faithful: "Right thoughts—right words—right deeds."

Priesthood is hereditary though not obligatory, and ritual plays an important part in Zoroastrianism as practiced by the Parsis. Much of this is centered around a worship of the physical elements: earth, air, water, the sun, and especially fire—a flame being the most commonly seen symbol of the religion. Houses of worship are called fire temples, and these places, inaccessible to any but Parsis, enshrine a flame which never finds extinction. Some of these sacred conflagrations have burned continuously for centuries.

I found it most interesting to learn that any newly created fire for ritual and sacramental purposes in the temple would require the joining of flames which had originated in over sixteen different sources, each of which must be purified and consecrated in many ceremonies. A few of the sources include (1) fire used in burning a corpse; (2) fire produced by lightning; (3) fire from the house of a king; (4) fire from the house of a goldsmith; (5) a soldier; (6) a brewer; (7) an ascetic, and so on. Combined ceremonies may easily extend well over a year before the flame is considered to have been completely sanctified.

With all the attention devoted to such scrupulous liturgical details there is no doubt that the physical blaze is but the outer symbol of the life force invisibly energizing the universe—the divine spark within each human being—a spark of the Great Fire, who is God Himself.

In Calcutta we had the privilege of photographing a *navjot* ceremony, performed for taking a child into the Zoroastrian religion. On this occasion a piece of woolen string is wound three times around the waist of a little boy not less than seven years of age. Henceforward, through life, the child and man will never be without this symbolically knotted thread—thrice wound and thrice knotted in remembrance of "Right thoughts—right words—right deeds."

Weeks later in Bombay we made Parsi contacts enabling us to photograph a real fire ceremony, a wedding, a thanksgiving ritual, and a truly inspiring prayer service held at the seaside, where the worshipers stretched out in a single line facing the sun over the ocean's horizon.

Though I wouldn't have expected it, there was something clean and ennobling about this reverence for the physical elements, especially when evidenced in the appropriate sphere, the out-of-doors. Such ceremonies as we saw, away from the gloomy mystery of cobwebbed interiors, and incorporating equality of sexes in every respect, had a wholesome, poetic beauty which radiated the highest aspirations of man. Mostly merchants by profession, the Parsis are a

clean, well-educated, progressive people, possessing quali-
ties which speak volumes for the underlying nobility of
Zoroastrian philosophy.

Their public-spirited generosity is commonly acknowledged in India and much of the rapid development of modern Bombay owes itself to Parsi energy and charity. They
claim that there is no poverty or destitution among their
own ranks.

Analysis of Parsi prosperity reaffirms the power potential
of a clannish minority. These nepotic rights have been
shrewdly protected by traditional exclusiveness. Although
anyone can study the works of Zoroaster or consider himself
a Zoroastrian, no one can join or become a Parsi except by
birth. Minor exceptions are found upon occasion of the
marriage of a Parsi with a woman of another faith who then
can partake of limited privileges. If a Parsi woman marries
an outsider, their offspring cannot be admitted to the
faith.

Twelve-odd centuries in India must have seen a good
deal of intermarriage on the part of male Parsis, for though
some people speak of recognizing a typical Parsi by distinguishing features, my poor dim Western eyes were never
keen enough to discern the fine distinction. In the main
they appeared very much like all other Indians to me.

Historically this non-proselytizing policy can be traced
to an agreement with early Indian rulers who were mag-
nanimous enough to grant sanctuary to the fleeing Parsis.
Still there would seem to be little doubt that they have
ardently and persistently maintained the exclusive features
characterizing their faith for the economic advantages
which accrue to any tightly knit minority rendering mutual

assistance in the midst of a loosely woven, unorganized majority. Evident advantages of this group unity are also seen in other parts of the world, including the United States, by the example of several economically successful minority religions and religious sects, although I know of none who is quite such an absolutely "closed corporation" as is that of the Parsis.

Beyond this singularity Parsi citizenship is impeccable. If they have none of the scriptural prohibitions regarding food or beverages so widely in practice among Orientals, they still conform in large measure to customs of the surrounding majority, thereby reducing friction to a minimum. Most are voluntarily vegetarian, few drink alcoholic beverages, and only a fractional percentage smoke tobacco. This last is caused in the main, however, by reverence for the sanctity of all fire. No emphasis is ever placed on ascetic practice and there are no monastic orders. Outside of a typical small, round hat—considered to be exclusively Parsi and often worn with street attire—there are no other visibly distinguishing features in their dress.

Perhaps the unique feature of Parsi religious rites is the traditional custom of exposing bodies of their deceased to be consumed by birds of prey in the well-known towers of silence. These flat-topped, circular structures about twenty-five feet high are found adjacent to most Parsi communities. In Bombay they occupy many acres atop a promontory in one of the city's most exclusive sections. Visitors are not permitted.

We were escorted and graciously allowed to photograph the towers in Calcutta, though there were no funeral services held during our visit. Here, amid a well-groomed park area, are two of the towers, surrounded by a high concrete wall. They are invisible from outside the park.

Details of the funeral service include one step in the ritual where a dog is held aloft and made to look upon the face of the corpse, presumably in line with an ancient belief that dogs, or certain dogs, have the mystic ability to discern true death. Dogs used for this purpose must have very distinctive markings, especially around the eyes.

Another distinguishing custom is manifested in the extraordinary precautions taken to prevent contamination while handling the corpse. Today many of these ceremonial demands are explained as being in practice for prevention of the spread of contagious disease. Gloves and special clothing must be worn while the body is washed—the corpse must be placed only on stone or metal—cow's urine (used in many purificatory rites and considered to be disinfectant) must be sprinkled wherever the corpse has lain or been carried. All utensils and articles of furniture made of wood, clay, or porcelain, being porous, are condemned as contaminated if they have made any contact with the body and must be disposed of. Clothing worn by the deceased and the pallbearers is burned after the funeral. No matter how distant may be the home of a deceased person, his body is always carried on foot to the tower on an iron bier.

While many such measures actually fall in with modern antiseptic methods, scriptural texts refer to the dangers as *nasu* or *druj* (evil influence), which likely indicate a fear of contamination that is manifestly spiritual more than physical. In addition, the generous usage of cow's urine, which in all probability actually has some septicidal ingredients and may thus be indicative of an ancient intuitive wisdom, could certainly be surpassed in all technical respects by the adoption of any modern germicide, if prevention of contagion were the only objective. But man has a deep affection for his venerable old traditions and few Parsi fire temples are without the back-yard enclosure which houses its sanctified member of the bovine species. Customarily this will be a spotlessly white bull.

Upon completion of the funeral ceremony the corpse is undraped and placed upon an iron grill atop the Tower of Silence. The savage birds of prey can dispose of the edible remains within a few hours—from a practical standpoint much more rapidly than any process of decomposition contingent on interment. Also, according to Zoroastrianism, this procedure prevents contamination of the sacred terrestrial elements, fire, earth or water.

The skeletal remains are assembled and cast down a central well in the tower—there left to molder and crumble into dust—symbolically linking high and low, rich and poor.

While I do not think that many parts of the present ritual would be acceptable in the West, there is no doubt that much of Zoroastrian theology, metaphysics, and philosophy is broad, noble and beautiful. It would well stand scrutiny alongside any other contemporary religious concepts.

There is a Zoroastrian high priest at present preparing a lecture tour of the United States. I believe it will be America's introduction to firsthand authoritative instruction. There will be a great deal in Zoroaster's teaching which can provide uplift and inspiration to many Americans.

Returning again to Hinduism, before leaving the States

I had been in touch with a branch of the Vedanta Society from whom I received letters of introduction to leaders in India. This organization is known there as the Ramakrishna Mission and is a reform movement within the Hindu religion. Main headquarters, including offices of the present, are located a few miles out of Calcutta on the banks of the Hooghly River at a site called Belur Math. Here a fine temple has been erected in honor of the founder, Sri Ramakrishna.

Within the last century, in opposition to the doctrine-graced privileges of caste and birth, several movements have sprung up in India with their own interpretations of Hinduism. Some, like the Ramakrishna Mission and Arya Samaj, have a commendably active program for welfare projects such as hospitals and orphanages.

It can be hardly said, however, that social efforts were the original purpose of these reform groups; rather, through reinterpretation and re-evaluation of Hindu scripture and its system of worship, attempts have been made to get down through these vast complexities to a more simplified analysis of basic fundamentals. This is similar in some respects to the efforts of certain Christian reforms in their "back to the Bible" movements. The Arya Samaj group, for instance, has turned back solely to the ancient Vedas for teaching and inspiration. It takes great pride in listing the number of Christian converts it has rewon to Hinduism— or the Arya Samaj branch of Hinduism.

There are six great philosophical systems in Brahmanism; one of the most generally accepted is the Vedanta. It is an interpretation of the Upanishads which implies that the soul of each human being is identical with the Brahman (the all-one) and, furthermore, that nothing except this all-oneness has any reality.

Man, however, in this earthly state is ignorant of his oneness with spiritual reality and can awaken his consciousness of truth only by searching into the depths of his inner self. When this has been accomplished and the knowledge attained, the soul's identity with the all-one will be seen and understood, as will the fact that everything which is not soul is illusion.

This theory was evolved in the eighth century by a Hindu scholar named Sankara, and if I have made any part of it understandable, it should be readily seen to be similar to the underlying theme of many of our Western metaphysical and mind-power movements.

In America and other parts of the world the Vedanta Society expends much of its effort in guiding students on the path to "self-realization." This includes training in moral discipline as well as philosophical enlightenment. Branches of the society are under the supervision of masters, or swamis, educated in mother institutions of the Ramakrishna Mission in India.

Proof that each phase in the many aspects of Hinduism is capable of varying degrees of understanding becomes apparent in the fact that Sri Ramakrishna—an uneducated but evidently a profoundly enlightened sage in the nineteenth century—allegedly received his illumination by intuitive means through intense contemplation of the Goddess Kali. His was the inspiration which gave impetus to the efforts of his brilliant disciple, Vivikananda, whose genius brought about organization of the mission and started it as a world movement. He also designed and drew up plans for the present elegant temple at Belur Math, which houses the marble image of Sri Ramakrishna seated in meditative pose. It was interesting to learn that this $800,000 edifice was built mainly by American donations.

I don't believe I have ever met a person who radiated a gentler disposition and kindlier personality than the organization's president, Swami Shankarananda. We had two delightful chats, the second of which was a filmed interview, on the temple grounds against a typical Indian background of slowly-grazing cattle. The swami was in no way reluctant to speak on any aspect of his philosophy or—in line with my particular interest—the relationship between Vedanta teachings and present world problems. It could hardly be said, however, that we were able to arrive at any singular component of Vedanta which might make a significant contribution to ecumenical questions of a collective nature, beyond the well-established ethical advice intrinsic to the teachings of all great religions, though these age-old gems of advice did have a more than ordinary quality of tolerance as a setting.

For instance, when I asked of the central teaching of the Ramakrishna Society, the good swami replied—and I quote from my tape recording: "The central teaching is the divinity of man and the *universality of religion*. The universality of religion means that each and every religion is true! God is but One. Men worship Him under different names and different rituals but He is the same God and He is manifested the same in all things. Christians know that God is all in all so, in one respect, being part of this Oneness makes every human being divine."

To a question regarding world peace he answered: "Real

peace can only come through renunciation and service. What we have in excess we should give to others who are in need. Without rendering service for the comfort and prosperity of others, peace cannot be established. When we come to believe in the divinity of each man we will forget our other enmity."

His concluding remarks were in reference to our obligation to fulfill Biblical precepts, "doing unto others" and "loving thy neighbor" being the unavoidable requisites for any earthly life of international harmony. More than this was not forthcoming—or likely to be—from a religious savant, I was beginning to surmise. After all, the primary concern of most religion is for the individual, stressing the value of the human soul. Particularly is this true in oriental attitudes, in which so much of life's hardship is looked upon as a cross to be patiently borne by earthly pilgrims advancing toward spiritual perfection and bliss through self-discipline, introspective analysis, and growth of spiritual perception.

I was curious to see the place where Sri Ramakrishna worked out his intuitive enlightenment, a development which presumably took place at another Kali Temple across the river from Belur Math, and about a mile downstream.

This temple does not have the importance as a center of pilgrimage that is held by the Kali Temple in the city of Calcutta. The result is a less-crowded, cleaner atmosphere with far more serenity. It's spacious, too, with a huge inner courtyard of well-swept flagstones, creating a sense of perspective which lends a surrealistic quality to the tiny figures wandering over its distant surfaces. Outside, by the bank of the silently flowing Hooghly, is the enormous banyan tree under which Ramakrishna, in the manner of Buddha before him, sat for many persistent years in determination to break through the veil separating man's mind from cosmic consciousness.

From what I can gather the central object of his concentration was the universality of the Goddess Kali's aspect of motherhood. I was told that, seated cross-legged, he could be heard at all hours as he cried aloud with emotion-packed pleas of "Mother, are you real . . . ? Mother, are you there . . . ? Are you real?"

It must be that the goddess finally yielded. Knowing the story of Ramakrishna, I sought out the enshrined image of Kali to see if she were perhaps depicted at this temple in a warmer, more conciliatory attitude. But no, she struck the same demonic pose, arrayed in skulls, standing astride the prostrate figure of her husband, Siva, teeth bared, tongue out. Such opposing moods are difficult for me to reconcile. That one frightful aspect of Kali I find hard to associate with contemplations of truth and beauty.

Yet whatever may be our conclusions or surmises, one cannot overlook the fact that the nobility of Sri Ramakrishna's character was so outstanding, his simple wisdom evidently so profound as to provoke the admiration and provide the inspiration for disciples the seldom-equaled brilliance of whom can in no way be denied. Beyond this contribution—the irrefutably valid contribution of encouragement toward consecrated effort—it is difficult to put one's figure on concrete endowments by Ramakrishna himself to the missionary program named in his honor, eleven years after his death.

Sri Ramakrishna had no particular respect for Western methods, Western culture, or any source of information beyond the "intuitive," yet the aims and ideals of the mission are undeniably Western in character. In 1951 centers in India and Ceylon totaled twelve hospitals, fifty-six outdoor dispensaries, eighty-two grade schools, night schools, clinics for laboring classes, educative tours into backward areas with lantern slides and recording, famine relief, earthquake relief, and many other activities social in nature.

It was Swami Vivikananda's aim to found an institution where young men would be provided the means of attaining liberation and of preparing themselves for service to humanity. He also insisted that admittance to the fellowship be unlimited by such externals as caste or color. In class-conscious India this was a daring move and Vivikananda had to fight for his ideals. It is a wonderful idea and it has worked out well.

I don't say that this movement borrowed in any way from Christian teaching with respect to man's responsibilities to his fellow. Such admonitions are amply recorded in their own texts, the Hindu scriptures. But if it is claimed that the basis for this particular welfare notion was born by intuitive means, then it only corroborates the rightness of idealistic goals in the West where down-to-earth efforts toward social uplift have long been far more prevalent than in the Orient. It is also true that Christian missionaries in the Orient were providing an eminent example of social consciousness centuries ago. I rather suppose it possible that these activities helped provide the impetus for self-examination and reform that characterizes the new-found movements in India.

Regardless of origins, surely the endeavors and aspirations of the Ramakrishna Society are right and true. If Christian missionaries provoked a sense of social consciousness in the heart of the Hindu, let these Christians now beware lest they be far surpassed in sincerity and consecration by those who are presently bringing into full expression an idea of which the Christian examples showed only a fractional part. In such matters yesterdays can be forgotten; it is the nows and tomorrows that count.

CHAPTER SEVEN

Other religious movements have long been working to overcome the prejudices of caste and color in India. Among these are the Jains. They have striven toward these ends since their beginnings more than twenty-five hundred years ago. It is strange how many great religious leaders came along about that same time.

First, Zoroaster in the sixth century B.C., and shortly thereafter Lao-tzu and Confucius in China; Gautama Buddha was also coexistent. And in the same land, working against the same priestly powers of Brahmanism, lived another contemporary genius, the sanctified teacher of the Jain doctrine, Mahavira.

The name Mahavira in Sanskrit means Great Hero, and Jain requirements for such a title are most exacting. It is their belief that only omniscient beings are able to outline the right code of rules for life. Such all-knowing individuals are not creators or rulers in the universe—not gods in other worlds—but human beings dwelling among their brothers and sisters. On leaving this life they never again have an embodied existence.

Qualifications for a Jain teacher—considered the ideal human being—are that he has overcome anger, pride, fear, and greed completely, that sex passion be extinct as well as any kind of physical or moral weakness. Further than this he will never need sleep, for sleep is judged to be a condition which obscures knowledge, consequently unbefitting to someone in a state of omniscience. Those who have qualified in the past are called Tirthankaras. There have been twenty-four of these in all. Mahavira, five hundred years before Christ, was the last.

Today rules of moral conduct even for the followers of Jainism are hardly less severe than Tirthankara qualifications, since the whole essence of the teaching makes it purely a religion of worldly renunciation and asceticism. Some have felt the Jain religion to represent a halfway point, theologically, between Hinduism and Buddhism. This may be.

Buddha and Mahavira were contemporary. They may very well have known each other. Both fought against the stifling restrictions of birth and caste, both accepted the Hindu doctrine of Karma, but where Buddhism tends away from asceticism and other moral extremes—seeking what is called the Middle Way—Mahavira's Jainism goes all-out on the theme of self-abnegation.

Within the first few days in Calcutta we were taken to visit an elaborately ornamented temple belonging to the Jains. Flower gardens, fountains, marble pools, and many pieces of sculpture surrounded a structure carved and inlaid with meticulous craftsmanship. Over-all cleanliness was in startling contrast to that of many Hindu temples we had seen so far. I became very curious to meet the sponsors, and it was conveniently arranged. I don't remember a more sincerely cordial, eager-to-please group of people more consecrated to their cause than the Jains.

According to rough statistics—and all statistics are exceedingly rough in India—there are somewhere between one and a half and two million followers of Jainism, all of whom are on the subcontinent. As in Buddhism, this membership is divided into two parts: the monks and nuns—known as *sadhus* and *sadwis*—and the lay followers; the latter can accept but cannot adopt the stringent self-denials, and I quote the pamphleted statement of an organizational secretary: ". . . on account of an inherent weakness caused by family ties or attachment with the world."

Unlike the Hindu concept of Maya, which insists that material substance is but an illusion, Jain cosmology teaches that the world is neither illusory nor a creation of imagination, but a fact existing in reality. Similarly to the Hindu idea of reincarnation and Karma, Jainism alleges that man is a slave to the lure of the senses and thus undergoes ever-recurring births in either human or non-human existences, according to the deserved reward of his actions. It is the aim of this religion to teach the process of freeing the soul from its bondage to materiality by a method of purification.

The first step toward this goal is a knowledge of eighteen types of sins, the first five of which are most vigilantly to be avoided, namely: (1) killing, hurting, or causing injury to any living being; (2) telling a falsehood; (3) taking that which is not given; (4) indulging in sexual intercourse; and (5) possessing property. The rest of the eighteen are mainly undesirable personal characteristics, such as anger, pride, etc.

Failure to overcome these ugly traits results in the continued attachment of their gross materialism to the human soul, adding a weight of impurity thereby and keeping the soul earth-bound.

Organization of the Jains at present consists of two large sects, with several minor divisions in each. Monks, of course, are most representative of the faith in both groups since the difficulty of reconciling the moral code with normal secular living is plainly evident, and some of those I saw went about as far toward world renunciation as I guess it's possible to go.

The first-named prohibition against killing or causing injury to anything is positively carried to maximum lengths. Not only are the Jains vegetarian to the fullest degree, abstaining from all flesh, fish, fowl, and eggs, but many vegetables themselves are taboo; root types and greens are avoided because the Jains believe there is too much life in these portions, as well as the insect or germ life surrounding them.

Tobacco and all wines or other intoxicants are forbidden completely, as well as the eating of honey and the wearing of silk, wool, or any other cloth, the making of which may entail some form of violence to living creatures. Water must be strained before drinking to prevent insects from being swallowed. Most monks will drink nothing but boiled water, though they will not do the boiling. It must be done by a lay person and then freely given to the sadhu.

Monks and nuns of the Terapanthi sect possess nothing and have no permanent homes. They wander about the country in groups headed by a master, staying a few days at a time in the homes of wealthy laymen. None sleeps longer than three hours in a night. They do not wear shoes in any season. The use of leather is taboo. They will not use a razor or scissors but will pluck the beard when necessary. Metal is never used. Quills serve as pens for writing. Spectacles are not worn.

Correspondence cannot be carried on because there must not be any contact with postal or telegraph services. Most of these prohibitions are to establish complete independence from society and the conveniences of civilization. Does it sound as though these people are antisocial? I'm afraid certain citizen groups interested in co-operative welfare projects might think so.

I wonder how some of our local civic-service clubs would look upon a colony of Jains? Poor citizens? Selfish? Yet they make no demands upon government facilities. They obey all laws which do not interfere with their religious vows. But no monastic Jain will ask police protection, nor will he testify in court for any cause.

As for self-defense, there is none, for physical resistance might lead to violence and harm to another. This is forever unwarrantable. Nor could any protection be offered to another—no matter how helpless or innocent—like protecting the virtue of a sister nun, for instance. Not only could no monk protect her from ravishment and bloodshed, but even she may not defend herself. Suicide is sinful, but there is mention of an instance—prescribed by Mahavira himself —in which the victim may strangle herself rather than submit. Some nuns carry strings for this purpose. (Before visiting the Jains I thought I knew something about "non-violence." By comparison I had only heard of the word.)

In the hottest weather they will not use fans because of alleged injury to life in the air. Stiff cloth masks are worn over the mouth *at all times* in order to forestall the inhalation of insects and to prevent vocal vibrations and gusts of expelled breath from harming these "living beings having air as a body."

A member of a Jain monastic order walks with eyes downcast, vigilant to avoid injury to any visible creature through carelessness. Furthermore a utensil similar to a wooden-handled household feather duster is always carried for the purpose of thoroughly sweeping any area before sitting or lying down. This procedure has nothing to do with cleanliness, but is done to decrease the possibility of smashing insects. Even the handle has a knob of string on the end so that when laid upon the ground, the shaft will make minimum surface contact, lessening possibilities of harm.

Among Jains of the Digamber sect less clothing is worn as age and saintly perfection increase, until the final Acharya stages—next in rank to Tirthankara—where no body covering is worn, ever. This drastic step in emulation of Lord Mahavira, who himself went nude, demonstrates maximum independence from material comfort, besides eliminating the peril of crushing vermin in the folds of the cloth.

Thus the whole concern of the Jain is in staying eternally alert to prevent a sinful transgression—an attitude which by most standards surely would be considered fairly negative existence. The doctrine of ahimsa is the keynote, one of the scriptures actually stating that "non-injury is religion." Like Buddhism, it is a metaphysical doctrine and a way of life which must be followed and adhered to by individual efforts alone. There is no God or gods to whom appeals for assistance and approval may be directed. It must be conceded that lay followers usually enshrine images of the twenty-four Tirthankaras in their temples and, without doubt, bow down and worship before them, seeking help as do those of any other faith. Yet for the sadhu there is only the law, no court of appeal, no dispensation, no gift of divine grace.

Members of the laity as yet unable to give up home, family, and property carry out the moral commands as much as possible. Because of the ahimsa doctrine no Jain will engage in commercial activity which in any way borders the usage of animal products. This eliminates most food and leather-goods stores, manufacture of cloth products, cutting of trees and plants, making carts, clearing jungles by the use of fire, drying up swamps and streams, brewing (which destroys a type of low-level life), making of any metals which will be formed for destructive purposes, etc., but it still leaves enough room for the Jains to find many lucrative sources of revenue. In the main they are a wealthy, influential people, much of whose income is spent on brotherly assistance and the construction of temples which are unsparing in precious materials and costly workmanship.

In all India few temples surpass the quality of those of the Jains, and particularly are they noted for the artistic excellence of their sculpture, though I had a wearisome experience trying to track down one famous example.

This was the gigantic, monolithic figure at Sravana Belgola, in the Hassan district of the state of Mysore. I had read of and seen photographs of this colossus for many years, but I didn't think I'd have the satisfaction of seeing it on the present trip. But I took a side trip to the south and while in Mysore—which I considered the loveliest part of India—I recalled that the Jain colossus was somewhere in the district. Upon making inquiries I found it to be a distance of some ninety-five miles to the northwest of Mysore City. Routes of transportation were most devious. It was out of season, and the usual bus services were curtailed, while access by rail meant several transfers, an all-day journey. Therefore, no means of arriving, visiting the monument, and returning to Mysore in one day were available, except via one of the few local decrepit taxicabs, vintage uncertain.

With a scheduled flight from Bangalore to Hyderabad just twenty-four hours away, I abruptly decided to chance a taxi trip from Mysore to the colossus and back in time to get the night train to Bangalore. I had met a driver with a dubious-looking piece of 1930 equipment who claimed knowledge of a short cut and full confidence of accomplishing the assignment, though it might be a little rough in spots, he admitted.

I had a quite detailed map of the territory and I kept trying to find some resemblance to our route, but after the third creek bed and second detour through farmers' back yards, I gave up and figured I'd have to wait for night and take a reading from the stars. One thing about India, you are never out of sight of man. At times like this it was a comfort, except, of course, that we had not one mutual word in common. The taxi driver would be my only oral contact and this was limited to a very few words.

One thing I must repeat is that of all India this territory for me was the most delightful. Perhaps not so grand and

143

rugged as Kashmir, but soft and rolling—and how very green. A lush, prosperous green, so different from the aridity of the north with its drought-stricken, famished inhabitants. An altitude of several thousand feet makes the climate of this plateau area more livable, too.

I had no idea of the surroundings in which the Sravana Belgola statue was located and when, after nearly five hours of driving, we finally burst through the foliage of this buxom countryside into the little village which bears the name, I could see a huge, smooth-stoned prominence rising sharply in the background. Suspicion quickly arose; there were signs of human construction way up there on top. "No, not again," I prayed, but in vain. It soon became obvious that if I wished to visit the image of Gommatesvara—the famous Jain colossus—I would have to climb five hundred feet up a flight of steps hewn out of solid rock, and without shoes or socks. As usual these would have to be left at the bottom of the hill.

Aside from the sting of the hot rock on the soles of my feet it was a thrilling climb with an unobstructed view on all sides of the smooth, dome-shaped mound. The surrounding landscape was magnificent.

Just below lay the village with several lovely temples and a sacred bathing tank that is known for its perfection of design and ornament. Far away I could see men and animals working in the fields. A breeze sprang up and it became cooler now as we rose above the plain. The clouds had thickened considerably and grown darker, too.

As we plodded along, I thought about the Jains. Many of them died on this sacred mountain, by the thousands, I'm told. They starved to death—voluntarily. Although suicide is not considered permissible, fasting is a virtue upon which no small emphasis is placed. All Jain saints have embarked on long periodic stretches during which they have taken neither solid nor liquid nourishment. All monks do the same today. It's a highly commended practice without defined limits. Presumably the longer the fast the greater the victory over flesh and the comforts of materialism. If, too, the fast should abruptly end in death—well, who can say that the intent was other than further prolongation of a prescribed practice? And thus we have a religion which condones death by self-starvation.

True it is that many Jain injunctions work toward the production of a highly moral character. Few followers are ever involved in criminal actions. One portion of their doctrine, emphasizing the individuality of each soul, is quite unlike the spirit of the East as a whole—closer to that of the West. Their attitude is tender toward fellow man and fellow creature. They have, in fact, organized several hospitals for the care of sick animals, an undertaking which, though seemingly unrealistic in India with its disease-ridden human population, still has an exemplary value under circumstances where animal cruelty is shockingly commonplace. After watching the treatment of beasts of burden by so many of their Indian drivers we solemnly averred that life's most miserable assignment must surely consist of being a horse in the land where only cows are kings.

But this is not a major fault. Rather it is the probable result of a beleaguered citizenry letting off the steam of frustration. In America such have-nots often fall into the violently antisocial, criminal class.

In the Orient there are far fewer examples of the aggressive selfishness so characteristic of the West. On the whole, one meets a multitude of easygoing, kindly disposed persons, especially in India among the plain people. I never got an inkling of that smoldering resentment encountered in so many other lands—except perhaps in the vicinity of Hindu temples. They are a good people by moral "Thou shalt not" standards, though it's hard to overlook the somewhat negative aspect of all this fanatic concern for self-vigilance. It makes one wonder if this is not part of the original underlying causes of the long oriental slumber.

Much of the same spirit can be found in other religions, Western as well as oriental, though Buddhism has the closest approximation of it. But if there is any merit in the lauded ability to exercise good judgment—if decisions concerning how little or how much makes a valid contribution to the growth and development of man's character in this drama of the universe—then might it not be said in all humility that the Jains go just a shade too far?

It also provokes conjecture on why a people should take such a lifelong gamble, accepting a faith which vehemently denies that which most of us look upon as self-evident good. At least it did to me, and I'd like to venture my own explanation for the inclination to other-worldliness which has long been so typical of most oriental philosophy, and why its doctrines have found such warm acceptance among peoples of the East.

They are unhappy and perplexed, underprivileged and frustrated. Overpopulation and underproduction have risen to a bewildering insolubility. Figuratively, at least, no one has a chance; the cards were stacked long ago. One could not get out and just be "aggressive" and "ambitious" as in the United States. There's no raw material to work on, no world to gain, by any methods, except on revolutionary proportions. It has long been considered wisest, therefore, to sit life out for the merest comforts of a full belly—or its closest approximation—until by now the spirit of resignation has almost become a racial characteristic. Actually I suppose it is Nature who makes that psychological decision for us when alternatives are reduced to nil.

Meanwhile there's the comfort of the doctrine of Karma with its theory of cosmic justice: "If we cannot live happily today, then let us at least take courage from this promise for another tomorrow." Were it not for such metaphysical reassurances, I think it likely there might have been movements toward racial suicide. As for the extremist Jains, hidden psychological factors have contrived to drive them further into warfare with the material elements which have baffled and thwarted the human need for a full and expressive life.

There are other factors at work in the motivation of asceticism, too. Perhaps because of having lightly trod the path myself it is very easy for me to be suspicious of those who willfully renounce material conveniences. There is the eminently satisfying reward of exciting concern, awe, and admiration from fellow men of lesser "will power." It's a passport to power, too, strangely enough. There are always those willing to follow the leadership of someone "strong" enough to forgo physical indulgence. "Is he not less gross than the others—closer to being God-like?" Remember Hitler's vegetarianism?

Couple this will-power factor with above-average intelligence and you've got the ingredients for a shrewd "reli-

147

gious" leader. He may do without many comforts; he may pass up a good many meals at fasting; but it's sufficiently gratifying to be called "master" or "Saint Somebody," and graciously receive the disciples fawning at your feet. Many personalities can feed sumptuously on such fare.

I wouldn't think of indicting the Jains on a charge of insincerity. I'm positive most of them are absolutely consecrated to the ideals and doctrines of their ancient faith. I don't doubt, however, that many of them have long ago recognized the civic values to be obtained from public admiration for any group in possession of a high moral code. The Jains broke away from the caste system. This left them socially stranded. Economic ostracism then could only be overcome by exhibiting certain outstanding or unusual characteristics as a counterbalance. The awe-inspiring stringency of Jain standards of virtue have afforded them a measure of respect from both Hindus and Moslems, insuring the sect of a hands-off policy for many centuries.

In the climb up Mount Indragiri to the Jain colossus, Gommatesvara, I had finally reached the first defensive wall guarding the ancient structures on top and we paused for breath beside a small shrine containing images to the twenty-four Tirthankaras.

My little guidebook gave a brief historical description of the huge nude statue I was about to encounter. "Erected sometime in the tenth century, this monument is more impressive on account of position, state of preservation, and size, than statues of Rameses in Egypt. It is bigger than any other monolithic statue in the world!

"It is completely nude and faces North. Its shoulders are

broad, waist small and there exists no support above the thighs. It is carved from light grey granite and looks bright and clean, as if having just come from the chisel of the artist."

According to legendary Jain accounts, the first Tirthan-kara had a son named Gommatesvara—this must have been thousands of years B.C.—who, in a struggle between his brother and himself for the empire, won the conflict, but then abruptly and generously handed over the kingdom to the defeated elder brother and retired from the world to do penance. Thus he became a saint achieving victory over Karma, and hence the statue. If he physically resembled the hazy little snapshot in the travel folder, he must have been a sturdy specimen. I would like to know what caused his sudden conversion.

We reached the main façade of the temple and continued our way up the impressive stone staircase. At a landing about halfway we paused again and, standing aside, I looked past one of the roof towers and there he was—Gommatesvara—peering at us from out of the central courtyard inside the temple wall.

Of course only the top of his head and part of one eye was visible, but it was a thrill to see this enormous giant gazing down upon us upstart mortals from his thousand years of rock-hewn immortality. It felt something like making an assault on Mount Olympus.

Here a temple guardian, perhaps a Jain priest, politely came forward and took over the duties of escorting us farther. We wound silently through a corridor, finally stopping at a window in the stone where the guard pointed up at another view of the image. I gazed—and gasped.

We were much closer to Gommatesvara now and he was visible down to the waist. That is to say, his waist would have been visible if there had not been some kind of structure of interlaced timbers all around him, from the neck down.

I was aghast. "What has happened to him?" I demanded to know. Naturally no one understood my English. I urged the party on toward the inner courtyard. Once inside the whole staggering truth became too excruciatingly real. It was a rough scaffolding—from the ground up—thick, heavy, and completely enshrouding the fifty-seven-foot colossus, right even with the end of his nose, and no one there could explain it to me.

I just couldn't believe it—and after all I'd told myself concerning the rewards for perseverance, too. I climbed all over the area, got on every roof top, trying to get a shot that showed something of the underlying contours, but it was a partial head close-up and nothing more. Finally I settled for a few angles of the whole thing just to prove I'd been there. Then we packed up and morosely started the long descent to the village. I'm afraid I tipped the little guard rather poorly.

We got down to Sravana Belgola ultimately and I hastened to find the taxi driver and get the answers about the scaffolding. After my excited description he made inquiries. We learned that Gommatesvara receives an anointing at odd intervals several times each century. It consists of compounding a variety of liquids and other substances such as milk, curds, ghee, sugar, dates, almonds, poppy seeds, coconut juice, and other fruits, plus flowers and coins, and pouring gallons of this mixture all down the face of the image.

A scaffolding is needed to get the offering up into place and, of course, they had to select the previous month to do it, leaving the framework so that workmen could later make assertedly necessary repairs in the granite.

Back in Calcutta we wound up affairs and prepared to move on to Benares. The last night brought us a complete worship service in one of the Jain temples. They opened all doors and showed us many phases of their particular liturgy.

So clean and elegant was the marble interior, with jeweled images and other priceless treasures enshrined, that an armed guard stands perpetually in the doorway with bayonet-tipped rifle at port arms. Needless to mention, he is not a Jain. The Jains themselves are non-violent.

Before approaching the altar for worship the Jain lay follower will enter a small chamber off the entrance for the purpose of bathing the entire body and making a complete change of clothing. Shoes are never worn inside.

One unusual type of individual worship consists of kneeling by a small table before the image and laying out an intricate design with grains of rice. When the figure is finished, it will be decorated with different fruits and nuts, forming a very interesting, often beautiful pattern, somewhat in the manner of a Navaho sand painting, though not as primitive or as colorful. Each element of the design symbolizes another promise of virtue. Each placement of a fruit is a dedication of effort and devotion. Some were bizarre, many fanciful; it was fascinating to watch these strange creations take place under the deft hands of an artistic worshiper.

Many aspects of worship by lay followers of Jainism are similar to that of the Hindus, from whom their faith originally sprang. One ceremony in particular is quite the same in character as the Hindu *arti*, a ritual in which the waving of a lighted candelabrum before the images takes a leading part.

At the time I hadn't seen the Jain version—or even the Hindu for that matter—and I'll never forget the first demonstration in the Calcutta temple. First, the worshipers assembled before the image in absolute pin-drop silence, while the candles were lighted. Then, without warning, from somewhere in the building several earsplitting conch-shell blasts were heard, followed by an overpowering din of drumbeats and bell clangings. The heavily carved, solid marble interior shook from the reverberations, for the drums were of enormous tympany size while the bells were of all diameters— three-foot monsters down to tiny hand bells which seemed to send forth a shrill, piercing scream. They were on every side, and yet so completely unexpected was the boiler-factory intensity that it brought on a desire to jump and run for your life.

We had been photographing in the temple for some time previously when the lid suddenly blew off on this last ceremony. At first it was positively terrifying, making the hair stand on end and the flesh crawl. Gradually our eardrums were deadened. I got a bit used to it and simmered down enough to start the cameras, although the bedlam continued strong as ever for fifteen or twenty minutes. During this time candles were waved ceremoniously before the images by each member of the congregation in turn. Bob and I had to work by sign language, for even the loudest shout was totally inaudible, like shrieking in a jet wind tunnel.

The reasons for such liturgy are not difficult to find. For one, it has tremendous emotional impact, shutting out any extraneous thoughts during the entire period of its furious unremittent intensity. A feeling of awesome fear is also produced, and prolonged continuance of the throbbing rhythm and inescapable clangor ultimately brings on a kind of hypnotic ecstasy visibly apparent in the facial expressions of the worshipers. It was an orgy of emotion well known in other religious groups, not excluding certain Christian sects.

So these were the Jains, a people embracing one of the world's most exacting moral codes. Good folk, assuredly; extremist—possibly. But a necessary ultimate on this wonderful planet of non-conforming humans. I had several more contacts with them later on during the stay in India, though that night was the wrap-up on Calcutta. We left for Benares in the morning.

The Hindus consider Benares the holiest city in the world. Thousands of pilgrims come every year to pass the rest of their lives at this sacred site, as it is believed that one who dies in Benares attains final salvation.

The Ganges is India's most sacred river and here in Benares, where the Ganges joins with waters from another legendary holy stream called the Asi, is the place of highest sanctity. According to tradition these waters have tremendous powers of purification, which, of course, primarily refers to the cleansing of spiritual impurity.

Many tales have sprung up, however, concerning actual germicidal properties of the Ganges for destruction of bacteria and other septic bodies. One reads unofficial statements about this or that test showing the incontaminability of the holy waters, referring in some instances to the "filtering action of the free silica," which no doubt does exist. Of course, in the absence of more authoritative information, a traveler is unable to make pertinent comment, but certain it is that stories of these purifying and antiseptic powers are accepted without question by the Hindus. The Ganges is the repository for the bulk of the debris of Northern India. Every scrap of unwanted or unusable trash—animal, vegetable, or mineral—is digested in the sinuous colonic tract of this insurfeitable monster, which gives back in turn the waters of life to those who dwell on its shores. Truly the Ganges should be the great god of the Hindus, for it is the power which both giveth and taketh away.

To us from the West, raised with such scrupulous regard for the dangers of infection and contamination, it is a startling sight the first time to watch the Hindus at their daily ablutions on the steps of the ghats at Benares, many in the form of strict ritual. Bodies are bathed, teeth and mouths scrubbed with fingers, water gargled, spat, or swallowed, while just adjacent will be the city laundry works, the sewage outlet, and a flaming funeral pyre, with constant consignment of bones and ashes turning the immediate waters a soggy gray.

Corpses of children under five years are not cremated at all; these bodies are simply cast into the Ganges and allowed to float away. Without searching, one morning I saw, and photographed, two such partially deteriorated cadavers drifting within a few yards of dozens of persons bathing and sporting along the riverbank, in the center of town. No one paid the slightest heed to a phenomenon which at home, we conjectured, would have brought emergency squads with sirens roaring full blast. It was another comparison on the value of human life between East and West.

Benares has much to offer someone seeking to understand Hinduism. Faithful followers of Lord Siva from all over India gather here on the banks of the Ganges (though the singular word "bank" should be used, for only one shore is considered holy). All Benares, therefore, is stretched along one side of the river. On the other is nothing but a barren, sandy waste believed to be the abode of Mara, the evil one.

Multitudes of the devout are gathered at all hours upon the steps and stone terraces of the bathing ghats, although dawn and dusk are the most appropriate and customary times for ablutions. Not so much bathing will be in evidence between these periods. Sadhus, holy men, cripples, beggars of all description gather in knots of discussion, perform all manner of Yoga and meditative practices, preach, pray, beg, bask in the sun, or loll in the shade in such numbers as to make walking through a matter of carefully planted footsteps.

I've visited a good number of medical installations in my day, but never have I seen such clinical examples of deformity and disease. Congenital monstrosities and bodies half consumed with the ravages of leprosy by the score, they are all attendant upon the traditional generosity of Hindu pilgrims until the time when death will transport their world-weary souls to the realm of paradise, the reward for having made the transition at Benares.

The sadhus and holy men there are to be seen in many

attitudes, following many kinds of practices. Most of them are dedicated to the worship of Siva and are distinguishable by the horizontal stripes painted across the forehead. Followers of Vishnu customarily wear three vertical markings.

Bodies are very scantily clothed—some altogether nude— long, shaggy hair is common, though it is the practice for pilgrims to have their heads shaved at the beginning of their rounds of ablutions.

We did a series on variations in individual worship, called *pooja*. This is the name for the daily ceremonies of each devout Hindu, consisting of ablutions, the recitation of prayers—sometimes called *mantras*—acts of purification, and offerings to the images.

A mantra is a mystic religious text assumed to have power to save the soul. It may be prose or poetry and sometimes consists of only one syllable, as is the case of the often-heard Mantra Om. The sound of this syllable, usually chanted with a deep chest vibration, will be sustained for long periods along with many breath-control exercises.

Hindu worship basically is an individual experience. In fact group worship is looked upon as an artificiality, and each Hindu strives only to attain self-realization. This means that he tries to awaken a direct sensibility of his true oneness with God, a teaching which is his spiritual heritage from the Upanishads.

Daily devotions, *pooja*, are usually performed on the riverbank, with the individual usually mostly facing east. Or, in the case of Hindus with independent means, it will take place in a small chamber of the home, called a pooja room. Before the commencement of these ceremonies a purifying bath must be taken and water is usually, but not always, the medium. Dust from the hoofs of cows may also be used, or sanctified ashes. Many of the holy men are frequently seen smeared head to foot with such ashes, or cow dung, which apparently is worn throughout the whole day.

After seating himself the worshiper embraces further purification by sipping water and sprinkling it around his area with a tiny brass vessel, similar to a teapot. He then prays, sometimes using prayer beads, practices his breath control, called *pranayama*, and meditates. If he is seated before an image, he must bathe it with any number of substances, such as water, milk, curd, butter, or cow's urine, depending upon the occasion. The image must be clothed appropriately too, according to season. It should be bathed often in hot weather with cooling showers and offered fresh, cool fruit. Hot foods are offered during cooler weather. During the ceremony every movement will be highly symbolical —the posture, the position of hands and fingers (which involves a whole sign language), exact placement of the offerings.

A word must be said about *pranayama*, for of all daily practices this is considered by many to be one of the greatest sources of strength. Control of the respiratory rhythm is of first importance in development of the powers of meditation. It is also a key to relaxation and physical health. It was part of my exercises when I studied Yoga and it became clear very quickly that proficiency in the art of meditation would be impossible without complete authority over most of the body processes.

The aims of meditation are to focus the mind on a single point or channel and keep it there until the doors of another, perhaps mystic, fourth-dimensional "spiritual" world are opened for the entrance of conscious realization. To reach the proper state of concentration and mental aloofness to insure a successful session of this, the mind must first be freed from physical distractions.

One must sit quietly in a posture bringing fullest relaxation *without inducing sleep*—this is the main reason for the familiar cross-legged position. It has been found to be most conducive and congenial to conscious mind control. In a soft easy chair one relaxes all right, but before he knows it he's snoring. Strength of will is necessary to keep the mind from wandering, but the body must be brought into near-quiescence or it will be impossible to resist the disturbing intrusions of the imagination.

For instance, you sit a few moments and then a desire to scratch some portion of the tingling anatomy becomes almost irresistible. Again, every time you shift weight for a tiring muscle, the spell is broken and you must once more struggle to regain the pitch of concentration. Bodily functions, too, such as digestive processes, are most disturbing. For this reason many schools of Yoga have long advised the adoption of a simple diet, eliminating all foodstuffs which could cause even mild gastric distress. This, by the way, is a truly ancient bit of lore, for as far back as 500 or 600 B.C. Pythagoras, in his school of philosophy and metaphysics at Crotona, forbade students and followers to consume the lowly bean in any form. Other vociferous vegetables, such as garlic and onion, have also been proscribed on many lists.

Consciousness of the heartbeat and pulse becomes another distraction; so does, above all, the breath. Those who have not attempted mystic meditation cannot guess the intrusion of respiration upon the efforts of mind and will. One

In Japan, terrifying figures of Nio stand at the entrances of certain temples as guardians against evil spirits and evil men which might bring defilement.

(above)—Nirvana-day celebration, Kyoto. The musicians' heads are hooded as a symbol of the desire to lose one's identity and to seek for unity with the divine. (below)—Japanese girls wearing the worker's costume of the Sectarian Shinto sect called Oomoto Kyo. Persecuted by the Imperialists during the war, this sect seeks for world brotherhood by promoting adoption of the universal language: Esperanto.

Both pictures are figures of the gentle goddess of mercy, Kannon (called Kwan-yin in China), said to have been the offspring of a tear shed by Lord Buddha at the spectacle of human suffering. She is often shown with many arms to illustrate her ability to perform numberless deeds at once.

The northern sect of Buddhism is the only one which retains a monastic order for women. These nuns are observing midday devotions in a convent high amid the mountains of Formosa. Despite the shaven heads some were quite beautiful.

(*above*)—Nuns standing before the Buddha of the happy world yet to come, called Mi Lo Fu—or on Formosa, Juloi. His spirit will reign over the long-expected "thousand years of peace." (*below*)—Taipei, Formosa. Figure of a judge presiding over one of the courts in the underworld. The native religion of China—termed polytheistic—has more powers and deities than ever have been catalogued.

(*above*)—"Selecting the God's answer." On Formosa one temple is entirely devoted to the problems and concerns of children. There are gods to be petitioned for each phase or sphere in the child's life. Separate gods guide child health, safety, talents, ambitions, even gods for the correction of wayward or disobedient offspring. (*below*)—Here I am enjoying the companionship of the descendant of Kung Fu Tsu (Latin: Confucius). He traces his genealogy back 4000 years—the oldest family tree on earth!

Another of the numberless deities in the folklore of China. This terrifying figure of wrath and vengeance can be found enshrined amid the incense-blackened interiors of temples on the Kowloon Peninsula.

(*above*)—In a newly constructed temple in Hong Kong are images of more than fifteen thousand Buddhas. The ultimate goal is to enshrine *one hundred thousand.* (*below*)—Seeing this portrait of Confucius convinced me I should return to Formosa for an interview with the 78th descendant.

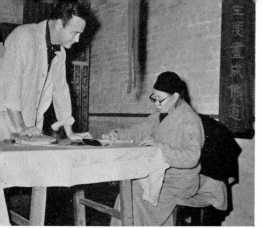

In a convent near Hong Kong we observed the daily routine of the gentle, scholarly sisters of Lord Buddha. This one was showing me her Chinese scriptures. (Frankly, I couldn't read them.)

(*above*)—I believe this is an image of Lui Jo, a kindly but powerful protector of man. There were so many figures of gods in some temples that frequently it even was impossible to learn their names from the attendants. (*right*)—In northern Buddhism tablets for spirits of the departed are usually placed near the altar, where they may be remembered and where they may find peace from the prayers.

(*above*)—In Siam all male Buddhists spend a portion of their lives in the monkhood. This group is chanting scriptures called Sutras. The object in the foreground is just what it looks like: a spittoon. Betel-nut is not used by monks, however, only laymen. (*below*)—Here I am in Wat Arun looking up at one of the many great bronze Buddhas in Bangkok. Seated figures represent the great teacher in meditation.

(*above*)—Siam. Reclining images of Buddha show him in a state of bliss —after entering Nirvana. (*below*)—The chief patriarch of the Buddhists in Siam. When I asked if a lifetime of monkhood had given him wisdom, he quoted Buddha: "Not by a shaven crown is one made religious, but by putting off great sins and small faults."

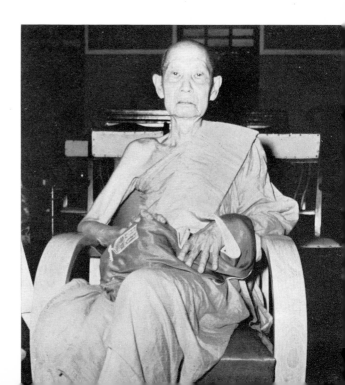

(*above*)—Although there is no monastic order for women in southern Buddhism, many live nearby and study in the wats. This one practices meditation daily. (*below*)—The fabulous fairyland architecture of the Siamese wats standing amid the traffic snarls of modern Bangkok gives them the appearance of celestial islands in a raging sea.

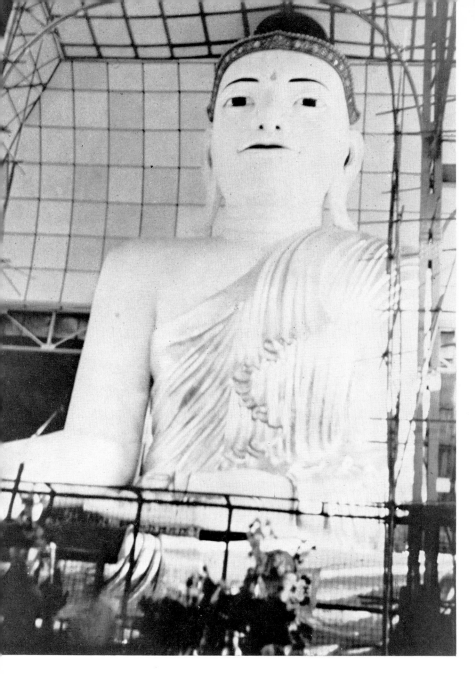

This giant Buddha in a modern temple on the outskirts of Rangoon is the
largest indoor figure I've ever seen. I was so stunned by its size I forgot to
ask the dimensions.

(above)—Headquarters of the Ramakrishna mission is outside of Calcutta on the Hooghly River. A beautiful temple, built mainly by private American donations, enshrines a marble image of the mystic founder. (below)—In Burma a young lady of fifteen years awaits an ear-piercing ceremony which will mark her formal acceptance of the Buddhist faith. An elaborate reception which might be likened to a "coming out" party will follow later.

(*above*)—In Southern India I encountered Archarya Shantisagarji, the foremost saint of the Jain religion. His absolute nudity is maintained during all hours of every season—as proof of his independence of material comfort. (*below*)—Nandi is the creature which carries Lord Siva about the heavens. This colossal figure of the Sacred Bull rests on a mountain in Mysore.

(*above*)—So sacred is Jewish scripture that even when worn it can never be destroyed. It must be buried in a cemetery. These are Torahs that were desecrated by the nazis and are now in a subterranean vault on Mount Zion, Jerusalem. (*below*)—Also on Mount Zion is the tomb of King David, the great spiritual leader who, as a boy, slew the giant Goliath.

must learn to breathe with absolute regularity—a far from normal waking habit—or face constant interruption and perpetual failure. Every time one lets the breathing impulse sink too low, a deep sigh will inevitably break in and shatter the spell. That's where Yoga, with scientific methods of learning to control mind and body, comes in. Most sadhus consider some Yoga routines indispensable.

Incidentally, the art itself is termed Yoga. One who follows the training and is an adept would be called a Yogi or Yogan.

We filmed an entire series of Yoga exercises as performed by an expert so slim and supple that in many instances he literally seems to tie himself in knots. Absolute mastery over every muscle—external or internal—was demonstrated to a point seeming almost superfluous for the sole end of meditation. And I suppose another trap on the path of self-development could be the placement of overemphasis upon mere physical accomplishment. At least, when questioned, this particular Yogi gave no tangible indication of having penetrated the deeper recesses of mystic discernment, even if his anatomical virtuosity was unexcelled.

It must be pointed out that other distractions besides physiological functions are equally, if not more, disturbing. Such things as mental and emotional serenity are imperative. Thus it is that much stress is placed upon maintaining conduct in accord with a very high moral code. One cannot seek contact with the divine while laboring under the burden of a guilty conscience. Persons sensitive enough to seek such communion in the first place would be far too sensitive to attempt approaching Deity without clean hands and a pure heart.

I used to wonder why those great teachers who sought to lead men into closer and more direct communion with divine reality often advised a single life and a break with family ties when the self-evident facts of man's nature always seem to cast a shadow of unnaturalness on celibate bachelorhood. Now I feel that this condition is suggested more for the peace of mind and freedom from responsibility that such a course usually offers than from considerations of morality or virtue. If you've never tried deep meditation, you'd be surprised at what a multitude of thoughts need to be subdued. Above all, such things as the responsibility and welfare of others can easily make the whole venture seem trivial or selfish.

Very few of the holy men are seen actually undergoing the rigors of self-torture one often hears about, though there was a man calmly bedded on a mattress of black thorns, haunting the main streets of Calcutta for several days. Mostly such adepts circulate around the country from festival to festival, like the human oddities at home who make all the county fairs. Many devout Hindus do not consider such demonstrations to be evidences of spiritual attainment, though one scholar explained his viewpoint of the matter and I confess I was more favorably impressed than previously.

He explained that he judged the outstanding contribution of Hinduism to the world to be the data resulting from centuries of man's efforts to break down all barriers and establish a personal relationship with the divine. He cited the fact that Hindus had tried every conceivable approach to bring about this direct contact; they have starved themselves, buried themselves, burned, frozen, and tortured themselves. They have stared into the sun, held limbs upright until they stiffened, gone nude, dressed in thistles, dwelt on mountain peaks, lurked in caves, refused to speak, sung without pause, chanted incessantly, eaten only fruit, eaten only grain, studied sacred literature, refused to read or write at all. They have tried by every imaginable mental or physical gymnastic, every emotional, intellectual device, to reach through the thick mist of material bewilderment and find the underlying bedrock of cosmic truth. To know truth, God, and themselves, not by faith or reason alone, but by direct experience: that has been the aim of Hindu religion, the practice of its followers. The results of these experiments, then, are Hinduism's gift to mankind.

From this viewpoint one cannot fail to be touched by the nobility of the cause, even if the conclusions are not overwhelmingly impressive. I would say it is always great comfort to those of us who "believe" when we encounter another scrap of substantiation. What faith does not need feeding, sustenance for its growth?

Though by reason we content ourselves with faith, who is so strong he would not welcome another grain of tangible confirmation? Are we not followers, in every instance, of religious leaders who claim this direct experience? Did not God "speak" to Abraham, and Moses, and the Prophets? Did not Jesus claim complete unity with the Godhead? Was not Lord Buddha "enlightened," as well as Mahavira? Did not Zoroaster receive divine revelations? Were not Mohammed's claims the same? On and on, to the saints and leaders of sects and smaller divisions, we call them God-inspired, awakened, enlightened, and those we believe to be so attuned we follow.

But what about the results of these Hindu experiments? Have they really provided man with foolproof channels to divinity? If they have done so, the answer is still remote as ever for most of us. If they have given us a route, it is no short cut, but long, hard, and demanding of much sacrifice.

And again, let us ask what changes all the experiments have made in the old methods. If the Hindu has been trying every conceivable approach to God, have these multifold efforts altered the old procedures in any way? Answers to this question are not conclusive, and not altogether favorable.

Brahman temple rituals and individual worship ceremonies are in the same ancient pattern, with the same objectives. New movements within Hinduism are largely social in character—combating the priesthood and caste system—though they have also done much to promote an understanding of Hindu philosophy beyond the borders of India and make it a recognizable world force. No doubt most of the authentic well-regulated Hindu courses of training in self-realization to be found in the Occident today can be beneficial to many types of persons. This Hinduism, indeed, is different from the Brahmanism of the caste Hindu. Dropping both the gods and the rituals while selecting a metaphysical doctrine and a portion of Yoga exercises, it stresses a sound morality and selfless ethic.

Whether its followers contact a "cosmic consciousness" is another question evoking slim answers, and considerably more critical interrogation from modern psychology. That it helps them attain emotional stability and a sense of inner calm is possible and often quite likely. That there's a short cut into the presence of the divine has not been convincingly demonstrated by word or deed of those assumed to be active practitioners. No light of extraordinary wisdom shines from these centers of mysticism. No results exceeding those of many other institutions concerned with the provisioning of man's emotional needs are visible.

Brahmin religious conventions have not appreciably altered in centuries, despite all the experiments in God-consciousness by their mystic pathfinders. Buddhists have continued the same methods of moral improvement and spiritual discernment that they evolved twenty-five hundred years ago. Except for monastic emphasis these are not remotely distant from modern Hindu cult practices. So, if it's possible that all the experiments—like Thomas Edison's nine hundred and ninety-nine—were just more methods which can be totaled with other trails leading nowhere in particular, then at least as data, if nothing more, they will not have been wholly in vain.

We continued exploration of Brahman observances in Benares for another week, but it was hard sledding. Though it is said to have been different a few years ago, visitors are now given only the barest peep into Hindu temples and camera resistance from devotees is at an all-time high. It was forbidden to photograph any portion of the cremation rites at the burning ghats or point a lens at the fulminating funeral pyres from any distance, even from the deck of the little boat we hired to cruise along the Ganges shore. As we came within two hundred yards, cremation officials strode scowlingly and watchfully to the water's edge, and there they remained until we passed and were well out of camera range.

Persistent quizzing finally brought out the answer. Evidently someone had made much ado in picture and print about the dogs which perpetually prowl the water's edge in search of grisly remnants unconsumed by the flames. This exposé had sufficiently embarrassed the civil authorities of Benares to cause them to pronounce the ban on photography.

The dogs, however, were still on the job when we visited, pawing about in the cooling cinders. I watched a couple of them snapping at each other over a bone fragment, as we floated downstream.

Later on, in Delhi, we completed photography on all details of the cremation ceremony.

The animals in Benares fascinated me. This was the first stop on the tour—and the first time in my life—where creatures I had seen heretofore only in a circus were domesticated. There were camels, up and down every lane. Elephants—enormous ones—shuffled along the main streets, with tiny brown men half-hidden behind their ears. Monkeys by the thousands scampered all over the city, into everything.

It is a part of the doctrine of ahimsa to leave animal life unmolested, but monkeys, because of their relationship to the monkey god, Hanuman—famous in the legendary story of the Ramayama—are treated by Hindus with an exceptional amount of forbearance, considering the mischief and damage they do.

They can be seen frolicking across the face of any apartment building, methodically entering every unscreened window, for heaven knows what fiendish deviltry. Still they are staunchly protected and the killing of monkeys is commonly regarded as an act of impiety.

For some reason hundreds of them have made the Durga Temple in Benares their home. They literally swarm all over the place, inside and out. The temple itself is not large, being a small shrine room within a canopied courtyard of marble, though the courtyard itself is extensive, with a high, thick surrounding wall.

We climbed atop the wall, watching and photographing the monkeys as they scampered from one perch to another, bedeviling and nipping at the worshipers whenever they knelt before the image. I saw one doughty old Hindu menacingly raise his staff as a group of the little chatterers approached. The monkeys began to get very excited and I thought we were in for a lively man-versus-beast episode. But then his companion spoke a word of reproof and the old man finally but reluctantly lowered his stick and moved along with customary Hindu sufferance, while the pesky little simians made flying passes at his heels.

Serpent worship is still very much in evidence in villages. These Nagas, or serpent deities, carved in stone are often found enshrined under some shady tree in a quiet corner of the town. Their aid is sought in conception. It seems appropriate when one remembers the account in the third chapter of Genesis. Snake worship may also be attributable to their deadliness—an omnipresent menace in India—and there is a belief that a person will be saved from snakebite if he utters the name of Astika, a famous wise man who interceded to save the snake Takshaka from being destroyed.

Few days pass, anywhere in India, when one does not hear the familiar drone of the snake charmer's oboe come drifting up to the hotel room from the street below. Like everyone else, we took pictures of a pair of them immediately. It was the hot season, and the snakes were as uncomfortable and ill-humored as the rest of us. The charmers seemed to have considerable trouble keeping them under control—or maybe it was part of the act, I don't know. Anyway, while being handled, the cobras could be observed striking and hitting the hands of their masters with frequency. We concluded that the fangs were removed.

CHAPTER EIGHT

Arriving in Delhi, I immediately became conscious of the importance of a religion which up till now on the tour had barely been discernible: Mohammedanism—Islam.

As the plane circles the city, one can see the domes and minarets of mosques, tombs, and other monuments erected by the onetime-prosperous followers of the Prophet. Right next to the landing strip is the famous Emperor Humayun's tomb, considered to be one of the most beautiful Mogul monuments. The contrast of its ruddy sandstone walls and white marble dome with the surrounding verdure makes an unforgettable first impression.

The sturdy grace of the 240-foot beacon of Delhi—the Qutb Minar—stands silently but enduringly symbolic of the power of Islam. Tombs, thousands of them of all sizes and in all stages of repair or decay, moldering slowly back into the red soil from which they sprang, are scattered across the countryside like the fragments of some gigantic fantasy, evoking a historical nostalgia at every turn.

There are Hindus and Jains in Delhi, of course, with their temples and sacred shrines. There are other religions, too, like that of the Sikhs, whom I was most anxious to scrutinize, but these other religious structures, with few exceptions, are inferior in all respects to those of Islam. For when the Moslem conquerors swept across these portions of the Indian Peninsula some centuries back, their fiery zeal for the cause of Allah and their detestation for all who violate the Mosaic command regarding graven images brought total destruction to nearly every religious temple or edifice in their wake.

They were, and are, particularly inimical to the idolatry of Hinduism and, as an observer, after a short stay in Delhi, I found it easy to believe the current opinion that the extensive contact between these two antipodal theologies at this geographical pin point forms a perpetually potential tinderbox. The present-day controversy with Pakistan also adds substantially to the fire hazard.

During our visit the annual month of Moslem fasting—Ramadan—was in progress. It was the hottest time of the year; tension was visible and tactile. Guided by the moon, the Moslem calendar shifts its months with no regard to seasonal changes; thus at present the thirty-day period of fast falls in the heat of summer.

Rules of the fast are that neither food nor water shall be taken during daylight hours. The strain this puts on those doing manual labor in these torrid days can well be imagined. Tongues and tempers become equally hot and dry. No one knows how many lost their lives in the rioting after Indian independence.

Friday is the important weekly day of prayer for Moslems. The first Friday after our arrival I got an impatient idea and abruptly tried, alone, to take my camera into the gigantic Jama Masjid—said to be the largest mosque in India, perhaps the world—to record the prayer service. I will confess I got nowhere. It was around one in the afternoon—temperature almost 120 degrees—when I trudged barefoot up the stone steps to the huge gate, tripod and Bolex on my shoulder, packed in between pressing throngs of panting, perspiring followers of the Prophet. How many thousands were on hand that day would be hard to guess, but the place was packed. I think the mosque holds around twenty-five thousand people.

I hadn't really started gathering material on Islam as yet, but this being a special holiday service, I thought it would provide a valuable demonstration of mass prayer. It would have, too. Unfortunately I didn't get it.

I first became aware of something peculiar going on when I seemed to feel the density of the crowd increasing substantially and bumping around me more than before. By the time we reached the top of the steps and were passing under the arch into the huge open courtyard inside the walls, I had felt several shoulder jolts that were distinctly sharper than the press of a normal clutter of pedestrians.

Glancing around, I noted several faces staring impudently at me and a few remarks seemingly passed in my direction. Not understanding a word and having no one along to interpret for me, I could only shrug and continue on my way. A few steps later I received a good stiff shove from behind which sent me piling into the people ahead who, of course, wheeled indignantly, glaring.

I started to explain, but gave up and turned back to see

what was the cause of the last block that was thrown at me. I was greeted by an angry-faced young Moslem, a man in his early twenties, gesticulating at my camera and shouting some incomprehensible demand. I simply stared back without speaking. He appeared to repeat his remarks and when I still failed to reply, two or three others joined in with him, pointing at the camera.

Then someone reached toward the camera and I pulled violently away, whacking the man back of me as I did so. Before I knew it, a little ring had formed with me and two or three youthful zealots as stars. Or rather, *they* were the stars—at least they had all the dialogue. My role consisted of firmly holding silent ground while I tried to think, meanwhile looking as stern and defiant as possible. I really can't say this was too effective—except perhaps in an undesirably antagonistic sense. The young hotheads were getting more steamed up by the minute. It wasn't difficult to gather that photography was near the root of the beef. My Occidental-fashion pith helmet probably didn't improve matters either.

Just as I was wondering whether best chances for resolution of the difficulty lay with an acquiescent or an adamant attitude—leaning a bit toward the latter because of the heat —a stalwart old patriarch, bearded and turbaned, elbowed his way into the circle, made a few blunt remarks to the youngsters, and, taking hold of my arm, escorted me to a small gate room in the wall. After seating me he left the room and I sat alone, watching the overheated, all-male crowd surge past the door, heads peering in at me from time to time. Moslems, incidentally, must be fully clothed at prayers, wrists and ankles covered regardless of high temperatures.

About five minutes later the old man returned with a mild-mannered Indian chap who spoke English. I stated what I wanted to do and why, but he looked aghast at the suggestion and, shaking his head, explained the impossibility of carrying out such a plan on a holy day of this importance. The place was packed with fervent believers, dehydrated from the sun and three weeks of fasting. The Moslem attitude of resentment toward graven images extends among most of them to paintings, pictures, or photographs of any kind. Thus for a lone Westerner to attempt setting up a movie camera in their midst during prayer service at this time, I gathered, would be like marching across the field between halves at an Army-Notre Dame football game waving a banner inscribed with the hammer and sickle.

He went on to say that mosque officials could not be responsible for my safety—or at least the security of my photographic equipment—though perhaps one day it might be arranged with an escort of proper authorities, arriving to get set up some hours ahead of time. . . . Maybe next year. . . .

I looked past the doorway at the sweat-streaked faces scowlingly eying my shiny camera gear—and got the man's point. It was no time for this fool to rush in, even though angels presumably in the mosque might be treading around in droves.

I thanked the gatekeepers and reluctantly made an exit which, I fear, plainly revealed my intimidation. Glancing back, I could see they appeared relieved and frankly, as I squeezed my way out amid the reproachful stares of the ascending multitude, so was I.

Efforts toward direct contact of Moslem authorities in Delhi were not especially fruitful. Nor could I seem to get much assistance through other channels that had previously been helpful. Everyone held a kind of hands-off policy on the matter, presumably because of the sleeping-dog situation between Moslem and Hindu.

I would not say that Delhi is a particularly appropriate place to study Indian religion anyway, being the political center of a regime with so many unresolved problems and instabilities. One gets the hands-off impression on any subject entailing the slightest controversy.

Naturally we visited all the important Moslem monuments, including the Taj Mahal. In a way this was a bit of a surprise: I guess because it so completely lives up to all the praises that have been sung over it. On the early morning motor drive to Agra I well recollect thinking that after all the years of lavish build-up on the poetic loveliness of the "monument to a woman," like anything overpublicized, it would be certain to fall short. Particularly it would do so to us in this hot season, after months of sight-seeing every temple, mosque, shrine, and tomb in many parts of Far Eastern and Southeastern Asia. After a brief stop to observe morning ablutions and *pooja* at the ancient town of Mathura (Muttra), once a great center of Hinduism and the legendary birthplace of Lord Krishna, we came to a halt before the entrance to the Taj about eleven-thirty in the morning. The sun was so blinding and the heat so intense we stumbled from the scorching leather seats of the car in a daze, clothing damp and wrinkled, groggy also from the long drive, which had started about four-thirty that morning, in anything but a mood to enjoy the "romantic" Taj.

Loading up with equipment, I mechanically made a deal with one of the local guides and started across the dusty forecourt to the gatehouse, unstirred emotionally by the sight of the familiar minarets, their tips visible above the high outer wall.

Very few visitors were on hand that day to obscure the first impression as we strode into the gatehouse and came into sight of the most Olympian piece of architecture I have ever laid eyes upon, framed in the archway on the other side. And I don't believe I shall attempt to describe it. Such a task belongs only to masters of the art of rhetoric, an assignment that's been fulfilled many times.

Besides what adjectives should one use? When I feel for them they all sound so hackneyed. Superb—shimmering—breath-taking—awe-inspiring—glistening—perfectly proportioned—cool and poised even in the noonday heat—etc., etc. Suffice it to say, it seemed to me the most idealized balance between architecture and landscaping, and impressive beyond words to one whose eye long had been jaded. Furthermore, it is not by any means of an unusual style, but quite similar to and typical of all other Mogul monuments to be seen in abundance in those parts. Yet the sheer magic of its proportionate lines and white marble contours makes it stand apart from sister structures as though it were placed somewhere as remote as, say, Squash Corners, Kansas.

It is seldom in life that one gets the feeling of perfection from something man-built, but for me, and I guess thousands more, the Taj Mahal radiates just that.

We spent several hours on photography, and though I failed to see the monument during the highly vaunted, much-publicized effect of moonlight, those who chance to catch the film will have the opportunity we missed—filters are ingenious devices. As we drove away, the one impression which kept me bemused all the way back to Delhi was that for once I could use a word, the pitiful abuse of which has long since caused it to become meaningless and trite. Beautiful.

Beyond visits to the great monuments I resigned myself to waiting until we entered wholly Moslem countries before further pursuing the investigation of Islam. I had received a cordial response to my letter proposing a visit to Pakistan from their public-relations office and was, in fact, contacted by their representative in Delhi. It would be the next stop after India and we would leave the study of Mohammedanism until then. There were more than enough other religions to be looked into here at hand anyway.

There are estimated to be about six million followers of the Ten Gurus in India. *Guru* is a common term among Hindus for a spiritual teacher or leader. The Ten Gurus were founders of the religion of Sikhism. *Sikh* means disciple.

We first encountered the Sikhs in Calcutta. They'd be rather hard to miss. For one thing, they have a distinctive custom of never cutting the hair on head or face. For another, they control all upper-class transportation facilities, monopolizing the occupation of taxi driving.

They twist their long hair into a knot on top of the head and wind a voluminous turban around it. Their beards usually are bound with a net which holds them tightly to their faces. This all gives them a look of strength, fierceness, and dignity. They also have a reputation for living up to their appearance, so people don't monkey around with the Sikhs or try any unnecessary flippancies with them, not even foreign tourists riding around in their taxis. Many of these chauffeurs are fairly good-sized men, too, and when they rumble to a stop, jerk open the taxi door and mutter the amount of the fare from the depths of a shaggy beard placed upon a pair of shoulders six feet high, it somehow finds one genially dispensing rather bountiful tips.

We photographed the daily routine of a Sikh business-man dressing hair and beard for normal street wear. It takes him at least forty minutes every morning and the complexity of the procedure would be a revelation to Hollywood hair stylists. It is very smart looking, too, in a severe sort of way. Of course the working-class Sikhs are not so meticulous.

Sikhism is considered to be something of a cross between Hinduism and the Mohammedan faith. Their principle sphere of influence lies in the Punjab, astride the boundary between the main bodies of these faiths. Yet, having their own leaders in the Gurus, the writings of these men for their sacred literature, their own observances and holy city distinctly make Sikhism a separate religion. What they have done is to borrow distinctive features of the two religions (which, in turn, may well have been borrowed from someone else).

For instance, from the Hindus the Sikhs have accepted the law of Karma, transmigration, and yet it is held that by trust and sincere worship of one God this continually revolving wheel of reincarnation can be halted so that the soul, whatever its imperfections, may return to God without needing to be reborn on earth. In other words, salvation by faith and grace.

As the Moslems have fervently embraced the Jewish idea of one God, so, too, the Sikhs cling passionately to the same doctrine. An outstanding difference between the two faiths, however, is the Moslem zeal for world domination and proselytizing, which has amounted to what might be termed fanaticism during certain historical periods. Sikhism has never striven for converts outside of India, though there are a few communities in other parts of the world.

En route by car from New York to Los Angeles, for example, we stopped for a visit at the Sikh Temple in Stockton, California, the only one in America, I believe. This is the center of a prosperous farming community formed by immigrants from the Punjab. They have a good-sized corner lot in a middle-class residential area and a modest, Western-type structure has been raised, which looks about like any average suburban church.

They received our unannounced call most graciously, permitting and co-operating in every way for photography of the evening service. And while the installation seems to fulfill the spiritual needs of their own migrant group, still there was no visible evidence of American conversions nor any intended program for the purpose.

Because Hinduism is such an all-embracing religion, some Hindus I spoke with try to claim Sikhism as a sect of their own faith. But this seems a broad assumption to me. The Sikhs have rejected any fragment of the caste system, emphatically stressing the "brotherhood" aspect and democratic principles of equality. All persons, including women and outcasts, are on a par. Pilgrimages are of no consequence; neither ascetic practices nor having food cooked and served in a particular way are of importance. The honoring of idols is eliminated, as well as many other observances firmly attached to the ways of the Brahmins, including vegetarianism.

Although the use of drugs, wine, and tobacco is condemned by Sikh teaching, the eating of meat—except beef—receives encouragement. This, coupled with moderation in all things and the emphatic view that men should marry and live in the world, has helped develop an especially sturdy, virile group of followers, whose exceptional physical courage and unsurpassed bravery in battle have become a universally recognized fact.

It is said that after an originally friendly relationship with the Moslems, enmity finally developed between the two religions, owing in large part to persecution of the Sikhs by Mogul emperors, who resented their refusal of allegiance to Islam. It was the second martyrdom of a Sikh Guru—over two hundred fifty years ago—which finally consolidated their peoples into a nation of warriors.

All converts henceforth were made soldiers, by baptism of the sword, and received the title Singh, meaning Lion—a name widely used by followers to this day. From thence descriptions of God revealed Him as All-Death, Great-Steel, etc., a martial aspect that was incorporated into many hymns and verses of scripture.

This warlike attitude evidently was fostered and abetted in large degree by the tenth and last Guru, the famous Gobind Singh, who inaugurated many of the customs of dress which have made Sikhs distinguishable for several centuries. Among these is the traditional wearing of five articles, the names of which all begin with the letter K: *kanga*—a comb; *kacha*—underpants; *kara*—steel bracelet; *kripan*—sword; and *kes*—long hair. Each item had a part to play in the military situation of the time, making the followers easily recognizable and never to be mistaken for others. The loyal supporters themselves were titled *Kalsa*, from the Arabic word for pure.

Today the long hair is the outstanding characteristic and I don't recall meeting a Sikh without his bracelet. The sword, modified to short dagger length, is still slung on the belt of many, though most of the merchants and tradesmen carry only a tiny replica of the weapon, perhaps attached to the comb which is embedded in the hair under the turban. This accounts for all but the underpants, the wearing of which I could only take their word for. The first group looked so sheepish when the subject arose that we desisted from causing the embarrassment of bringing it up. The Sikhs also consider themselves "whole-bodied," being unshaven, as the Hindus, and uncircumcised, as the Moslems.

Guru Nanak, born 1469, is considered the founder of Sikhism. At the early age of nine he rebelled against his Hindu heritage by refusing to accept the sacred thread at a presentation by the Brahman priest and, after a series of incidents extremely disturbing to his parents, he left home to wander about the country singing ballads descriptive of his own version of religious faith.

He must have had an engaging voice and a persuasive personality, for he collected many followers who were converted to his theology and philosophy of life. He also set the style for the subsequent liturgy of Sikh worship. To this day the singing of ballads forms the major portion of Sikh temple services. During every one of my visits a singer with an orchestra of four or five men kept up an almost continual round of lyrical compositions.

I found them very pleasant listening and, because of the oriental penchant for minor modes mounted on a strong rhythmic background, they had a seductive, slightly hypnotic quality. Although the East has not yet developed a sensitivity to harmonic complexities—and even its lines of melody seem for the most part sadly limited—there is yet no doubt of their indisputable mastery of the third aspect of musical expression, rhythm.

After frequent opportunities for hearing a variety of musical performances throughout Asia I came away with profound admiration for the percussionists. As a onetime member of orchestral percussion groups myself—being an old guitar-and-banjo player from way back—I can unhesitatingly vouch for the virtuosity of all oriental drummers. Playing with finger tips on the heads of small tom-tom-like drums, they have no terrestrial equal for depth of rhythmical concept or fabulous dexterity of execution. The changes of time and tempo alone would probably stump comparable artists in the West. There were beats I tried to pick up on occasion, ranging into every conceivable odd number of quarter notes to the measure. Time divisions such as five-four and seven-four were elementary, less than commonplace.

Regarding the melodic line in Eastern music, I had always heard much about oriental scales presumably ranging into quarter tones. Because it is a pet theory of mine that in order to enrich harmonic possibilities, Western music must—ultimately if not soon—embrace finer gradations of interval in its chromatic scale, I made every effort to verify the assertions concerning oriental ability for breaking in between the half-tone scale to which our Occidental ears seem locked. At this point, after assiduously bending an ear for months, I regret my inability to confirm or deny the claims of enthusiasts in the cause of the oriental musician's tonal versatility. Frankly, I could never quite tell whether the flatted vibrations were intended or accidental, and I don't think I'll ever truly know until I can hear the tones purposely placed against a strict harmonic pattern. Except for formal operas and ballets oriental orchestras are always so confusingly casual—like jam sessions where each takes his turn at self-expression to the nth degree of his imagination. In this sense I know they do roll off into a quarter tone or even an eighth tone now and then, but hardly more effectively than a real cool jive-hound.

Besides two or three percussionists the Sikhs—who did not happen to use quarter tones—would usually have but one simple melodic instrument in unison with the ever-constant voices, which could always be heard anywhere in the vicinity of the temples. One reason for this was the fine acoustical resonance; another was that nearly all temples now use a public-address system; I never became altogether accustomed to the sight of several thousand barefoot, bearded, and beturbaned Asiatics sitting cross-legged around a quartet of their members who calmly took turns at a stint before a chrome-plated microphone with the non-chalance of any modern crooner.

But then, such is modern progress—one sees the same confusing inconsistencies no matter where. I recall stepping on the wrapper from an "Oh Henry" candy bar down in one of the deeper chambers of Angkor Wat. And I remember, from years ago, the Eskimo boy way north of Nome who, when removing his little parka in an igloo, revealed a sweat shirt with Mickey Mouse printed on the front.

The headquarters of the main body of Sikh followers is in the Punjab, about three hundred miles north of Delhi at the city of Amritsar—a word meaning Tank of the Waters of Life. It is a very colorful place, founded by Guru Ram Das, still far from the embellishments of modernization and typical of all anciently designed oriental cities. Tourist accommodations or other facilities for Western living are practically nonexistent.

We had left Delhi about sundown and traveled by automobile along the narrow, partially paved highway that stretches through the desertlike portion of the southern Punjab. I repeat, it was hot; it was a heat which failed to abate as the darkness covered us.

Our vehicle was a loose-jointed, open convertible, with top down for the first fifty miles. After that I managed to persuade the driver to put it up. The extreme dryness of the wind tearing at our faces during higher speeds seemed to wrench every drop of moisture from the body. Our lips and tongues became so cotton dry in the first ten minutes that one could scarcely speak.

With the top up the journey was much more bearable and so we sped on, Bob and I with our equipment piled in the back seat, two colorful turbans streaming from the front. The pink one belonged to the driver, while under the white turban on his right, seated with ramrod immobility, was the President of the Sikh Gurdwara of Amritsar, the top-ranking official of the religion. A large, handsome man, perhaps in his sixties, he had the kindliest eyes you ever saw. We had already filmed an interview with him the day before in Delhi. He was now our escort on a visit to the Sikh capital. He speaks English well, slowly and carefully, thoughtfully choosing each word in a voice that is low and soft.

I asked him what he felt was the specific contribution of Sikhism to the world at large. His answer, according to my transcription, was: "The contribution of Sikhism toward humanity is manifold. Firstly, Guru Nanak, the founder of our faith, preached that there should be no feuds between religions. He chose the very first disciples, one from Hinduism and the other from Islam, and started his pilgrimage of Hindu places of worship and Moslem shrines, including Mecca, to preach his gospel. I'm sure if he was alive today he would try his utmost to bring all the religions of the world into a common front. Secondly, Gobind Singh, the last Guru, infuses the spirit of democracy in the religion. He first baptized his five followers and then got baptized himself from them, and this spirit is still going on in the Sikhs. Every human being, irrespective of any creed, caste, sex, or religion, can visit our places of worship and can join in our prayers."

He finished and sat quietly holding the handle of the long sword that stood upright between his knees. I then told him that most everyone thought of the Sikhs as a rather warlike people and asked if they were really interested in world peace. This was done principally for a potential movie audience, because his answer was bound to be more or less obvious.

"Yes, definitely," he said; "we are for peace and we always try to maintain peace. Whenever we have to fight, we fight for a righteous cause."

Now as the car sped northward through the sultry night air, we continued the conversation from time to time, on an informal basis. Most of my questions had to do with the history and functioning of Sikhism.

He spoke of the Sikhs having risen and girded themselves as a bulwark against intolerance and fanaticism. Though he did not name them, it could be assumed that he meant the Moslems, for there is little friendship existing between the two groups, even in the present day. Amritsar lies but a short distance from the border of Pakistan, only thirty-five miles from the Moslem city of Lahore, a city once entirely controlled by the Sikhs. But the Sikhs are there no more, nor indeed anywhere in Pakistan, not since the Moslem-Sikh riots at the time of Partition, when they almost equaled the intensity of the Hindu-Moslem riots at Delhi.

While in Amritsar I wanted very much to visit Lahore. It would have been such a short step over and back. But because of the customs involvement of visas, and permission to take equipment in and out during the present period of ill-feeling, we abandoned the idea until making official entry into Pakistan at Karachi a month later. The subsequent flight to Lahore and back then added at least fifteen hundred miles to the journey, a project which could have been accomplished earlier by a forty-minute taxi run. Such are the problems of a world where territorial borders separate peoples stirred to mutual hatred by political, ideological, or theological differences of opinion.

In some instances unbelievers were undoubtedly pushed

around by Moslems. On the other hand, when visiting Lahore, I was shown unmistakable evidences of desecration of Moslem monuments, allegedly incurred by the Sikhs while they were in control of the territory. For one thing, they built temples immediately adjacent to the mosques and would interrupt Moslem prayers by their rhythmic music and loudly voiced hymns. Like the Moslems before them, they had also expropriated valuable building materials from other religious structures for their own purposes. In this case they took marble from the mosques.

And here we see again the ever-recurring, ever-human expressions of resentment and retaliation. Few can seem to rise above them, though it appears more than ever obvious that unless and until we do there will be small likelihood of attaining the peace we all hunger for. The spirit of retaliation is as unending as the sequence of the seasons.

Now, with the Moslems once more firmly seated in Lahore, no Sikh dares show his face there for fear of his life. The Sikh temples are still standing, but our official Pakistan tourist guide forbade my even taking the picture of one of them. So great was his distaste for the followers of the Gurus that he seemed to turn ashen gray whenever the word Sikh was mentioned. If the Sikhs have many stories to tell of Moslem inhumanity, the Moslems have an equal number.

Speeding northward in the car, the president also spoke of how the early Gurus fought Hindu idolatry. He told of an instance during morning ablutions when a Guru was bathing in company with a crowd of Hindu devotees. While they all splashed water toward the sun in honor of their ancestors, the Guru was seen to splash water sacrilegiously in the opposite direction. When asked why, he replied that he splashed the water to his home and fields one hundred miles distant since they could observe him equally as well as the inanimate, unseeing sun.

Like so many things, however, it's easy to point the finger of accusation at another's weakness without sensing it in ourselves. In the case concerning idolatry I refer to the Sikh scripture, the Granth Sahib.

When Gobind Singh, the last Guru, approached the end of his days, he announced that for the Sikhs the succession of Gurus was over. Henceforth the accumulated writings of these inspired teachers and leaders—the Granth Sahib—would be the center and guide of the faithful. And so they have been.

Enshrined in an elevated position at the center of all Sikh temples is the Holy Granth, so revered as to have been given the oriental title of respect—Sahib.

Usual temple copies of the book are large three-foot-wide editions which, when not in use, are covered with many layers of the finest tapestries and embroidered fabrics. During the service these coverings will be ceremoniously removed from the scripture one at a time and replaced in the same manner at conclusion of the reading. While one man reads aloud with a chanting intonation, someone always stands beside him swinging a horsehair plume to keep insects from besmirching the sacred parchment.

It is also forbidden to turn one's back upon the Granth during any time it is uncovered, like the attitude anciently displayed toward ruling monarchs. I was unaware of this last bit of protocol until, at an outdoor tent celebration in honor of one of the martyrs where we were photographing the service by express invitation, I was roughly grasped by the shoulder and jerked around to face a wild-eyed fanatic jabbering away in Punjabi like mad. I was completely baffled until someone whispered the facts to me. You can imagine the complexity of the assignment from then on: trying to photograph the service, or more particularly the reactions of the assembled followers, and still never completely turn away from the holy book.

This ceremonious oral reading of the Granth takes place somewhere in each temple for the better part of every day, usually in small side rooms. In the Golden Temple at Amritsar it amounts to about twenty-two hours out of each twenty-four, ceasing only between midnight and 2 A.M. Not a few times have I heard the Sikhs accused of an idolatrous attitude toward their sacred book, though it would be hard to say that their reverence surpasses that of the Jews for the Torah.

We stopped several times that night between Delhi and Amritsar, trying to satisfy the body's insatiable demand for liquid, at villages with unpronounceable names. Though small in size, they were not so in population. Narrow streets were filled with pedestrians and tiny shops, like concession booths at a carnival—with one big difference: few of the shops stand flat on the ground. Instead, most of them are placed on supports about three feet high and the owner simply sits or squats on his haunches inside amid his wares. There would not be room enough for him to stand erect or for customers to enter; merchandise is passed outside to them. We used to speculate on the condition of our Western leg muscles if we were to remain in this position for an eight-hour day.

Until a late hour the streets are filled with restive, socially inclined citizens, laughing, talking, nibbling at cheap oriental sweetmeats. But in this scene there is another variance with cities of the West—no women. None. In all of India, as far as public thoroughfares are concerned, one hardly has the impression that the female sex exists after dark, unless at an exclusive social gathering of non-Hindu, non-Moslem peoples like the Parsis.

Particularly is this true in Moslem countries, where you can walk abroad at night for miles through the crowded streets of a large city like Karachi and never see one woman, old or young.

In the small towns it is the same. Society is male. No wonder marriages are arranged by family agreement. It is difficult to imagine how boys and girls would otherwise ever get together. Certainly there are no accredited social agencies for this purpose. And for the most part the two sexes just never come into contact until after the nuptial vows. Thence, the woman's world is narrow indeed.

Amritsar has a population of about three hundred ninety thousand. The narrow, crooked streets were well filled with pedestrians hastily moving, we presumed, to and from the temple, which is right in the center of the city—or at least so we had heard. After considerable driving I began to wonder. We wound and twisted, backed and turned, until it was evident the driver did not know his way. I didn't blame him.

Like most oriental cities—or any other pre-machine-age towns in the world for that matter—streets are wide enough for one vehicle at most. Those on foot squeeze past by flattening against the walls of the one- and two-story shops.

Either because our antecedents craved variety or because they built along the trails of wild animals, or for some other mysterious reason, no street seems to follow a straight course for more than fifty yards. If there are names and numbers they probably cause more confusion than not. Few lanes or avenues maintain the same name for more than a couple of blocks. Even in modern cities like Tokyo finding an address—even for a taxi driver—is a matter which requires several personal inquiries. You get only a general idea of location from the number itself.

In Amritsar our Sikh driver evidently had too much pride to ask his way to the Golden Temple. So we searched, and searched, around and through the labyrinth. We tried to follow the pedestrians, but always made some false turn and wound up back on the outskirts—as in a dream of frustration. Finally he gave up and asked—and asked again—at least three different times.

It was about 4:30 A.M. when we halted with a sigh of relief at the entrance to the sacred area. Artificially lighted, the place was jammed and at this outer point the temple was not yet visible. We removed our shoes and unloaded the equipment, which brought the usual encirclement of curiosity seekers.

Loaded down, we made our way over to the marble water trough where feet must be dunked before entering the hallowed grounds. This is a must—with a crowd of fifty or sixty of the faithful at your heels it would be a little awkward to skip. Men and women watched as we immersed our feet and rubbed the soles on the lip of the trough. All men are heavily bearded and I even noticed a few elderly patriarchs wearing the ancient costume of elite guard of Guru Gobind

Singh—unusually colorful garments—and carrying a long pikestaff. They made me think of Don Quixote.

From there we proceeded along a broad marble walk, passing under several arches until we arrived at the shore of a small artificial lake, in the center of which is placed that most exquisite piece of three-hundred-year-old craftsmanship and design, the Golden Temple.

Actually the lake is like any oversized Hindu bathing tank —adjacent to all Brahmin temples for ablutions—being square in shape with stone bathing steps leading down into the water from the four sides. As we came to the edge, many persons of both sexes were dressing, praying, or bathing, though some fragment of clothing was apparently kept on at all times.

All Sikhs in this area have a moral obligation to enter the holy lake each day if possible, and a pleasant debt it would be, for it is the cleanest place of its type that I saw in all India. Looking into the clear water, I could see large carp-like fish gliding about while the current rushing in from underground sources causes a turbulence on several points of the surface. A tempting relief it might have been for dusty, road-weary travelers, I can assure you. But not knowing the obligations, I didn't yield. It might have officially made me a Sikh for all I knew—or have constituted blasphemy.

Turning our attention from the bathers, we started around the water's edge, walking barefoot on the wide, cool marble walk which circumscribes the watery area. Thousands of devotees, silently and reverently passing to and fro in that still-darkened hour, made one think this must be a special festive occasion. It was difficult to imagine such

wholesale enthusiasm being generated every single day—
though I have no doubt that it is.

As we walked, our attention was constantly attracted, of
course, to the spotlighted temple out in the center of the
lake. It is not large, rather like a small enclosed white marble pavilion out in the water. The name Golden comes
from the gold-plated domes on the roof. From all directions electric beams are cast at its jewel-like loveliness, and,
in turn, reflected thence back to those of us on the shore of
the lake, thus suffusing the entire surroundings with a soft,
unearthly luminosity. Such theatrical effects, coupled with
the chanting lilt of the hymns being broadcast throughout
the area over loud-speakers, made it difficult to imagine a
more celestial atmosphere. At no time, in no place, have I
felt quite so "out of this world."

To enter the temple, one must go halfway around the
lake—opposite the main entrance, and out upon the penin-
sula-like walk leading from the peripheral edge to the sacred
portal. This ramp, or bridge, also of marble, is wide enough
to accommodate about four persons abreast in either direction. When we arrived, and during the several hours of our
stay, this walkway was absolutely jammed with crowds of
the faithful moving both directions in a slow, orderly
fashion, under the direction of traffic supervisors.

Because of the limited capacity of the temple and because
all Sikhs must make a daily visit if possible, the length of
stay for each worshiper is kept to a minimum, perhaps ten
or fifteen minutes being the time allowed to complete the
necessary acts of homage.

Guards alerted for our arrival escorted us along the ramp,
through the dense throng, and finally up to the main door

of the little temple, though there are open doorways on each of the four sides of the building, symbolizing the fact that God's abode is everywhere and that He may be found in any direction. The inside of the temple is divided into several smaller rooms or chambers. The main sanctuary itself, being open on all sides and quite small, is only large enough for an altar to enshrine the holy book plus sufficient space for the readers, musicians, and various officials who seat themselves around an embroidered cloth on which offerings may be deposited. Other rooms in the temple are in the nature of vestibules, an anteroom, and a mezzanine where, as mentioned, less sacred copies of the Holy Granth are read aloud during many hours of the day and night.

Shortly after our arrival we heard several trumpet blasts heralding the arrival of the holy book and in a few moments a highly decorated golden palanquin arrived at the entrance. Unfortunately for me we were as yet unprepared to turn cameras on the spectacle. Trying to find proper electrical outlets for the photo-floods—an eternal problem—held us up for some thirty minutes. By the time we had made contact the ceremony of installation was completed.

This, however, did not prevent our getting the highlights of all following parts of the liturgy that morning and I believe it to be some of the most interesting film taken on the journey.

Music within the temple is continuous except for short intervals while the Granth is read; actually no lectures, talks, or discussions of any sort are permitted. The unveiling of the book, incidentally, was fabulous. It must have been draped on this occasion with at least twenty different coverings and in the film it is like a concerto in Kodachrome.

With the exception of a few officers, including the president, seated cross-legged on the floor, none of the faithful was permitted to linger in the sacred chamber. Instead, they were slowly herded past the altar, jammed within the confines of a roped corridor, squirming and struggling for a glimpse of the book, and each casting his coin upon the silken robes in front of the shrine.

One other feature distinguishes Sikh temples: holy bread. This is a dark, pasty, doughlike mass which is sweet, rich, and quite palatable, made of flour, honey, dried fruits, and nut meats. Men with huge bowls of the concoction use their fingers to dole out little pats of it to each of the devout who ask for a share. I never saw one fail to obtain his portion, but upon occasion I saw the servers turn down several persons who evidently were angling for seconds. It must be good; at least it is eagerly sought after by all Sikhs passing through the temple.

Beyond this the Sikhs take great pride in the maintenance of the free kitchens. In these kitchens food is supplied free to all who enter and sit in rows upon the floor, without distinction of caste or creed. We visited several at feeding times and also while the food was in preparation. It is simple fare, but wholesome: flat, tough, tortilla-like cakes and a thickened vegetable stew, consisting mostly of beans.

In ever-hungry India a charitable enterprise of this magnitude is quite an undertaking, but I never saw more persons in attendance than they seemed able to take care of. I did not, however, see any who were not Sikhs and of course they could not possibly feed all others who might be likely to need food. Although the offer of free food to all is claimed, the primary benefit is doubtless intended for destitute Sikhs—a worthy enough accomplishment at that.

I was told that the institution of the *Langar*, or Free Kitchen, was started centuries ago by the first Sikh, Guru Nanak. Another Guru, Amar Das, made it a rule that no one could see him unless he first took food at the Free Kitchen.

The story goes that once the great Emperor Akbar came to visit the Guru and wanted to be an exception to the rule, but he had to sit and dine with the common people before Amar Das deigned to give audience.

The Sikhs were strong indeed in those days. And they have continued to be a sturdy group of people, proud of their democratic ways. There must have long been an element in priest-ridden India that hungered for an organization which championed the things that the Sikhs now stand for. The spiritual cleanliness, simplicity, and wholesomeness of the faith is remarkably visible.

They were not always treated by other Moslem rulers with the deference shown by the tolerant Akbar, however. The Golden Temple was desecrated and the lake filled in a number of times by bigoted invaders and rulers. At one time the Sikhs were declared outlaws with a price upon their heads. They were hunted and killed without the slightest compunction and forced to take to the jungles and wilds.

During the year 1739 a local Moslem official named Massa Ranghar turned the holy precincts of the Golden Temple into a stable and made the inmost sanctuary a nautch house.

One of the outstanding deeds in the annals of Sikh heroism concerns the action of two of their members, who entered the temple at that time in Moslem garb and, sighting the presiding official as he was seated smoking and enjoying the dances of public women, fell upon the man with a broadsword and cut off his head. They then took advantage of the followers' stunned surprise to make good their escape. There are many other similar stories, all worthy of conversion into flamboyant movie plots.

Dawn finally broke that morning at the Golden Temple, followed by yellow sunlight which squelched the puny glow of our man-made photo-floods, but the service did not slacken. The rhythmic hymns continued and the devout still pressed their way past the Holy Granth as we folded up the equipment and wandered outside. Taking one camera, I found my way up onto the roof of the temple for some sunrise panoramic shots. I also took pains to examine the quality of the covering on the domed pagodas. I guess it really is gold-plate.

As the sun ascended, the heat rose with it and we gathered our gear and retired to the little hotel to rest and await the cooler evening hours for the drive back to Delhi. During the afternoon the president paid a call to inquire if I had covered every phase of the Sikh liturgy that was desired. I assured him we had, with the exception of the ceremonial arrival of the Holy Granth. Of course we could have photographed that by staying another day, but I had already made several engagements for the morrow in Delhi, including a wedding with the Arya Samaj group at 6 A.M. Thinking about it at the time, I couldn't help musing over the fact that in oriental religion everything seems to take place at dawn. In a way it was a bit like army life—throughout the entire trip I don't recall sleeping past six-thirty on a single morning.

Back in Delhi we had several more contacts with the

Sikhs, resulting in a good sequence of film—about thirty minutes in the edited version.

In Delhi also we continued the investigation of Hinduism, visiting temples and ashrams. Short one- or two-day tours included the holy cities of Hardwar and Rishikesh, where the Ganges emerges from the foothills of the Himalayas. These places are inhabited by innumerable *sadhus*—holy men—lounging, preaching, or indulging their personal ceremonial and meditative practices. This is similar in many respects to the situation at Benares, except there are far fewer lay pilgrims attending these more remote shrines.

I watched groups of them in more secluded spots preparing food. Much of the atmosphere was similar to our own erstwhile hobo jungles: a kind of vegetable mulligan would be simmering on the open campfire and raw contributions to the community pot seemed to be required before a newcomer came in for a share of the more palatable potpourri.

In many ways it is a carefree existence in a land where familial obligations must be endlessly burdensome. India has been accused of harboring numerous beggars or charlatans under the guise of a holy man. It wouldn't be fair for me to try to render a generalized opinion on the score; my acquaintance was too sketchy. But surely many I saw had all the earmarks of love of indolence. At any rate, if a Hindu had a hankering for a life void of responsibility, it would be an easy out. One need not join an order or be called into account in any way. You just dress the part, avoid the barber or shave every hair completely, and hit the open trail—making the rounds of the holy places in due season, either to join in with gatherings for local special events or, from what

I could ascertain, to find the most agreeable climatic condition in accord with the procession of the seasons.

Of course there are sadhus or monks belonging to certain cults or centered around a spiritual leader. We visited and photographed one such group making its headquarters in Delhi at the temple to the Goddess Lakshmi, while about thirty of them were at vesper service. This ceremony starts with a fierce clanging of many bells, lasting about ten minutes—to attract the attention of the deity—and is followed by hymns, prostration before the image, and a consecration of flower petals which are then carried away by the participants with great reverence. Later we were presented to the leader, or swami, and permitted to take scenes of him seated on a dais receiving the adoration of his disciples as they bowed before him.

During the entire time we were there his total attitude was almost trancelike, with a wide-open, unblinking gaze. His stare into the lens is most peculiar; I believe it may even have a hypnotic effect on some members of my audience.

From what I gathered these sadhus, who were meticulously shaven of every hair except the single lock which is permitted to grow at the crown of the head—called a *sikha* by Hindus and regarded as the symbol of a resolve to face life unmoved—attend to the maintenance of the temple and participate in the usual rites. These are similar for nearly all Hindu cults, held thrice daily, at sunrise, just before noon, and again exactly twenty-four minutes before or after sunset.

Beyond this the monks study their scriptures and follow various Yoga routines to gain body control and work for the enlargement of their powers of meditation, under the guidance of the swami, who is presumed to be a fully developed and already emancipated soul adept at the practices of mysticism.

From here on we were able to visit and record many Hindu temple ceremonies, a privilege that had been denied previously. I will admit that temples which gave permission for photography were not the more important shrines, and many of the rituals were obtained in the less sought after, less conspicuous holy places, but I'm sure they are identical and valid in every respect with those carried out in the pilgrimage shrines, authentic and comprehensive.

The climax of my stay in Delhi was an interview with Dr. Radhakrishnan, the Vice-President of India, an outstanding contemporary scholar and authority on Hinduism and, in fact, religions of all the world. We had two meetings, a common occurrence in my interviews. The first was usually to form an acquaintance and let the person know my ideas, aims, and probable questions; the second would then be for the filming itself.

A kindlier, more sweetly dispositioned man I have seldom met (nor a vice-president under such informal circumstances: he was in bed. Not ill, mind you, just resting, nightshirt and all, about four in the afternoon on two successive occasions). We were ushered into his combination study, reception, and sleeping quarters without hesitancy upon the precise hour of our appointment. Nor was the unusual circumstance of the reception ever mentioned as far as I can recall. In every respect it was simply an example of complete informality, perfect trust in the ability of a foreign stranger to understand.

Dr. Radhakrishnan is not an ancient sage, yet my guess

would place him somewhere around seventy. He is in command of himself and surroundings and secure in his knowledge of human nature. Receptions conducted with such informality by a person of the doctor's rank can only be flattering to either friend or stranger.

I tried to explain my mission and he seemed sympathetic, willing, and agreeably interested. We set the approximate questions for an interview next day, but as was so often the case with those I sought out, they seldom seemed to understand that the event was to take place not only for microphone, but camera as well—or vice versa.

Upon arrival the following day the good doctor was still abed—cheerful, chatty, but reluctant to withdraw from his snug harbor. We conversed amiably for some time until I began to worry about losing daylight, and missing out on the film. I began to press the point about the outdoor interview, for I knew that Bob, out in the garden, would be all set up by then and beginning to fret over the vanishing sunlight.

Still the Vice-President was reluctant to go out-of-doors. "Why couldn't we just bring the microphone in here?" he wanted to know.

"But it's photography as well as sound," I urged. "It's for a film—to be shown on the public screen."

"Well, why not pictures right here?" he insisted. And at this point I was on the spot, for, thinking that the previous day's agreement had made clear the desirability of an outdoor setting, I had failed to bring photographic lights.

It called for a bit of fast thinking then, for our interview time allowance had only fifteen minutes to go. Other appointments were waiting in the anteroom. If I sent someone to the hotel for photo-floods we'd probably miss the boat all around. So I pulled a slightly unfair shenanigan on the good doctor by implying that lighting facilities were among our equipment and that coming inside would present us with no great problem, *but* . . . supposing those seeing the film with him in bed or at least so informally draped should begin to whisper that he was perhaps invalided or incapable of withstanding the physical rigors of his high office. What then?

Or further—think how sturdy and zestful he'd seem being interviewed in the beautiful, tranquil garden of his home . . . (and what nice Kodachrome, my silent, selfish subconscious whispered) . Especially would his vitality—or lack of it—be conspicuous in comparison to that of his physical-culture-conscious prime minister, Mr. Nehru! I think this last may have turned the trick, though I recall rattling on with similar fragmented arguments until the doctor silently rose from his volume-strewn coverlet, called for an extra garment or two, and we proceeded directly out to the side lawn.

Before going into the house we'd picked out a sundial as a likely place for the scene, and on coming out I found Bob, light meter in hand, ready and waiting for us.

Leaning the doctor against the pedestal and placing myself so that he'd play into our lens, I picked up the microphone and asked my first question.

Dr. Radhakrishnan speaks softly, very quickly, glibly, I would say, with a decided British accent. He made no hesitancy in his answers as I find them on my precious rolls of magnetic tape. The following conversation is indelibly etched, verbatim:

Ayres: "Dr. Radhakrishnan, we have discussed certain similarities between some faiths—would you say that there is what might be called a 'central core' common to all religions?"

Dr. R.: "If we get behind the forms, the ritual, the myths, et cetera, and try to understand what really constitutes the essence of any religion, you will feel that that essence consists in developing what may be regarded as the spiritual dimension to man's existence. Take the Upanishads, for example—the central postulate there is, 'That art thou.' In other words, there is a divine light or a divine seed or a divine impulse located in each human being. Similarly, the Buddhists declare that it is possible for each individual to grow to be a Buddha. Similarly, too, you find Jesus telling us the Kingdom of God is within you; or the proverbs—'the spirit of man is the candle of the Lord.' *The religious life consists in enabling that inner light to grow in you so as to overcome the darkness and make you the representative of that religious impulse.* That, in my mind, constitutes the central core of all religions."

Ayres: "And a very tangible core it is. Thank you, Dr. Radhakrishnan. Well now, Doctor, earlier you were speaking of a new world order. Do you feel that religion could in some way act as a basis for this new world order?"

Dr. R.: "We are trying to build this new world order on economic and political relations. Important as they are, the new world order can't be sustained on them alone. We do require a psychological coherence, a kind of spiritual unity, to sustain it, but religions as they are functioning today actually present more obstacles than help to the building up of such an order. So, first, what we need is a better kind of understanding between religions. That's what we require at the present moment. If we believe that the divine light dwells in all, then we must also believe that there's nobody in this world, whatever be his nation or race, in whom that light does not dwell. Therefore, if we give up the conception of the chosen people based on national existence or racial inheritance—if we adopt the view that man as man, to whatever race or to whatever nation he belongs, also is the offspring of God—if we adopt *that* principle in building a new world order, then this world order can be sustained . . . not otherwise."

When the doctor finished his statement, I found it hard to explain to him just why it was necessary to repeat the routine in another, closer angle. But he finally consented, putting the answer in another set of equally potent words. This time when he finished, however, he simply turned on his heel and strode away, flinging back over his shoulder, "See you in the house for tea—right away." These words are on the tape too!

Here is a man of faith—a Hindu in every sense of the word—and yet how far his attitude and manner of expression seem from the many devout Hindu worshipers encountered in the various shrines and holy places.

At tea Dr. Radhakrishnan spoke about the breadth, depth, and latitude in Hindu worship. It was plain to see that he represented the highest form of Hinduism, unquestionably a religious attitude compatible in every respect with that which would be necessary to inspire the new world order.

I'm certain that the doctor would not deny Brahmanism and yet his statement regarding the spark of divinity in each man, although not inimical to Brahmanism, is contradictory in Western eyes to the commonly encountered spirit of peoples under the caste system. If the average Brahman does not deny the divinity in each man, his actions in terms of the Occidental understanding of equality scarcely, or seldom, lend the flavor of realism to his words—a criticism which in the end, I suppose, could apply in degrees to most of civilization, under whatever religion or ideology.

Strangely enough, it was not until reaching home and playing the tape over again that his meanings began to endear themselves. While actually working my mind was always so involved with other aspects of the situation, such as film and the recorder, getting the V.I.P. to speak into the mike, the weather, and a thousand mechanical things, that my end of the conversation required a terrific effort of concentration. These were times when I envied the quick-witted ability of the familiar man-on-the-street radio and TV interviewers, who are never at a loss for words!

A few more contacts with the Jains and Sikhs and we were off for Bombay. Bombay, incidentally, is quite a change from other cities on the subcontinent. It's cleaner, more modern, and, of course, still strongly charged with the atmosphere of its British parents. This was noticeable, not only in such obvious ways as city planning, architectural lines, and transportation equipment, but also in mass attitudes and procedures in business, commerce, and public office as well. These functionings seem to reflect what must have been British procedures and customs during colonial occupation, making a distinction from British business customs in their homeland.

If the Indians learned the mechanics of a more modern, democratic way of civilization from their newly shaken European masters—and I guess with all they've suffered they would at least find it necessary to make such an acknowledgment—they also picked up some bad habits.

When I've criticized India, I've done so with not the slightest intention of lessening our compassion or responsibility for these darker-skinned brothers. Their faults have hurt no one but themselves and the flaws are the result of a system that has been thrust upon them for many centuries. They are a good people: civilized, gentle, sensitive, deserving of every possible help on the road to democratic maturity. Their needs are great, and we must help them in many ways: above all, they must have our patience and understanding.

Before leaving Bombay I want to tell of one incident with the Jains. From time to time across India I had recorded a number of their ceremonies in different locales. Representatives of one sect, the Digambara (Sky-Clad), had seemed anxious for me to pay a visit and observe the consecration of some of their monastic members, who publicly go about in the nude. There was one saintly group of them in particular, which I felt would give an effective climax to the whole Jain sequence.

However, since these devout believers have no permanent home and simply wander throughout India, staying in the smaller towns and villages, they are hard to locate on short notice—even by officers of the headquarters for the faith—and I was obliged to wait patiently for word from them as to the whereabouts of the group. It wasn't forthcoming and

finally after six or seven uncommunicative weeks I'd practically abandoned the idea.

For a number of reasons—mainly the mechanical condition of our equipment—I made the aforementioned week-
long swing through Southern India, returning to Bombay
by air one morning about ten, pretty well bushed from the
singlehanded adventure. Among the correspondence at the
desk of the fine old Taj Mahal Hotel was a telegram dated
the previous morning:

MYSELF IN MHASVAD TOMORROW WITH ACHARYA SHANTI-
SAGARJI STOP DORECT FILMSTAR LUIAIRS (sic) MHASVAD
SATARA DISTRICT STATION KOREGAON SOUTHERN RAILWAY
—TALAKCHAND VENICHAND SHAH PLEADER

At last it had come: the summons to meet the famous
Jain saint.

Acharya (which means spiritual teacher) Shantisagarji
is the most highly venerated of all the Digambara Jains. He
is an aged man, and I had heard much about him. I leafed
through a large congratulatory volume printed on the occasion of his eighty-first birthday some years back. It carried
testimonials and inscriptions by every high official, statesman, and diplomatic representative in Southeast Asia. On
the roster of those most emancipated from the world's materialism this man stands in highest rank and, in my project,
to miss an audience with Shantisagarji would be like an
art historian in Paris overlooking an interview with Picasso.
I was very eager to accept the invitation.

Problem number one was to find the place; no hotel informant could locate Mhasvad on any available map. However, from a timetable of the Southern Railway we did find

Koregaon Station about three and a half hours south of Poona, a total of seven hours by rail from Bombay. Because of schedules there was no way of completing the journey in one day, so I would have to leave immediately, spend a night in Poona, and head for Koregaon in the morning.

By four that afternoon I was aboard the train for Poona, arriving there in time for a bite of dinner—the usual gristly mutton—at a tiny hotel that evening. It was off-season and my one recollection is that the unscreened room I was given must have been without human occupants for a long while. A lumpy mattress, mice, bats, and myriads of birds roosting and fluttering about the inside beams and partitions kept me in a semiconscious state a good part of the night.

At five the next morning the porter called me; I was grateful to dress and get out, leaving the field to those earlier, local inhabitants. Minutes later I was pacing the station platform of the Southern Railway—or I should say, threading my way across, for it was packed with worker-class families seated among their personal boxes and bundles upon the floor, where in most stations everyone sits if he sits at all. I wondered where they all were heading, but, of course, beyond sign language there was no means of communication with anyone on my part. Not knowing what the day might bring, I picked up a few emergency rations on the platform—dry biscuits and damp chocolate. A quart of water was in the equipment bag; it would have to do.

I think it may have been a little before 6 A.M. when my train wheezed in. It was a two-class job, ancient, limping, puffing, with a blood pressure which must have been well over 250! I began to understand why the schedule showed Koregaon to be three and a half hours from Poona, when it appeared only a little more than seventy-five miles distant.

Aside from the main-line routes trains in India thunder about in a pitiful state of repair—bearings burn out, boilers burst. Schedules are but vague outlines of connections that can only be hoped for. Waiting an additional hour or two is commonplace. Upon occasion I've cooled my heels a good four and five hours.

As the cars squealed to a halt that morning, the crowd rose as one, gathered their voluminous gear, and began a tumultuous boarding. I was grateful to find a seat in the sole second-class compartment, for the third-class cars were positively bulging with passengers and baggage. There was interminable pause and finally, in a spasm of shuddering lurches, we were off, eventually rising to full cruising velocity of perhaps twenty-five miles per hour!

We were so packed in that many passengers, unable to find space, clung to the outside steps and handrails. Then, we were scarcely out of the station when the off-side compartment door was opened and a cluster of ragged stowaways swarmed up from somewhere below and took over the entire floor space of the compartment, without objection from any of the paying passengers. I would say there was quite a substantial gang of us on that little puffer-belly and we were cozily clustered together for quite a while.

I kept wondering when the bulk of the party would find its destination and debark to give the rest of us a bit of room to stretch out, but everyone stayed right on; we even gathered a few more boarders at some of the way stations. It was a long seventy-five miles!

It was almost five hours later, I'd say, when Koregaon hove into sight. At least that was when a tiny station appeared outside the windows of our overstuffed contraption. No town was visible on the flat, dusty terrain. "Well, at least I'll be out of this tight pickle," I thought as I gathered my stuff together, but it was an inaccurate surmise.

Everyone else got off too, while I stood, like a lone rock in the rapids, as they boiled and swirled around me on the platform. There were hundreds of them, gabbling, chiding, flustered, excited, all headed for somewhere here in the Koregaon area. Exit from the tracks meant single file through a narrow turnstile, and with the mass impatience of the group I elected to wait until after the crowd had gone through before leaving myself.

I had sent off several wires the day before announcing the time of my arrival, but both names and addresses were indefinite and I had no assurance of contact. After a thorough search it became certain no one was on hand to meet me here in Koregaon, so I began an inquiry as to the whereabouts of the village of Mhasvad; I thought it was probably within a mile or two.

It was not easy to get an answer; I kept repeating the name, getting nothing but blank looks, until finally one of the railway men seemed to understand. He pointed across the horizon and made finger signs with a couple of English phrases which seemed to indicate that Mhasvad was somewhere about fifty miles to the east! I was aghast.

This is quite primitive country by modern standards; it is way off the tourist path. There are dirt roads, of course, and no accommodations of any kind. It's the type of countryside where one goes by sturdy car, carrying his own supplies. I was not equipped for such an expedition with my vanilla cookies and candy bars!

Besides there seemed to be no transportation whatsoever. There was no automobile of any kind around the station, just two or three oxcarts with their chargers stomping around in the heavy dust. I made additional frantic inquiries concerning transportation to this Mhasvad place and finally someone indicated that a conveyance of some sort would be available about a half mile distant, toward what might be the town of Koregaon.

I picked up the camera gear and started out, following the line of my fellow passengers down the rutted country road. As usual it was hot. I'd say the temperature was easily in excess of 100 degrees. It was quite a grind and it was a welcome sight when a little cluster of crude buildings came into view. I could see some kind of a truck or bus standing there, too.

Hurrying, I sought out the bus driver and was directed to a tiny ticket office. "Mhasvad?" The reply was affirmative and I plunged into my pocket for money. But when I looked up, the man was shaking his head.

"What?" I asked. "What's the matter?"

He had one word as he pointed to the disreputable shambles of an outdated autocar: "Full."

If I have ever seen a "filled" vehicle, this was it. The arms and legs of all my erstwhile rail companions protruded from every window, every crevice. The top was piled high with crude baggage surmounted by additional passengers to the point of endangering the over-all balance. Several last-straws were trying desperately to get aboard somehow. It was the most blatant bawling clambake I have ever seen, bar none.

"When is the next bus?" I inquired.

"No more bus today," was the answer.

"But there must be some kind of transportation to Mhasvad—some other bus, taxi, truck, private car. Something, somewhere, around here!"

I got no reply, only a negative shrugging.

"Well, then, I must get on *that* bus—I must get to——" I had started to become a bit frantic, when, looking up, I saw that the bus was just starting to pull out. This brought on an automatic reaction which propelled me alongside the bus in a few strides, grasping for a handhold, when I happened to realize that all my photographic materials were piled on the ground by the little office.

And that was that. There were no other available vehicles at any price—absolutely none. Nor was there a train back to Poona until nightfall. There were just a few scattered villagers now that the emigrants had departed and no one with the slightest concern for my predicament. There was no solution anyway.

Assembling my gear, I sat down for a breather in the fragment of shade from the slight eaves of a weather-beaten shack, while a couple of naked kids stood staring at me. This could be called the low point of my tour, the nadir.

I realized now that I was tired, very tired, and that I'd been tired for some weeks. I had been going almost five months without a pause, not a day off that could be recalled. There was pressure all the time, worry over a dozen things, and plenty of discouragement. I thought of all the interesting items I'd missed: the Red Swastika group in Hong Kong, the Jain statue, my visa for Indo-China, festivals that had taken place the week before. They piled up, and got gloomier and darker by the moment.

I also recalled the sage advice of good old Charlie Skouras when I had called upon him at home for a letter of introduction to the Orthodox authorities in Greece. He gave me a wonderful letter, too, but, shaking his head, expressed doubt and misgivings as he said, "You want to show films of people's religion but I don't see how you can. It's too sacred and too touchy a subject. Still, maybe if you stick at it . . ." He paused and then continued, "Three years ago I build this Cathedral of St. Sophia. I pay for it with my own money and it takes years of my time. Now it's finish and everyone agrees a very beautiful job—but if I would know at the start how much pain and torment I go through to build it, I would never have started. I say this so you be prepared to face plenty grief and disappointment—yes, more than you guess!"

And then it happened. There was the sound of a motor and from out of nowhere a car swung around the corner and stopped. I could not believe my eyes. It was not an old car, nor was it like any car I'd seen for a long while in these or any adjacent parts. It was a brand-new, bright blue Chevrolet Deluxe sedan! The chance that such a gasoline buggy was in existence within a radius of two hundred miles was a thousand to one.

A small dark man stepped out from beside the driver. He had a telegram in his hand. "Is a Mr. Aye-res here? We are sorry to be delayed. Your telegram did not come until this morning," he apologized as I was loaded into the empty back seat of the sedan, which at the time felt like a Rolls-Royce town car. The door slammed and we started over the rough, rocky road to Mhasvad—two ruts stretching through gullies and ravines.

About fifteen miles out we encountered the bus; one wheel had fouled up in a dry wash. Most of the passengers were standing around trying to help the driver extricate the vehicle.

My escort said, "Happens all the time, but he'll be up and along again soon. Takes the bus about four hours to get to Mhasvad. We'll make it less than two." I was so glad I hadn't caught the bus and I was inwardly embarrassed for allowing myself to get into that sulky, gloomy mood.

To whom did the car belong? Just one of the more well-to-do Jains who happened to be in the area for a day's visit with the saint, and when my telegram finally arrived, he was kind enough to send for me.

Mhasvad is a typical small Indian town, with narrow oriental streets and low adobe buildings with inner court-yards, reminiscent of Spain and Mexico. A new Jain temple had been built and there was quite a crowd milling about the streets. These were mostly pilgrims from near and far, who surround the Archarya and his entourage wherever their wanderings may take them. One has the feeling that their existence is in the mood of a perpetual gala occasion.

It was now midafternoon and I was taken directly to a low building with a good-sized interior, which was jammed with standing crowds of people. Shoes were removed at the entrance; in fact, though I didn't demand it, special permission was accorded me in order to wear shoes upon the streets. I may sound pampered, but I'm certain I could not have stood the heat from that sun-baked surface.

In the center of the crowd, on a low platform, sat the saint, cross-legged, nude, and surrounded by admirers making deep bows and presentations of gifts of food, such as fruits and coconuts.

As I watched from the side lines, I noted that the aged man made no acknowledgment or any attempt to communicate with anyone in any way, nor did anyone speak to him. He simply sat, unblinkingly, as I had seen so many of these religious devotees do in the Orient, and he looked nowhere.

T. V. Shah, the sender of my invitation, had come forward when I arrived and was now acting as my interpreter. The suffix "Pleader" on his name indicated he was an attorney and he was a very cordial, intelligent man. He escorted me to the dais and presented me to Shantisagarji in what may have been Hindustani. I bowed. The saint allowed his eyes to drift toward me, but made no other sign. I mentioned something to the interpreter about a question on the matter of the world's state of unrest, but when he spoke to the aged man no reply was forthcoming and it was suggested that this was an ill-timed moment for discussion.

I could see, too, that this was an old man whose consciousness of his present world was wrapped in haziness. Perhaps the years of earthly denial and mystic meditation had already attached his mind to other spheres.

I was then permitted to take several flashlight shots of him and no one ever had a subject which "held it" more obediently. I still wanted motion pictures, however, and I made a strong request that the saint be removed to a better-lighted spot. After much discussion by Jain authorities it was finally arranged, although I did not observe anyone consult the saint about it.

In the Digambara sect permanent nudity is arrived at as

the final stage of a series of steps wherein the Jain monk wears less and less clothing. In this particular group of about a dozen monks and an equal number of fully attired and robed nuns Acharya Shantisagarji was the only person who was totally "sky-clad." The other members of his immediate staff wore G-strings as the only remnant of worldly garb before entering the Vanprastha, or saintly, state. It is considered that no one can wear clothing and become sainted, nor can Nirvana be attained without renunciation of all apparel and worldly goods.

Nudity has sometimes been the mark of saintship in other lands in ages past and we read of several instances in the Old Testament where prophets denuded themselves at the Lord's command. Christian saints are presumed to have done likewise, including a St. Mary of Egypt and numerous Moslem mystics and monks.

The Greeks spoke of gymnosophists: "These men went about naked, inured themselves to hardships and were held in highest honor—every wealthy house was open to them, even the apartments of women."

Marco Polo said, "Some Yogis went stark naked because, as they said, they had come naked into the world and desired nothing that was of this world. Moreover, they declared, 'We have no sin of the flesh to be conscious of and therefore are not ashamed of our nakedness.'" Many Hindu sadhus similarly go in the nude to this day.

According to the Jains, no ancient religious practice can be stopped by any government in the world; certainly the practice is protected in India. I do not know what the position of the authorities in the United States would be if the Jain saints decided upon a visit to America, but I presume it would create quite a controversial stir if they managed a visa. I don't believe, however, that there are Jains anywhere outside of India and the foregoing is a most unlikely problem. They just don't gravitate toward material, skyscraper worlds.

Besides the nudity Jain saints cannot accept food or an invitation to dinner from anyone by appointment, nor do they eat if food be taken to where they may be staying. Food must be given reverently and respectfully and it will be eaten on the spot, for the saint cannot carry it elsewhere.

They do not drive or ride in any conveyance and must cover a certain distance on foot every day. They do not spend more than five days in any one town except during the rainy season, when they will remain in one locality for four months continuously.

This last rule shows the importance of the weather on religious attitudes and surely demonstrates that nudity as a religious observance would not exist in a less gentle climate. It is one of the likely reasons why Westerners are startled at such a suggestion.

Within an hour a special procession of nuns and monks, including the saint, had been arranged and I was able to capture the whole affair on my movie camera. It would make a fitting climax to my sequence on the Jains.

That evening I was returned to Koregaon, where I left after a four-hour delay in schedule for a nightlong journey, interspersed by several transfers, back to Bombay. The next day we were busy wrapping and shipping film. We mailed home over fifty pounds of religious books, pamphlets, and notes that had accumulated during two months in a land that puts more importance on religion than perhaps any other place on earth.

Many wonderful things about the Indians in general would remain with me forever: unique gestures, mannerisms, and that wonderful gentleness which prevented even the slightest feeling of apprehension, no matter how alone or in what remote part of the country I was stranded. There's also a kind of sweet, naïve sincerity that gets down under one's skin and makes you want to see them get a better break out of life than they've had in centuries past. They've got it coming.

The following morning flight took us mostly across water on the route to Karachi—or so I was told. I slept the greater part of the way, and for an inveterate window-looker-outer this was unusual.

CHAPTER NINE

The people of Pakistan, a nation with two unconnected land areas, are like the family in the big house who were left with one bedroom and the garage. Naturally some adjustments can be made. The Pakistanis have put a hot-plate in the bedroom for cooking and have planted a few vegetables along the driveway to the garage, but economically it's a comedown from the old setup and twice as much labor for what they get.

The unfortunate part is that the now-divided householders, having everything else in common, allegedly separated primarily on the basis of one point: a point which, in the case of both sides, basically seeks to inculcate the spirit of unity rather than disruption, harmony and love rather than strife and estrangement. And that point is religion.

Otherwise they are alike racially, emotionally, and culturally. You can't tell a Moslem Indian from a Hindu except occasionally by clothes or hair styles. Their divorce is a misfortune, for they need each other very much.

216

The inhabitants of Pakistan are fine people. From my first encounter with Moslems at the mosque in Delhi, I got the impression that photographic information on Islam would be a difficult problem. It was not, however, any more difficult than gathering the material on Hinduism. There were a few instances of camera resistance; this situation was bound to arise when so much emphasis is placed on the Mosaic command to refrain from forming a graven image. To the zealous Moslem any image, whether graven or merely photographic, is an anathema. On the other hand, we sometimes took cameras and the recorder into the most highly sanctified shrines, making pictures of the most intimate rites without interference.

Of course, to accomplish this, we needed an escort and appointments, for these recordings had to be prearranged. And this is where my experience in Pakistan differed from India; in Pakistan I had government assistance and supervision at all times. Before leaving the United States I had laid my plans before the Pakistan Embassy. They, in turn, were most cordially responsive to the idea and we kept in contact until my arrival. I must say they maintained their end of the bargain magnanimously. From the moment I set foot on their soil at the airport in Karachi until we departed three weeks later the public-relations officers of the government of Pakistan extended themselves tirelessly in behalf of my project. No one could have been more co-operative. I shall be eternally grateful to them.

As I have mentioned before, it is one thing to feel one has an acquaintance with the fundamental theology and dogmas of a religion; it is another to know how its rituals and especially the sacraments are practiced in different regions. Customs differ greatly from place to place and are affected by ancient local practices as well as climate and products of the land. Unless one has expert, concentrated guidance in locating the performance of these rites, it could take many, many months before one stumbled onto them.

For those needing an introduction to the religion of the Mohammedans, let me briefly state that it began on the Arabian peninsula about six hundred years after the inception of Christianity and it was originated by a man named Mohammed, born in Mecca in A.D. 570, often referred to simply as "The Prophet." Mohammed did not consider himself divine; he performed no miracles, and he never permitted anyone else to deify him, so the term Mohammedan is never used by his followers. Instead they term themselves Moslems or plurally Muslimen, meaning "those who submit." This refers to the name given the faith by its founder: Islam, signifying surrender to the revelation and will of God.

No, Mohammed never thought himself a god, but he readily proclaimed that he was the recipient of direct communication from either the angel Gabriel or from God, termed Allah by the Moslems. These divine injunctions were dictated by The Prophet to scribes, who set them down on such materials as stones, pieces of leather, and palm leaves. Later Abu Bekr, the first Caliph, had them collected and compounded into a single volume, known ever since as the Koran. This book, believed by Moslems to be completely infallible, is the Islamic guide in matters of doctrine, morals, manners, civil law, etc.—the sacred literature of what has been called the fastest-growing religion in the world, a faith numbering perhaps more than 350,000,000 adherents.

Two reasons are usually cited for the success and rapid growth of Islam: its simplicity and its fanaticism. Actually these could be reduced to one—simplicity—and the emotional enthusiasm that a simple, easily comprehended idea can generate.

During the time of my contact with the followers of Islam I wanted to illustrate one of the five requisites for fulfilling the requirements of the faithful by getting permission to visit Mecca during the annual time of pilgrimage. I tried every means, high and low, to accomplish this, without success. I cajoled, entreated, argued, and implored, through channels diplomatic and political, but the steadfast rule that no unbeliever shall enter the center of Moslem sanctity steadfastly remained an impenetrable barrier to my efforts.

Finally one official said, "Well, you know, Mr. Ayres, if you honestly desire to enter Mecca, it really can be accomplished very easily."

I perked up and waited expectantly. "Yes," he went on. "All you have to do is become a Moslem."

It would be so easy. To join Islam, all one need do is declare before witnesses the words "*La illah ha illillah, Mohammed era sullillah . . . ,*" a phonetic spelling from the Arabic meaning, "There is no God, but one God, and Mohammed is His prophet." Admittance to the brotherhood then follows without question. Of course, after such a declaration one must demonstrate the sincerity of his proclamation by living up to the moral and ethical demands of the Koran and conducting his life in accordance with Moslem ideals.

These obligations fall roughly under five major headings,

sometimes known as the five pillars of Islam: (1) Daily repetition of the creed, (2) giving alms, (3) prayer, (4) fasting, and (5) pilgrimage.

With Moslems charity and the brotherhood of man come next to love and devotion to God. In fact brotherhood struck me as the outstanding characteristic of the religion. Democratic equality is emphasized in far greater degree than among Christians in the Western world. This, I would say, is also one of the chief reasons for the present high rate of expansion of Islamic followers and is particularly noticeable among darker-skinned races, such as the various peoples of Africa who traditionally have suffered discrimination at the hands of Occidental whites. This is also the reason why Islam would have an excellent chance of becoming the unifying religion of the yellow races.

Brotherhood is vigorously demonstrated in prayers at the mosque, where private concessions such as the reserved pews found in many Christian churches are nonexistent. "First come, first served" is the rule of the mosque and there are endless tales concerning the plight of high-ranking dignitaries whose tardiness at prayer service forces them to perform the symbolic acts of submission while bareheaded and barefooted in the broiling noonday sun of the courtyard or amid the stacks of footgear in the entryway.

The simultaneous co-ordination of Moslem mass prayers, which are repeated five times daily, is itself a perpetual symbol of equality and brotherhood. Old, young, rich, and poor alike—facing the direction of Mecca—nod, kneel, bow, and abase themselves in a vibrant unison of worshipful reverence for Allah. These prayers, which take four or five minutes and are always similar in routine, may be performed in private when unavoidable, although attendance at the mosque is strongly urged as a means of keeping brotherly affection a vital concern. Most Moslems attend at least once a day.

Officials of the mosque include the muezzin, who makes the call to prayer; the imam, who leads the prayer, and the khatib, or mullah, as he is called in Pakistan, who does the preaching. There are no priests as intermediaries between man and God, nor any ecclesiastical hierarchy. No collection plate is passed in the mosque, no offerings received at prayer time. Before prayer in the mosque elaborate ablutions must be performed, usually in a tank or fountain provided for the purpose. Hands, arms, and face, including mouth, teeth, and nostrils, are thoroughly scrubbed. It is interesting to note that when water is not available, as is frequently the case in desert regions, sand or dust may be used in its place.

The fourth pillar of Islam is the act of fasting. Principally this reverent observance takes place during the Moslem month of Ramadan, when neither crumb nor drop must pass the lips throughout the long hours of daylight. Here again, love of fellow man is expressed by the dropping of quarrels and forgiveness of wrongs. As the end of the month of Ramadan draws to a close, multitudes of the faithful can be found at sunset scanning the western sky for the first sign of the new moon, which will herald the conclusion of their grueling fast. Until this object is visible the period of privation cannot be concluded; therefore, no advance date of this event is ever published.

In olden times—mostly in isolated communities—clouded skies might have prolonged the harsh term for several days, but there is no chance of such a misfortune today. We have movies of Moslem officials being sent aloft into the evening sky by modern aircraft for the sole purpose of rising above any cloudy overcast which might make the new moon invisible to observers on the ground. Who says the Moslem peoples are not progressive?

The last of the pillars is pilgrimage or Hajj. This journey to the holy city of Mecca is a moral obligation for all Moslems financially and physically able to do so. It need only be taken once in the lifetime of each believer, although repetitions are considered to add spiritual merit.

Again we see the emphasis Islam places on brotherhood and unity, for this occurrence annually takes place during a single month of the year and assembles on equal ground Moslems from all corners of the globe. Without regard to color, wealth, or accomplishment they meet together with bared heads and in simple white robes to renew vows and restate their faith in the teachings of The Prophet.

Since the Moslem calendar is based solely upon cycles of the moon, its months slowly shift around the zodiac without regard for seasonal changes. A matter of a few years may alter the time of pilgrimage from winter to summer. In the barren land of Arabia any climatic extremes can be uncomfortable to the scantily clad pilgrims, but especially torturous is the heat of summer when temperatures are probably as high as or higher than anywhere else on earth.

We did a sequence in July on a pilgrim ship setting sail from the harbor of Karachi. It was an old freighter, temporarily converted for the purpose of conveying these mostly elderly rural people fulfilling at long last the dream of a lifetime. Life aboard was a primitive affair with crude ovens on one side of the deck and live goats, for fresh meat, corralled on the other. Bundles of personal belongings, bedding, and household effects were carried in the arms of aged, bearded patriarchs, while their wives, covered from crown to toe in the smothering burka, struggled to keep a footing on the steep gangplank.

The whole proceeding was filmed as a finale to the chapter on Islam. Later a discussion arose as to the probable experience in store for these pilgrims, and I have had detailed accounts of the whole complex routine undergone by the faithful visitors to Mecca. It was a shock to find it considered likely that many of those now setting sail would never return; that frightful midsummer Arabian heat, beating mercilessly down upon these aging, uncovered pilgrims over the period of days required to fulfill ritual demands, has always taken a staggering toll of human lives by sunstroke and heat exhaustion.

No infidel is allowed within a distance of several miles of the city. For an outsider to risk crashing in by disguise would be to court death at the hands of innumerable fanatics. Moslems themselves have smuggled in cameras and a few legitimate photographs of the ceremonies have been made in recent years, but I do not know of a non-Moslem who has ever visited or photographed within the walls the Kaaba or the sacred Black Stone. This stone has been the center of adoration and reverence since long before the time of Mohammed.

In explaining Moslem concepts to me a zealot in Lahore once enthusiastically described Mohammedan attachments as purely spiritual, and it is true that mosques contain no images of any kind. He pointed out an odious comparison to this in the predilection of certain Christian sects for the abundant use of images in their churches. "Idolatrous," he called it. "We Moslems worship only the one God who is great. We teach of no idols or sacred relics."

However, when I asked about the Black Stone in Mecca, he had absolutely no answer.

I do not know a religion of any notable size or age, regardless of its dogma or doctrine, which has not had to make compromises with what are evidently certain instinctive urges in its followers. These urges, when properly channeled, can gradually be transferred from idolatrous immaturity to respect and appreciation of significant symbolism.

I don't believe we covered the sacraments of any religion more thoroughly than those of Islam as practiced in Pakistan, starting with the rite for a newborn child in the delivery room, where the baby is customarily placed in the hands of a mullah who whispers the first phrases of the Koran in the child's ear. These beautiful verses, called the *Azahd*, are also used by the muezzin when calling the faithful to prayer at the mosque.

Another charming ceremony called *Aqiqa*, which takes place during the child's seventh month, consists of prayers, naming the child, and a ceremonial head-shaving, followed by festivities and the sacrifice of a goat, the flesh of which goes to the poor. The origin of this rite must have arisen in pagan practices.

The wedding ceremony we attended is, by all odds, the most unusual I've ever seen. It was the type popularly in use among ultraconservative Moslems living principally in rural areas where the boy and girl never see each other's faces until after the ceremony.

Courtship, in these cases, is restricted to negotiations between the parents and the wedding takes place while the participants, both heavily veiled with fruit blossoms, are seated in separate rooms. It is all primarily a legal transaction, with the groom signing a written contract guaranteeing certain monetary settlements in the event he ever seeks a divorce. The amount of money agreed upon depends on his idea of the bride's desirability and, frequently, will be placed at a very high figure just to prove the groom's intense ardor or to boast of his youthful pocketbook. It is also part of feminine vanity to be able to impress female associates with a high masculine estimate of her charms.

Sometimes these chivalrous, unrealistic promises have proved a strong obstacle to divorce and Moslem humor in this respect deals with many instances where the irate husband curses himself for his folly in placing the promised settlement so high. "I'd love to divorce you, if only I could afford it" is the gist of his complaint. Divorce consists simply in stating one's intentions publicly on three different occasions at intervals of thirty days. Thus the customary stipulation of a protective settlement in behalf of the wife is necessary.

After the marriage contract has been accepted and signed by both parties, the groom enters the bride's chamber and, lifting a corner of her veil of flowers, uses a mirror to catch the first glimpse of her face. Then he returns alone to his former quarters for a celebration with male comrades.

Moslems are given burial in cemeteries where all graves face at right angles to Mecca. The head of the corpse is then turned upon its right side in order to face forever the symbolic spiritual center of Islam. No grave is elevated above the surface of the ground and there are usually two simple gravestones—one at the head, one at the foot.

Islam is divided into several sects, the largest being the Sunnite. This group accepts a body of tradition called the Sunna, which for them supplements the Koran. Also, many followers of this sect seem to gravitate toward practices not in accord with strict Islamic teaching, such as the veneration of sacred objects. For example, many of their large mosques have each a chamber containing relics, such as hairs from the beard of The Prophet, articles of his clothing, and the like. I have seen devout followers in an attitude of profound worship before them—and scarcely to be blamed, I might add—if the relics actually be genuine.

Tombs of famous saints are another magnet for those with strong instincts of supplication. In Lahore, at a shrine called Data Gang Baksh, we visited the tomb of St. Azrad Sayed Ali Hajewali, the saint reputed to have brought Islam to the Lahore district some nine hundred years ago. It was absolutely packed with devotees caressing and groveling before the stone grille surrounding the central portion of the consecrated area. Similar activity may be found at other shrines.

This is not to say that all Moslems concur with the spirit of such demonstrations. My particular guides, who were also Sunnites, remained calmly aloof from any such participation; they were even, in fact, slightly disdainful of it. But there is no doubt that if a faith, however ironclad, is to have a wide appeal in this world, it must have simplicity, it must be tolerant, and it must make reasonable compromises with man's immaturity and his craving for self-expression.

After the Sunnites the next largest group is the Shi'as.

Followers of this sect declare an allegiance to Ali, the cousin and son-in-law of Mohammed. The Shi'as are set apart from other Moslems by the doctrine of the imam as head of the state, considered to be chosen by God either directly or through a previous imam. Besides Mecca they have their own objects of pilgrimage at holy places in Iraq.

I also visited and photographed a religious service in a mosque belonging to the Ismaili sect. This is the group whose spiritual leader is the Aga Khan, and I must say I was more favorably impressed by what I saw of them than by any other sect of Islam.

Mainly it was the modern, progressive spirit of the Ismailis which seemed so much in advance of many other groups. For one thing, women attend prayer services at the same time as the men, which is a most unusual occurrence with Moslems, although even here they do not actually sit together, but rather each sex has an equal half of the mosque with a railing dividing them. There appeared to be more of a community spirit, too, with something of a social program for members. At one of their mosques I remember refreshment stands and a parklike atmosphere surrounding the area. Also, the prayer service had a less formal aspect than that usually found in other mosques and included portions of the liturgy where members shake hands with all those near them.

For many years I had heard of His Highness, Prince Aga Khan, the leader of this Moslem sect, and I always wondered how a man in this position of spiritual responsibility could remain in Europe or other parts of the world, separated for such long periods from his flocks in Asia.

I was told that his position of royalty is hereditary and

that his means are completely independent. He is fabulously wealthy and receives no financial support whatever from his Ismaili followers. When he is presented with an amount of diamonds or other precious materials, His Highness invariably donates the entire sum to charity. Among Ismailis of critical discrimination I found the Aga Khan to be held sincerely in highest esteem. They readily enumerated many of his worthy deeds and accomplishments, which are unknown for the most part in the West.

He has unquestionably done a tremendous amount for his followers and amply fulfilled any moral responsibility in the eyes of his people. And yet, how great still is their need. Perhaps the Aga Khan has done all that anyone could. He is old and infirm now and not to be blamed for seeking peace and quiet among surroundings of his own choosing.

Possibly, by the devious workings of God's purposes, much of the Aga Khan's attachment for the Occident has been responsible for Moslem reforms beyond those of sects whose leadership has remained rooted in the East. One outstanding feature lies in the fact that Ismaili women do not wear the burka. As far as I know, they are the only unveiled Moslem females in Pakistan. Aside from Ismailis and a few workers in remote rural areas one takes for granted that unveiled women are either Christian or Hindu.

There is one exception: a tiny, brave band of women in Pakistan at the present time who are working to overcome this stifling custom. They are Moslems, yet do not wear veils. But they are indeed few up to now—and courageous, for the most part. Primarily they are European-educated women of high social or political standing who are being encouraged by the modern government of Pakistan to break loose from backward ideas with the hope of adding more national energy and releasing additional man power for the critical days ahead. I photographed some of these courageous ladies at a religious song service in a private home, during which none showed the slightest embarrassment at our presence in their unveiled and bejeweled midst.

Outside of this handful of pioneer suffragettes I could not give the foggiest description of the physiognomy of a woman of Pakistan, for the burka is far more than a veil in the Occidental sense of the word. It may be of varying materials and colors, but absolutely opaque; there is no gauzy contour coquettishly obscured by some flattering filminess. There is only a human-size shape, which moves along the avenue and streets of modern Karachi completely enshrouded to the toes with a garment shaped like a bedsheet. Seeing is done through a tiny mesh eye port in the precise manner of a child playing at ghosts. To encounter a whole nation of women attired thus was the most startling thing I experienced in all Asia. Until my visit I naïvely thought that veiling would be solely confined either to modest maidens or harem favorites.

Today it has made a strange situation for the whole nation—a most interesting psychological problem. First of all, the veiling of women is not necessarily a Moslem religious custom, although it certainly is practiced in most Moslem countries and supported by many religious leaders. It is not considered that women were so draped at the time of Mohammed, though they had far fewer rights before his time. The Prophet is said to have enacted strong measures to ensure their protection.

Rather the custom of veiling seems to have risen in later

centuries as protection for both husband and wife from brigands or libidinous sultans who in earlier times were often prompted to seize upon any tempting morsel of femininity who happened to have physical appeal. Stories of the insatiable appetite for variety which animated some of these old-time lupine neurotics reveal scoreboards that are fantastic; they are alleged to have had harem populations numbering way up into the thousands. So the women in Mohammedan countries are now hidden from public gaze anywhere, any time. The burka is removed in the privacy of her home, but at no time during the presence of any man other than her husband.

In fact she is seldom seen at home with or without the veil; when visitors appear, the woman usually goes to private quarters. During any of my visits to private homes there was naught but males present. But nearly always, with sharp eyes, you could catch the movement of an inner door opening just a tiny crack, and then you'd know some justifiably curious female was pathetically trying to get a glimpse of the life in which she never plays a part.

The women of town and city sit indoors, steeped in introversion, running a strictly limited gamut between kitchen and couch. Few indeed find their way toward even an elementary education or a life which offers the opportunity of fulfilling a function beyond that required for motherhood in most other species on our earth. Of course some masculine support for continuance of this state of subjection does exist. Mainly it comes from an ultraconservative, religious orthodoxy twisting scriptural admonitions for virtue and modesty among women into justification for these medieval and present-day extremes.

This hidebound element is headed by a loosely knit group of informally educated, rural preachers called mullahs, many of whom allegedly present a dogmatic barrier to modernization at the introduction of every new idea and have been a thorn in the side of progressive governmental action on numerous issues.

While I was in Karachi, traces of huge political signs with "COMBAT MULLAHISM" could still be seen here and there, recalling the recent temporary victory over this element which constantly seeks, among other things, a return to outmoded scriptural laws, like those which prescribe the amputation of a thief's right hand—a practice still extant in Saudi Arabia.

Certainly the charge could not be leveled against all mullahs, but there is very little doubt that many of these elders, spiritual leaders, and guides in rural areas are motivated to a degree in their subtle, undeclared war against the forward march of the East by the desire to maintain personal stature and a position of power over the lives of simple folk.

In Lahore we visited the headquarters of another sect, the Ahmadiya, which claims among its followers the noted statesman, Sir Zafrulla Khan. This sect is not on good terms with most of the rest of Islam; it is indeed considered heretical.

The outstanding claim of the Ahmadiyas is that their leader and founder, Hazrat Ahmed, who passed away in 1908, was the long-awaited Messiah, sent to rally the whole of mankind under the banner of Islam. I have his photograph: a bearded man in turban with strong face and piercing eyes—evidently a forceful, persuasive leader. The sect now reputedly has about a million followers and missions in many parts of the world, including one just a few city blocks from my present home in Hollywood.

Followers of Hazrat Ahmed think of the Sunnites as unbelievers and refuse to say prayers or permit intermarriage with them. Incidentally, there is a legend among Moslems around Lahore that Jesus, whom they consider to be a prophet but not divine, somehow escaped from the cross and fled to Kashmir, where He dwelt quietly for many years before His death.

Although Moslems do not accept either the Old or New Testament, many Biblical stories as well as much of its law and teaching have found their way into the Koran. Some Old Testament prophets are also recognized as well as Jesus and John the Baptist.

Unlike Hinduism, Islam is not nearly so conscious of the practices of mysticism. Efforts in this direction are comparatively slight, but as with all religions there are some groups indulging this universally found inclination, which seems to make mysticism one of the strongest bonds of similarity between all religions. Proponents of a universal religion would do well to study the psychology and philosophy of all mystics. They can provide a connecting link. One of these sects among Moslems is called Sufism—a name presumably taken from the Arabic noun *suf*, meaning wool, and referring to the coarse robes affected by ascetics.

Sufism arose in the eighth century, spurred perhaps by ascetic examples in Christianity and Buddhism; by the tenth century it had penetrated every corner of the Islamic world, but not without persecution by conservative elements reacting against any drift in the direction of individualism. After many struggles the movement gained grudging recognition and tolerance from the conservatives, and thereafter numerous schools, with monastic orders roughly similar to those in Christianity, sprang up in different centers.

Aside from the philosophy of asceticism and various mystic exercises arising out of Sufism it is said to have been responsible for inspiring the artistic as well as the spiritual evolution of Islam. Sufis, devoting much time to meditation about God, were consequently drawn correlatively into a contemplation of beauty—a course which stimulated many artistic works, particularly in the field of literature and poetry. Emphasis on this outlet was vastly caused by the Moslem orthodox ban on all pictorial representation, a prohibition which stultified and effectively squelched most efforts at painting and sculpture.

Music, too, has played a not inconsiderable role in inducing ecstasy in Sufi practices and I had several visits with an eminent Sufi monk in Karachi who sang endless numbers of chants and ballads for my recorder. Though I did not understand the words, I knew they must have been the means of rapturous transport to the monk, for I've seldom seen a face so ecstatically radiant as his when he sang. Ultimately he actually seemed to sing himself into a short, trancelike state.

Another branch of Sufism using music to stimulate spiritual emotionalism is the order of dervishes, a sect reputed to have somewhere in the neighborhood of seven million followers throughout Mohammedan countries. In order to induce a state of excitement and sensitivity the circular movements of the body used in a dancelike rhythm to music have given them the name "whirling dervishes." I recorded some of this music and surprisingly enough found it usually to be of slower tempo than one might imagine.

In Cairo I had an interview with Ahmed Surry Dede Baba, the supreme patriarch of all dervish orders. He is a sweet-faced, eager-eyed old man who dwells in the monastery of Tekiyet Solimania, a refuge hewn out of sandstone in the cliffs overlooking the city. He willingly consented to don his ceremonial robes for my photographs. He also took it upon himself to pose with an enormous water pipe, or hookah. I considered this to indicate that dervishes hold a liberal attitude toward some of the minor habits frequently frowned upon by orthodox elements. Also, he is a married man with many children; he obeys the rule of celibacy only while in monastic life, as do many other monks and followers.

After a substantial discussion, through an interpreter, I got the impression that the "whirling" part of their mystical practices is only a minor segment in the over-all aims of a sect whose efforts are directed at spiritual enlightenment and a closer relationship with God. According to the patriarch, the underlying doctrine of the dervishes is that, in order to know God, you must first know yourself.

"You come to know yourself by carefully studying all your thoughts and actions. Then, knowing your faults and weaknesses," he said, "and, above all, believing that God *always observes* you, you will be far too uneasy to err under His scrutiny." Further, he said that, to be happy, a person must be rigid in the observation of rules of cleanliness, maintaining clean mind, clean tongue, and clean hands.

Later he escorted us on a short tour of the lovely gardens, which incidentally contained an elaborate, recently completed tomb, patiently standing in readiness for the day when it will receive his revered patriarchal bones. Such is the devotion of the dervishes to this gentle leader with the boyish smile.

The study of Islam in Egypt, by the way, was made most difficult by the constant surveillance and supervision of all our efforts by officers of the Tourist Bureau. This was the only place on the entire world tour where we encountered real obstacles to the project. Upon our arrival an officer was assigned ostensibly to facilitate my research, but after a couple of days of constant company, I could only conclude that his primary function was to prevent photography of anything which might be construed as casting an unfavorable light on the present government.

We were permitted to photograph a few of the finer mosques as long as vendors and other peoples on the street did not show. One interesting sequence was allowed on the preparation of the annual carpet for the Kaaba, used during the month of pilgrimage in Mecca, and we got a couple of long shots of the Pyramids, irrelevant to the study of Islam. Except for my interview with the dervish patriarch—the highlight of all—that about covered it.

The idea of doing a piece on the religious life in the villages was frowned upon. I wanted to try to illustrate the fact that Moslems are almost one hundred per cent teetotalers by taking an atmospheric shot of men conversing and sipping coffee at one of the street cafés, but I was refused permission . . . no street scenes, no people, no weddings, funerals, or other ceremonies. We were not given access to religious schools or permitted to photograph mosques, many of which had interesting stories and legends surrounding them. Perhaps they were not kept in what the Tourist Bureau considered the best repair.

It did not take long to ascertain that a motion picture on Islam, as practiced in Egypt, was impossible at the present time. So after only four days in Cairo we took leave for Jordan, but not without describing the exact content of our meager packet of undeveloped movie film plus an additional obligation to submit all celluloid to the Egyptian Embassy in Washington, D.C., for censorship after printing—the only example of such an extreme measure encountered on the whole journey. After being personally accompanied during every daylight moment this seemed a bit excessive, but of course we finally complied, if not without some protest.

In Pakistan no restraint was put on lens or mike, and if the net result on film is not wholly glamorous in every instance, it is truthful, human, and pulsating with the breath of life. Assuredly it will put Americans closer to an understanding of the heart and spirit of the average Pakistani than my long shot of the Sphynx and Pyramids will do for their brothers in Egypt.

In pursuit of my study of Islam one question bothered me at the start. Why didn't the Arabic countries embrace Christianity? With six hundred years in which to do so, why didn't Christianity catch on? Why does it not do so today? Without ever arriving at a pat answer I have finally found satisfying reasons for this—some of them were in textbooks, some came from conversations and personal observation of the people in Moslem countries.

At the time of Mohammed, Arabia was inhabited by fierce tribes of nomads and Bedouins who, like the American Indians, were unrestrained in warfare and pillage among themselves by a central authority or government. They were an illiterate, lawless lot given to gambling, drunkenness, disorder, and vice of all kinds. Their women held the position of abject slavery, while religion, if any, was a primitive idolatry filled with many depraved, distorted practices.

Christian missionaries were sent to these people in the early days, but achieved a mere smattering of success. Apparently the tribes were too scattered and antipathetic to bring about the adoption of a purely spiritual doctrine. The savage tribesmen of Araby needed higher spiritual concepts, but they also needed a civil code and someone to maintain order. Such a combination was not strongly co-ordinated in Christianity, which has always looked to the state for the establishment of justice and keeping of the peace.

Then Mohammed was thrust onto the scene. This strong-willed, brilliant man, who spent his earlier years as a merchant, felt keenly the deep needs of his people. In middle life he came to be the recipient of prophetic visions of such astonishing magnitude and matchless wisdom that he became convinced that he carried a message from Allah, the one true ruler of the universe. He gathered followers, fought pitched battles, and finally swept across the desert lands of Arabia in complete victory for the cause of unity, lawful order, and Islam—a multiple achievement which surely could not have been accomplished any other way or by a less positive personality.

I was amazed to learn of the astounding rapidity with which Mohammed completed his reforms. For one thing, the Arabs were great wine drinkers and, at the time, drunkenness was a deplorable weakness of the whole population. It is said that two years after the advent of The Prophet not a single wine flask could be found on the entire Arabian Peninsula and they have never returned to this day. Gambling was halted, usury outlawed, idols smashed, and civilization introduced into an area which, like Scythia, could never have been reduced by Roman legions or ever persuaded to more moderate ways by the gentle doctrines and concepts of Christianity.

Previously I mentioned the simplicity of Islam. This was and still is responsible for the success of the faith of the Moslems with certain peoples. Surely the concept of One God is easier to grasp than the mysterious dogma of Three in One.

During an interview I was fortunate to have with the High Mufti in Istanbul he stressed Moslem repugnance to the whole idea of the Holy Trinity, and then blandly asked for my opinion on the subject. I replied that my personal view was irrelevant, since no Christian was expected to be responsible for the explanation of a dogma which admittedly transcends human reasoning.

This answer, of course, gave the Mufti no satisfaction whatever and he continued by assailing the idea of God becoming incarnate in the person of Jesus Christ and again demanded my personal opinion. This time I could only answer that I had never fully been able to reach an unequivocal decision as to the kind of divinity abiding in the Nazarene, that I had no certitude whether He differed from other men by the inherent quality of His spiritual nature, or if it were simply a matter of degree. I continued to explain that I saw great beauty in either concept but that I felt inclined toward the latter, which gives all men a share of the divine nature with the glorious possibility of developing and expanding that portion residing within himself by his own efforts.

I tried to create a feeling of tolerance in the Mufti for the first concept, however, by citing the indescribable beauty of a teaching which reveals a God of love so compassionate of the pains and misery of His creatures that He would willingly reduce the power in a portion of His nature, take upon Himself the imperfections of a fleshly existence, and undergo all extremes of mental anguish and physical suffering in order to convince man of His infinite capacity for tenderness and affection.

When I had finished the Mufti was silent for a moment, and then, shaking his head, said that God did not need to take the corruption of flesh upon Himself in order to convince man of His love and compassion—there was enough evidence in life itself for that. "Besides," he went on, "to Moslem thinking, such a concept is idolatrous, pagan, and unthinkable."

"Well—so be it—I still contend it is a doctrine of rarest beauty," I said doggedly, and later contented myself by reflecting that even had the Mufti agreed as to the aesthetic excellence of the concept, he could hardly admit it. Was he not, after all, the highest official of Islam in Istanbul?

CHAPTER TEN

From Pakistan and Egypt my quest of Islam continued into the Hashemite Kingdom of Jordan. In a stalemated condition of war with Israel, Jordan was the only state which demanded that an affidavit of religious affiliation from a Christian ecclesiastic be displayed in order to obtain a permit of entry. Like Egypt, it also exhibited grave apprehensions concerning the intentions of transient Westerners.

This Arab country, lying longitudinally astride the inland border of the state of Israel, has many sacred Biblical shrines which are revered by Moslem, Christian, and Jew alike. The presently patrolled line dividing Israel and Jordan cuts through the very heart of Jerusalem. Most of the newer sections of the city are in the hands of the Israelis. Jordan controls all of the ancient walled city with its historic shrines, except a high point in the southwestern corner called Mount Zion. Seizing this portion during hostilities was a great moral victory for the Jews, since it contains the tomb of King David, the spiritual leader who, as a boy, slew the giant Goliath. This tomb, upon a not wholly un-disputed site archaeologically, is for Israel perhaps second in spiritual importance only to the place of Solomon's Temple —a shrine they are not able to visit now.

Bethlehem, a rapidly developing community, lies a few miles south of Jerusalem, within the Jordan border, but the Israelis have cut the highway connecting it to the city and the new Arab route skirting the road block is almost three times as long as the ancient way. There are innumerable instances of such wasteful inconvenience for both sides along the whole length of the present illogically haphazard border.

For those who have not previously read descriptions of present conditions surrounding the Christian shrines in the Holy Land, let me explain that nearly all important histori-cal landmarks in the life of Jesus are commemorated by altars and plaques completely enveloped under the struc-tures of mighty churches.

Foremost of these is the Church of the Holy Sepulchre in Old Jerusalem, under control of Jordan. This building, maintained by Roman Catholic, Greek and Armenian Orthodox, and Egyptian Coptic sects, houses the alleged site of Calvary, the place of Jesus's crucifixion, and the tomb in which He presumably was laid. The church is an enormous, dimly lit structure, containing many ornate chapels and dark, circuitous passageways. It was not crowded during our visit and tourists were granted full privileges of staying as long and photographing as much as they pleased without supervision or charge.

On the site of Calvary in the Holy Sepulchre is a broad altar covered with valuable vessels of precious metals. In back of the altar is a life-size painting of the crucified Christ and at the side a marker which indicates a crevice in an up-jutting boulder, said to have been caused by lightning in the great storm which raged over the land after Jesus's death.

We heard a story that a thief had hidden himself in the sepulchre within recent years to plunder some of the valuable sacramental vessels. Somehow, during the midnight hours, he was apprehended directly before the holy altar of Calvary by monks, who are permanently quartered on the precincts. It was said that these monks slew the thief on the spot, literally tearing him to pieces in the violence of their indignation.

The Church of the Nativity in Bethlehem is a huge building possessing a main entrance not more than five feet high, which rightfully causes all men to stoop before entering the presence of the hallowed ground. The precise spot assumed to be where Mary gave birth to the infant Jesus is indicated by an elaborate marble monument in a lower, crypt-like portion of the church. Nearby another small marble chamber marks where He was laid in the manger.

The Rock of Gethsemane is another holy landmark that is now enshrined in a large Catholic church, as well as the presumed site of Christ's heavenly ascension atop the Mount of Olives. The exact location of this momentous event is in dispute by at least three different religious groups: the Roman Catholic, the Orthodox, and Islam. Each has its own monumental structure on a separate spot which it considers to be the one and only possible place from which Christ arose.

South of Bethlehem, at the village of Hebron, is the tomb of Father Abraham, the Patriarch of the Hebrews—a shrine that is also very sacred to Moslems. Our government guide would not permit us to take photographs on the inside of the mosquelike building housing these alleged tombs of Abraham and his sons, where pious Moslems stand in prayer throughout all hours of the day. Nor were we permitted to photograph the exterior of the tomb as long as any Arabs were in sight. In fact this prohibitive rule against photographing was applicable to all human beings in native dress, wherever we chanced to visit in Jordan. And a distressing restriction it was, too, for the countryside is replete with the most interesting Arab types and characters, all picturesquely arrayed in robes of the exact style with which we are familiar from illustrations depicting Biblical times: Bedouins with camel trains, shepherds with their flocks, peasant women carrying water jars from the well in the fashion so frequently described by scripture.

One youthful, well-educated Arab—a bright, usually pleasant young man—complained to me with no little amount of annoyed vehemence: "Bedouins, Bedouins, Bedouins—wandering nomads—that's all Americans and Europeans think we Arabs are! And it hurts our cause in the dispute with Israel, too, for it strengthens the world's belief that the Jews can and will bring greater development to this backward area than we are able to do!"

So I understood, and maybe he was right too—at least he had a point—although it seems to me that improved social conditions, scientific agriculture, and industrialization would be hard facts for an opposing propaganda machine to obscure. If such things did not exist, it would be equally hard to simulate before the scrutinizing gaze of any well-informed visitor, regardless of custom or costume.

So we didn't get any shots of Bedouins in Jordan, although later in Israel, where modern progress unquestionably exceeds that of Jordan by many self-evident degrees, we got all the Bedouin pastoral scenes one could desire. In fact I do not recall photographic restrictions on any phase of Jewish life—agricultural, industrial, cultural, or religious.

Wandering about the narrow, colorful streets of Old Jerusalem is an unusual experience compared to that of most oriental towns, because of the high state of cleanliness. This is maintained principally by the law which bars pack animals or other beasts of burden from any of the narrow stone avenues within the ancient walls. Motor vehicles are not allowed either and although it must be a chore for shopkeepers to carry in all merchandise by hand or to hire one of the generally available porters for the purpose, these restrictions have done much to preserve the commercial potential of an area that had long since grown too crowded and outdated for any but pilgrims and tourists.

Even during the heat of summer the little streets, many of which support roofs forming an arcade, are cool and fragrant with the exotic aroma of incense, strange spices, and dried fruits. I have visited a good many primitive or ancient villages throughout the world—European, Asiatic, Latin American—and any suggestion for visiting the "quaint market places" long ago lost whatever romantic visions they once may have conjured up; debris, dung, drosophila, and just plain dirt have definitely effected their deadly deglamorization. In Jerusalem this uniquely was not the case.

The summer weather too, by the way, was just great. During the whole of our five weeks' stay in the Holy Land I could not have asked for a more pleasant climate. The altitude in the Jerusalem area is in the vicinity of 2400 feet; the days are hot and bright, but the nights cool and dry. There is no stickiness such as one feels down on the Mediterranean coast.

After a lifetime of associating Jews with Jerusalem, I found it odd that none now resides in the old city at all nor do Jews visit there. On the site where once stood Solomon's famed temple—the latest reconstruction of which was destroyed by Rome in A.D. 70—now stands a very holy Moslem shrine called Dome of the Rock. This mosque is believed to be set upon the spot where Mohammed's spirit ascended to heaven, although his death took place hundreds of miles distant.

On one side, at the base of the temple area, there is an ancient wall built of large blocks of stone. Called in later years the Wailing Wall, this structure legendarily built by pennies of the poor is said to be the actual foundation of the temple itself and the only remaining part. It was long the custom for Jews to rend their clothing and strew themselves with ashes there, sorrowing over the evil days which had befallen their nation and their scattered people. When we were there, it was a desolate spectacle indeed, for the area is shunted by Moslems and forbidden to Jews.

Just outside the walls of the old city there is another monument of interest to Christians: an old garden with a tomb which was uncovered within the last century and believed by many to be the true site of Christ's last earthly resting place. From an accumulation of data substantiating many scriptural descriptions of Golgotha and for those seeking archaeological verification there is enough corroboration here to make the place a strong contender for being the likely site of the real tomb. It raises a denominational controversy, however, and it seems highly improbable that such a recent discovery could ever batter down the century-old walls of tradition no matter how logical the ammunition.

Just out of curiosity I inquired which crypt site was favored as seeming to be most authentic by local Moslems, who are by no means excluded from the Church of the Holy Sepulchre and, in fact, are official custodians of the keys thereof. Results of my meager personal survey showed that the local Arabs, for some reason, lean strongly in favor of the new tomb.

Completion of the photographic work on the film for Islam was now almost accomplished, although I will again repeat that one could profitably spend years with each religion, as it differs from area to area, and still leave oceans of material uncovered.

Several weeks later, at the Cave of Elijah near Haifa, we recorded the music and dancing of a group of Druses celebrating the advent of a new son to an overjoyed father who had made a sworn promise at this holy place that he would bring all his neighbors back for a day of joyful festivity if God saw fit to reward his prayers with a healthy male offspring.

This kind of pact is commonly found all around the globe among certain elements in every religion; promises, made to the god or gods, will only obligate fulfillment in the event of receiving the answer to some heartfelt request. It may not fall in with the spirit of true religion, but its spirit is truly human.

Druses, by the way, are Moslems, a sectarian offshoot of the Ismailis found mainly in Syria. One oddity is that while Druses must love truth, it applies only to relations between themselves. A Druse may tell a falsehood to someone outside the faith if he confesses his sin to one of his brethren at first opportunity. Also, with them, a metampsychosis or reincarnation is an accepted doctrine.

Traveling into Israel from Jordan or any other Arab country is kind of an adventure. In fact I'm not sure one can legally make this journey except through the Mandelbaum Gate in the heart of Jerusalem. There are no airlines or other kinds of transport between Israel and its neighboring states. Embarkation to the Jewish homeland must ordinarily be made from some neutral country. Of course Israeli visas must be arranged beforehand, but we were not allowed to display them in our passports, for then no Arab state would have permitted entrance to their territory at all.

The procedure is to call upon the proper authorities in Jordanian Jerusalem, stating your wish to cross into Israel. Arrangements can then be made for the transfer to take place at a specified time several days hence. It is strictly a one-way deal. Once you have crossed the temporarily quiescent line of hostilities, there can be no backtracking or retracing of steps. They'll let you go all right, but for the time being the Arabs are through with you. Evidently they want no friend of Israel within the bosom of their hospitality regardless of whether you pay your own way or not.

From the time you state your intention of crossing everyone in Jordan seems to know about it. "Going over to the other side, eh?" says the hotel clerk next morning—a remark that is repeated by your guide and the waiter in the dining room. There is no particular menace to the tone, just disappointment. Another American has let them down. From then on, until the transfer is made, there is an atmosphere of uneasiness; all Arab relations grow just a trifle chilled.

There is no public transport crossing the line. A taxi will cart you bag and baggage up to the Jordan immigration patrol but from this outpost to the counterpart in Israel—a distance of about sixty or seventy yards when we made the crossing—you are on your own, without benefit of porter service. Knowing that desultory firing flares up without warning every few weeks along this border area didn't add to my comfort as we trotted back and forth several times, toting equipment and personal effects across the well-exposed, shell-torn strip between check points.

Wondering how this unique gate happened to be called Mandelbaum, I inquired and learned it to be simply the name of the proprietor of a little store that chanced to sit astride the now devastated area. Poor Mr. Mandelbaum—I hope the honor gave him some consolation for his loss.

Once over the line and through customs, it is another world—a world with a more familiar atmosphere than we had known for many months. I felt the strong influence of Europe for the first time; it was no longer the Orient.

In Jordan, outside the historic old city itself, Jerusalem is clean, with quite a number of new buildings, but quiet. Very quiet—exuding the feeling at night of being in some small resort village. While throughout the day merchants of all kinds walk the streets crying their wares behind donkeys and small carts.

The Israel side, however, bustles with modern traffic.

Shops are more sophisticated; the merchandise is Western and, above all, there are women. Unveiled, clear-eyed women going about normal, everyday affairs, shopping in the stores or on the streets with or without male accompaniment. Until Israel I'd forgotten how barren civil life had become without them. In the evenings and on late Sabbath afternoon to see young men and women strolling along arm in arm was a sight I had not known since the far Far East, and then rarely.

Food, too, in Israel took on a more familiar Western character—despite all the kosher restrictions. Good Yiddish cooking, I'd say, and clean! For the first time in months we began to relax some of the ptomaine precautions. Some items are scarce for the Israelis though, like meat; there is very little of that.

The King David Hotel, perched on an elevated plateau overlooking the old walled city on the Jordan side, is first-class, despite bullet holes in the plate-glass windows and here and there across the eastern façade. Some of these are quite recent—pitted proof that a cease-fire agreement always has to make allowances for temporary temper tantrums. We saw them in Jordan, too. Incidentally, the hotel also overlooks the valley of Gehenna, referred to in the New Testament as a place of punishment, or hell. I was told that before the arrival of the Israelites this valley had been the site of repulsive pagan rites, including the sacrifice of children.

The assignment now was Judaism, the last religion to be covered on the present schedule. As I unpacked my letters of introduction and began making the usual contacts, it felt good to know that photographically the project was on the home stretch. Here it would be government assistance again, for the Department of Religion plays a considerable role in the State of Israel. We needed the Public Relations Office, too, mainly for facilitating any suggestions of the Department of Religion.

Whenever possible I tried to show all ceremonies of importance in the life cycle of each follower. In Judaism this became no small task; Jewish life is filled with ritual. I also tried to pick out for emphasis the important fundamentals of each faith. In Judaism I started with their strong adherence to the concept of One God, using the exhortation from Deuteronomy as the keynote: "Hear, O Israel, the Lord Our God Is One."

Judaism being the root of both Christianity and Islam, I wanted to show some of the important ideas permeating all three. For instance, many of our concepts of morals and ethics as well as theology have their origins in the first five books of the Holy Bible, called the Pentateuch—or according to the Jews, the Torah—Genesis, Exodus, Leviticus, Numbers, and Deuteronomy.

To the Jews the Torah is by all means the most important part of the Bible and it is kept separated from the other sacred books, usually on hand-written parchment scrolls in the central part of each synagogue, within an enclosed cabinet called The Ark. Since service in the synagogue is held twice daily, enough of the Torah is read each day to complete the whole by the end of a year. So sacred is Jewish scripture that even when worn out it can never be discarded or destroyed. The volumes or pages must be given proper burial, usually in a cemetery.

I presume the heart of the Torah would be the Ten Commandments. Certainly this is true to Christians; they are the ethical and moral foundation on which civilization must stand, or by neglecting fall. Moses is presumed to have lived about 1200 B.C., and that the light of such wisdom should have shone forth more than three thousand years ago can only be attributed to divine inspiration.

It is interesting to speculate on the social benefits from just one of these: the command to rest on the Sabbath day. Nowhere in the world do people rest one day out of every seven, except where they have been influenced by the Jewish Sabbath laws. Today this original Mosaic command brings a period of rest to all the peoples on earth.

To see how Jewish people practice their religion, I found it necessary to take note of the word "observant." This is a key word, for it divides the Jews into three general groupings: the Orthodox, the Conservative, and the Reform (sometimes called Progressive). These differ only as to how many of the 613 religious laws they observe.

Israel is the land of none but Orthodox practices, although certainly few, if any, of the devout actually maintain observance of the whole 613 laws. Of course I couldn't begin to make pictures of all the various observances, or even enumerate them here on paper. I hope it will suffice if I speak of a very few just to give an idea of the life of an observant Jew.

Roughly speaking, the daily routine of every mature, pious male starts when he arises at dawn. First, he washes his hands in a basin usually provided near the bedside, during which time a prayer is said. Then articles of clothing are donned, including a small vest-like undergarment called the *tziot-tziot*. This has sacred threads commemorating scripture which are reverently caressed.

Next, a prayer shawl or *talit*—always worn in synagogue and for praying—is ceremoniously placed about the shoulders. Then phylacteries are carefully wrapped around the left arm and tied to the forehead. Called *tefilin* in Hebrew, these are just little boxes containing scriptural passages. The reason for wearing them comes from a verse in Deuteronomy, which says of the texts, "Thou shalt bind them for a sign upon thy hand and they shall be as frontlets before thine eyes."

After the *tefilin* a skullcap, or *yamaka*, is placed on the head and a twenty-five- or thirty-minute prayer is read while facing in the direction of Solomon's Temple. This same morning routine may also be carried out in synagogue; it should be, in fact, if possible.

The yamaka is one of many of the perpetual head coverings worn by observant Jews as a never to be forgotten sign of reverence before the God to whom they owe all affection. Usually these caps are put on indoors after hats are removed, but I saw many of the truly devout who constantly wore the yamaka securely fastened to the hair with a bobby pin, under their hats, so that even a windy mishap would never catch the person without head covering.

Morning prayers completed, there is another ritual washing of hands as the man approaches the breakfast table, where, after a bite of salted bread—symbolic of the salt of the covenant anciently used on the sacrifices—food may at last be eaten. When the meal is finished, there is another period of devotion and thanksgiving.

At sundown the above routine—which, if not absolutely

accurate, is a very close approximation—is repeated in full. More devotions take place before retiring.

Like the yamakas, another mark of piety is found in the fact that most of the true Orthodox never shave; this because of a law which forbids that sharp steel touch the face. Also the sideburns are allowed to grow until they can be twisted into slender curls, which will be maintained from birth to death.

For me one interesting aspect of Jewish religious law was the insistence upon a literal interpretation. If a person can find a way of circumventing the laws and yet fulfill the state requirements, he seems to fall under no condemnation. For instance, the law about shaving is frequently modified without censure by using an acid or a special cream which softens the hair so that it may simply be scraped off the face with a wooden stick.

Having so many laws traditionally surrounding their lives at every turn has clarified in my mind why so many Jews enter the law profession and are known for being the possessors of keen legal mentalities. Rabbinical courts, both low and high, render decisions for Jews in many spheres of human relations, particularly marital problems. I was fortunate to have an interview with the Chief Justice of the Supreme Court—a man who is also the Chief Rabbi of all Israel—Rabbi Hertzog. Although I think he's originally Polish, he immigrated to the Jewish homeland from Ireland and, curiously enough, seems to have brought just a suggestion of that famous national twinkle with him. He proudly showed me all his antique Torah scrolls and religious *objets d'art* and he seemed equally interested in my photographic and recording gear. He then read a short statement: "It is our deep faith that the Jewish people will renew the prophetic call to the whole of mankind for universal, everlasting peace based upon the eternal principles of the brotherhood of Man and the Fatherhood of God." I got a warm, wonderful feeling from this gentle, fatherly man. His words are used as a climactic summation in the film.

Sabbath with the Jews is observed on Saturday, which is truly the seventh day of the week; or rather it should be said they observe Sabbath from sundown on Friday to sundown on Saturday, and nowhere is this day observed as piously as in Jerusalem, where everything stops. No store of any kind is open, not even for medicine or drugs. No restaurants are open; there is in fact no cooking of any kind in either public or private establishment, including hospitals. Food is prepared the day before and will not even be rewarmed. No public transport or other conveyances are in operation, although limited taxi service has been made available for tourists. Few if any of the true Orthodox will answer the telephone in their homes or as much as flick a light switch.

Dinner on Friday evening is a family affair surrounded with beautiful and meaningful ritual. It is followed by a generous period of hymns, sung by all present. I found family life among the Jews to be a most vital phase of the group existence, much more so than that of many other nations and faiths.

Unlike Sunday in America, Sabbath in Israel is not a time for recreation, but for rest, devotion, and synagogue alone. Just before sunset on Friday horns may be heard proclaiming the advent of the holy day and thereafter a spirit of quietude reigns until late Saturday afternoon, when the streets suddenly become alive with dignified but good-humored crowds engaged in a neighborly promenade. Automobiles do not emerge for several hours, as a rule, and the holiday strollers fill the avenues, sidewalks, and streets from building to building.

Service in the synagogue is a matter of strict ritual with worshipers always facing Old Jerusalem. And here the rabbi plays a very small part, most of the liturgy being led by the cantor or respected laymen. The rabbi is considered to be a teacher or guide, but not in any sense a priest. Since olden times the rabbi's scholarship has been largely confined to a thorough knowledge of the Bible and Talmud and in much of Orthodox Israel this is still true. In Western countries like America, however, where the rabbi provides leadership in many civic and community affairs, he must have a well-rounded education, with his rabbinical degree conferred by a seminary.

Since destruction of the temple in A.D. 70 there have been no priests in Judaism. However, blood descendants of the ancient intercessors—often found in families using the name Cohen—still carry on the one priestly function of blessing the congregation. After having their hands ritually washed by a Levite, all Cohenim in attendance at synagogue cover both head and hands with the prayer shawl and pronounce a divine benediction. In Jerusalem this is performed every day, but in America I think it is done only once or twice a year.

I have listened to discussions speculating on functions of the priesthood in the event the great temple should ever be restored to Judaism. Surely grave questions and grave decisions would arise at that time: as, for instance, the position of modern Judaism on just the one subject of animal sacrifice.

At Orthodox services, although women do not sit with the men or participate in the liturgy in any way, a special place is reserved for them, usually at the rear on a balcony, where they may observe all that takes place without being seen themselves.

Religious teaching is an integral part of Jewish education. We visited one school in the district of Meah Sherim and did a sequence on a class of little eight-year-olds with side curls and yamakas, being instructed in a portion of the Lamentations of Jeremiah. Actually it amounted to an exercise in group chanting, for both the Bible and the Talmud are traditionally chanted.

This, because of the rhythm, is usually accompanied by a swaying motion of the body which is carried out by Orthodox people of any age during liturgical prayers and readings of scripture anywhere. Some claim this custom originates in a verse from the Psalms which says, "All my bones should say, who is like unto thee?"

Second to the Torah and Bible is a collection of philosophical and theological dissertations, epigrams, anecdotes, laws, and commentaries by rabbis and ancient sages, all gathered together into a number of huge volumes called the Talmud.

There are many Talmud schools, called Yeshiva, throughout Israel. We visited some on several of the *kibutzim*, or collective farms. These collective farms, by the way, have been the answer to the tremendous surge of lately returned refugees wishing repatriation in the ancient homeland. There are several kinds of administration to be found, ranging from those with complete and distinct private property, grouped merely for social purposes and mutual use of machinery and utilities, to those farms which are run on an economic basis of pure socialism.

And what a gamut of facial characteristics are now visible among these peoples. There are swarthy Yemenites and those born in Northern Europe who are the blondest of the blond. One would be hard put to select a type that could be considered typically Jewish.

Of course we had to visit more of Israel than the Jerusalem area, so an auto tour was arranged for most of the central and northern part of the state; farther south, the Negeb Desert was just too hot in summer season. The tour included the Yemenite village of Taoz; the collective farm at Yavne, where I recorded the graduation exercises of men from the school for kosher slaughterers, called *shohet*; then Tel-Aviv, which is, of course, very modern, with a fine sea walk for promenades. The school at Kfar Batya came next, where the boys and girls did some magnificent choral work. Another school, Kfar Haroe, and from there we traveled north through Nazareth, a village built precipitously in very hilly country, on up to Safad and the tomb of Simon Bar Jochai, where well-aged scholars spend their lives in continual study.

Simon Bar Jochai is considered by many to be the father of the mystic science of Cabala and to have written the Zohar, known as the Cabalistic Bible, although modern research places the date of the Zohar much later. Cabala is a secret system of interpreting scripture based on the assumption that every word, letter, and number has an occult meaning. It is believed that knowledge of many mystic symbols—especially the names of God—will enable one to do miracles.

Several days were then spent in the area around Haifa with its charming Mount Carmel district—truly a place to tarry awhile, if one ever has time in this world to tarry! We took occasion to spend a few hours at the Bahai shrine, strolling amid verdant gardens overlooking the bay. The Bahais are members of a religious organization who consider themselves a world faith, for they accept the teachings of all great religious leaders as the progressive revelation of One God. Therefore, one need not renounce his original faith in order to become a Bahai unless that faith teaches exclusive infallibility.

The founder of this group, Baha Ullah, a nineteenth-century Moslem from Persia who was severely persecuted for his broad-minded views and exhortations for religious tolerance, is considered by Bahais to be "the manifestation of God for our time." Some of the basic principles emphasized by Baha Ullah are the equality of races and sexes; the importance of truth over tradition and prejudice; the union of religion with science; the need for an international language; compulsory education for all; the abolition of extreme poverty and extreme wealth.

There is no priesthood, professional clergy, monastic order, or mystical doctrine in the Bahai faith. Its administrative order has grown steadily the past half century until today, I understand, it is already established in nearly one hundred countries with supporters that are Christian, Hindu, Jew, Buddhist, Moslem, and Zoroastrian.

As a contributing factor in any movement for world peace the importance of such an organization cannot be overestimated. The aims and principle as set forth are, to me, above reproach. They present a beautiful and mature ideal of world fellowship in the broadest possible aspect.

In continuing the accumulation of data on religious observances in Israel we made a brief survey of kosher laws and koshering processes. Kosher is a word of approval meaning that an article is in accord with laws of the Bible and Talmud and therefore available for use or consumption by observant Jews. In the line of foodstuffs there are several things a devoted child of Abraham absolutely may not eat, such as wild birds of prey, horses or other animals lacking the cloven hoof, lobsters, shrimp, fish without scales, and, above all, pork.

Perhaps because of man's inherent inquisitiveness into the "why" of things, reasons for these prohibitions have been discussed and analyzed for many centuries. Scientific answers have been sought to justify the term "unclean," as usually given by scripture, and some are quite logical, especially those which deal with efforts of the early Israelite leaders to repress all inclinations toward perverted, idolatrous practices current in the pagan world surrounding their people at that time.

Many answers, however, attempt to attribute the ancient leaders with an insight to physical laws of hygiene and infectious diseases far in advance of common knowledge of those ancient times. Although such answers can hardly be credited with being more than personal conjecture, few will contend with those who wish to accept them. It must be admitted that a great deal of those things which constitute religious dogma and ritual are impossible to rationalize empirically. In the heart of the devout Israelite his observances are the command of God; nothing else matters.

The eating of wild game is taboo, unless these animals can be killed in a certain way. There can be no hunting with rifle, sling, or bow by observant Jews. Animals must be killed by bleeding at the hands of qualified, accredited slaughterers. To become a shohet, a man must have good moral character and be a credit to his community. Among other requirements of his profession is a knowledge of how to maintain an acute edge on his knife blades; they must be honed to perfection. In the school we saw the instructor test all edges with a fingernail and it was claimed that the merest suggestion of a burr or nick would send the student to the foot of the class. At an actual slaughtering any animal killed by an imperfect instrument would not be considered kosher and thereby inedible to the observant. Certainly this is a humane rule.

After the animal is slaughtered it must be carefully examined for any sign of disease or imperfection, particularly in lungs and liver, before it can be given the first stamp of approval. But this is only the beginning.

The hindquarters of the animal are not used at all. (Here the "unclean" must have had a sexual connotation.) Then all large bones are removed and large blood vessels are cut away. Pieces of the meat are then soaked thoroughly and subsequently hung and rinsed with a hose. After this they are salted and allowed to stand for many hours before another soaking, hanging, and rinsing. Principally such meticulous concern in the preparation of kosher meat is to remove all traces of blood from the flesh, for it is blood that is specifically forbidden.

The reason that butter and cream are seldom to be seen on dinner tables in the homes of Orthodox Jewry is because of another kosher requirement which forbids that meat and dairy products will ever be eaten at the same meal or be permitted to touch the same dishes and utensils. Two complete sets of cooking ware, serving vessels, and eating utensils must be kept forever separated in each home. Also, these dishes must be washed in separate basins, while special soap containing no animal products will be used on the dairy service. I was told this restriction is founded on a law forbidding that an animal be cooked in its own or its mother's milk.

Known to the world since ages past and used since time immemorial by the Jews for ceremonial purposes is a fermented product of the fruit of the grape called wine. It takes knowledge and experience to make good wine and the Jews have both; they are masters at the art.

Grapes have grown on the plains of Judea for countless centuries and today they flourish as never before. During August mile upon mile of vineyards were heavily laden with bulging clusters of juicy, delicious globules. We carried bunches of them for constant nibbling wherever we went.

But not just any wine will be able to pass kosher requirements. It must be made according to very rigid specifications. At the winery a rabbi will be in charge. His principal duties will be to see that the process fulfills all demands of scripture and that the workmen, above all, are observant of the Sabbath. Violations in this respect might mean contamination of the whole vintage and dismissal for the em-

ALTARS OF THE EAST

ployee. When all requirements have been compiled with and approved, the net result is a variety of products with which the whole world is familiar: kosher wine.

But for the vintner observance does not stop here. In ancient times it was a law that one per cent of all Hebrew wine must be given to the priesthood. Today no one receives the wine; it cannot even be given or sold for charity, but one per cent of the output of all kosher wineries must be poured out and destroyed. In the case of the particular Israeli company where we observed the gushing libation being swallowed by the sewage system it amounts to about five thousand gallons per year. Some vintners have tried to combat this exacting demand without avail. For the Orthodox it is a law ordained by God and who can bring about an amendment?

To the vintner I voiced my assumption that doubtless he at least was able to use his lower-grade product for the sacrifice, but he refuted this vehemently, stating that such an evasion would find the Rabbinate refusing its stamp of approval. According to him, the requirement was for a cross-section or average grade of the whole product; a demand which would see the discard examined by laboratory test tube if an evasion were suspected.

The term kosher applies to other considerations besides foodstuffs. For instance, it is a law that linen and wool cannot be mixed in one garment and there are approved laboratories for the sole and distinct purpose of determining the exact make-up of all wearing apparel. We photographed the procedure in one of these shatnez, where the technician used chemical solutions and a high-power microscope for his analysis of the tape and interlining of men's suit coats.

Since a state of war still existed in Israel, I wanted to see something of army life, particularly its religious aspects. Of course a draft law is in operation for both men and women. Everyone is liable for basic military training and a stretch of service. Uniforms are a common sight everywhere. Also, my wartime association with the chaplaincy in the U. S. Army whetted my appetite for a glimpse into the functioning of this branch of the military setup in Israel.

I found that while presently there may be a period of lull in the hostilities, there is no relaxation of vigilance on any score particularly in matters of religion. The Israeli Army provides the reverent soldier every opportunity to maintain his precious observance. While in uniform he will be given all manner of ritual materials. Supply depots are well stocked with prayer shawls, phylacteries, Torah scrolls, Bibles, special service plates for Passover.

As in civilian life, the soldier retains separate eating utensils for meat and dairy products; in this case two sets of metal mess gear are provided. Even in field kitchens or chow lines large cooking and serving vessels are plainly marked meat or milk.

He attends synagogue whenever possible, or if in the field, a portable ark will be hastily set up and this place then becomes a synagogue, for it is Jewish teaching that God is everywhere.

At an interview with the Chief of Chaplains of the Israeli Army, I asked if he thought army life decreased a man's faith in God. Chaplain Goren replied, "No, if spiritual guidance is properly provided to the Army, the individual's faith is strengthened as a result of the dangers he encounters."

From my own experience in the Pacific theater in the last war I find myself unable to corroborate Chaplain Goren's statement. While I think that real danger will cause almost anyone to turn for help in whatever direction his desperation will bring to mind, including prayers to the divine, I do not believe that the battlefields of war promote the growth of faith or enlarge spiritual understanding any more than any of the other puzzles, predicaments, or experiences of life.

There is one qualifying comment applicable here, though, concerning the fact that men amid the dangers of battle are brought abruptly face to face with the realities of life and death in its harshest aspect. This experience of any duration must cause them to think more seriously on the mysteries of life at an earlier age than they otherwise might, possibly inclining them toward religion if they were predisposed in that direction. On the other hand, I've seen the bitterness of an unrewarded prayer cause cynicism, too. Here, of course, the basic spiritual concept must have been at fault.

We tried to cover most of the sacraments in Judaism, but we got only the rite of circumcision and funeral services in the State of Israel. The marriage ceremony and a synoptic roster of the sacred holidays were observed after returning to the States. These were taken from the ceremonies of Conservative Jews who stand at some mid-point between the all-observant Orthodoxy and the ultraprogressive spirit of the Reform.

The wedding ceremony has a number of beautiful symbolic moments, including a sip of wine in commemoration of the happy days to come, followed by a crushing of the glass under the feet of the groom as a reminder that sorrow can come in the midst of joy—sorrow for the house of Israel and for the afflictions of all mankind.

The Jewish holidays we were able to include started with Rosh Hoshana, celebrating the New Year. The Jewish calendar begins with the act of creation, a date which ecclesiastical computations place 5716 years ago. The ancient ram's horn, or *shofar*, is sounded in this ceremony.

Then came Yom Kippur, the day of atonement—called the Great White Fast—which is observed by a day and night of fasting, seeking a return to God and goodness. Here we recorded a splendid rendition of the Kol Nidre.

The spirit of Hanukkah is charming. A happy time, lasting eight days, it recalls the victory of the Maccabees. Until recently this was a relatively minor holiday, but with the victorious establishment of the State of Israel it has become somewhat synonymous with the triumphant spirit of Zionism. Also, the fact that this joyful celebration falls during Chrismas season and contains certain traditional elements, such as gay household decorations and gifts to children, similar in spirit to the great Christian holiday, has caused Hanukkah to be emphasized for the benefit of Jewish children in Western countries during this highly publicized, sentimental season.

Succoth, the Feast of the Tabernacles, held in memory of the harvest period when the ancient Israelites dwelt in the desert, is the oldest of Jewish holidays and presumably served as a model for American Thanksgiving Day.

Finally, we did a sequence on Pesach or Passover. This wonderful ritual, highlighted by a ceremonial dinner in

private homes, commemorates the liberation of the Israelites from Egypt and their birth as a nation. Presided over
by the head of the household, it is a lengthy feast filled with
much beauty and a variety of moods, including one touching moment when the sacramental wine cup is diminished
by ten drops, symbolizing sorrow for the afflictions of the
Egyptians when visited by the ten plagues. There is also a
prayer for the peaceful future of all mankind.

Upon completion of this series of holiday celebrations I
became aware of one whole element in Judaism which has
unfortunately been omitted in the establishment of the
ceremonies of most other religions, and that is family ritual:
elaborate ceremonies held in the home, performed and presided over by members of the household, to the exclusion
of rabbis or other church officials.

Unquestionably this has done much to strengthen the
notable unity of Jewish family life, a factor that is rapidly
sagging throughout all the rest of Western society. Looking
back, I find myself amazed that family ritual should have
been so sadly neglected in Christian liturgy. Aside from the
saying of grace at mealtime or a little Bible-reading in some
homes there is little else.

At Passover nearly every member of the household has a
part to play in the symbolic acts of commemoration. It is an
event filled with moments both sorrowful and joyous. It
would be almost impossible for those concerned not to feel
drawn together in an uplifting, emotional experience upon
this yearly occasion. Undoubtedly family ritual is a great
institution and one for which the Jews should be especially
grateful.

Another important rite for Orthodox women is that of the monthly ceremonial bath. These are taken after the menstrual period in public ritual places called *mikvah*, where mechanical arrangements are made for catching and storing rain water, a necessary ingredient of the ceremony. The act is simply one of total immersion in a marble or tile-lined pool which has a small open pipe near the surface allowing the bath water to be mixed with rain water from an adjacent storage tank.

A Jewish woman friend, of the most progressive group, once told me about her only experience in a ritual bath. She had made a childhood promise to an elderly relative who was of the strictest orthodoxy that she would visit the special tank for brides-to-be some time before her wedding. Someone reminded her of this only a single hour before the ceremony when she was already primped, powdered, coiffured, and couturiered from head to toe. However, wishing to fulfill her sworn obligation and thinking the ceremony to be merely a light, symbolic sponging, she consented and was taken straightway to the mikvah.

She painted a glowing portrait of her rude awakening when stalwart matrons staunchly removed all cosmetics, including nail polish, trimmed the nails themselves, and then dunked her to the utmost tip of an elaborate four-hour hair-do! Surely all womanhood can sympathize with her travail as she embarked on a tearful, bedraggled march to the altar thirty minutes later!

In Jerusalem, within the past year, a determined young Jewish woman has finally succeeded in overcoming an age-old edict of the Rabbinate that marriage could not be legalized without female submission to the premarital rite

267

of the mikvah. I understand that her plea of unconstitutionality was upheld by the courts of Israel. She has not started a strong movement away from the mikvah, however, and presumably among the Orthodox it will long remain.

The ritual acts enumerated thus far are but few of the many observances maintained by devoted followers of Judaism. We soon see that to the pious Jew religion is more than a church; it is a way of life. In his eating and drinking, his work and play, ritual plays a never to be forgotten role. The primary objective of this appears to be sanctification and the desire to fulfill God's commands. It is also a fellowship and an experience with great emotional beauty. Further than this, ritual has probably meant survival for the faith and for the group. Without ritual the Jews long ago might have lost their identity.

Today, in America, a strong reform movement maintains the important holidays and rituals, but has eliminated numerous observances which seem to conflict with commonly accepted Western customs. Articles of clothing and hair styles peculiar to Orthodox Jewry have been dispensed with, as well as many of the kosher laws. Women are also seated with men in the temples. Even in Israel there is a progressive element, especially among the younger people and those in government circles, where manners of clothing and hair styles are definitely Western. Prayers, rituals, and worship in the synagogue seem still to be quite Orthodox, however.

And my reaction to the State of Israel? From what I saw I should say it's definitely here to stay. It's a clean, healthful country, whose new inhabitants are putting forth a tremendous effort at development in every necessary walk of civilized life. Scientific agricultural programs have made many sections of the country into garden areas. The increase of water supply is phenomenal. Jews returning to the homeland from cultural centers in Europe have invested Israel with Western manners and methods. This, plus many American contacts, has put the country much closer in spirit to the Occident than are most of its neighbors in the Near and Middle East.

We were only a few days in Istanbul, for I felt the present photographic stage of the project was about over. Although my health was good, I was tired. We had moved so fast and so constantly I seemed to get sea legs whenever we paused for breath.

I was tired of sight-seeing, too. I had really been tired for months. It was like spending too many hours in a picture gallery, where the eye becomes fatigued with the sight of an overabundance of beauty and loses its power of discrimination. Monuments—the very word had always given me a romantic tingle—were now falling under the personal scrutiny of a mind which found itself preoccupied with dreams of hamburgers, ice cream, and a quiet cabin somewhere in the Sierras.

We did visit St. Sophia and other world-famed points of historical interest in and about the environs of precipitous Istanbul. The general terrain and architecture of these, incidentally, is so alive with good composition that it gave me a tremendous urge to return one fine day with my sketchbook and oils. Mostly, however, I just wanted to sit on the hotel balcony and enjoy the panoramic activity of the numberless craft moving about the dramatic entrance of the

Golden Horn on the Bosporus. I have never counted so many boats or so many kinds of boats as were congregated in the bay.

I have mentioned the interview with the Mufti; we also called on the Patriarch of the Armenian Church. He was a friendly, humble, little man whose face and personality radiated sincerity and simplicity of heart.

The Armenian Church is not in communion with any other Christian church, although it is similar in many respects to the Orthodox Church of the East. Its priests marry and the language is Armenian, but its membership has been uncertain since the incorporation of Armenia into the U.S.S.R.

In response to my request for a statement on the attitude of his church toward world peace the Patriarch obligingly prepared the following reply: "The world is in want of peace—not of the peace which the leaders of the nations pretend to procure and preserve by arms and by sinuous and erroneous ways of diplomacy—but of that peace which has become established and secured by the bright light of brotherly love.

"It is with this love that Christ came to give us his peace. It is only by the religion based on this love that it will be possible to bring the nations together and realize the kind of peace which will be first in the hearts of each individual —and afterward in the enlightened consciousness of mankind.

"Above all confessional varieties and differences, there is a warm and living faith inspired by love. This faith can create harmony among the nations and thus realize the great ideal of one flock and one shepherd. Every attempt for peace made without the consciousness of this simple truth will be condemned to remain fruitless."

I also obtained a presentation to the Supreme Patriarch of the Greek Orthodox Church, since he too has his headquarters in Istanbul. He is a handsome figure of a man: a bearded giant standing surely not less than six feet six inches in height. During an unhurried private audience his personality was the very soul of genial hospitality. He commended the purpose of my tour, asked that I convey his cordial greetings to friends in America, and offered me a taste of a special sweet prepared on some nearby island. This was like soft, vanilla frosting and was eaten with a spoon from a small bowl.

In answer to my request for a recorded interview he asked that I return for the answer next day and, accordingly, I did, bringing Bob and the equipment just in case. But to my disappointment and chagrin His Holiness informed me that the board of councilors had advised against the voicing of a public statement at that time and, of course, I could easily understand this reluctance on the part of a person who carries the responsibility of speaking, in a sense, for the millions of followers of the Greek Orthodoxy. He graciously suggested the possibility of an interview at some later date, if I should return to Istanbul. For this I thanked him deeply and withdrew.

And that about wound up the short sojourn in Turkey. Originally I had intended visiting Greece while in the neighborhood, not only to observe the religion of the Greek Church, but because of a long-standing sentimental attachment to the ancient land which conceived and gave birth to Western culture and its beloved philosophy.

Now, however, having postponed the massive task of a documentary on Christianity until the present material had been assorted and evaluated, and because of a traveler's fatigue I knew would dull the enjoyment of fragmented sculpture and additional historic landmarks at this time, we booked passage for the States.

Epilogue

It has been asked consistently if the experiences of the tour have caused me to change my viewpoint in any way— if my own religious convictions have been altered, expanded or, perhaps, become confused. This is not easily answered, because most changes take place so gradually they're indiscernible in short perspective.

Before the trip I was acquainted with the fundamental doctrines of the various faiths we covered. Each of them has much that is admirable. Direct observation of the practices of those faiths showed many more facets to be admired.

For years I have conscientiously inquired into every religion, religious concept, or sect of a religion known to man, but still regret my personal persuasion not to form an unequivocal alliance with any one of them. That is not to say I never will or that I am in the least way critical of any person inspired, elevated, and content in the warm embrace of any of the great religious institutions in the world today. I find truth and beauty in them all. But I have found some aspects of each incompatible with my own inner spiritual demands.

My personal faith is just that—personal. My principles and precepts are eclectic, chosen from many sources, yet in a simplified form compatible with nearly all. I do not advocate my method of spiritual recognition and worship, my faith, for everyone. For this there are many reasons. Also there are many reasons for retaining and strengthening the world's present religious institutions. I would not be one to tamper with them. I do believe there is much good in my position of non-organizational, non-sectarian neutrality at the present time. I'm sure it has given me an entree into the presence of liturgies that may well have been denied the proponent of a particular creed. Certainly I have been able to arrange and comment on my material without regard to the bias of any particular group.

I have felt no strong urge to join in wholehearted acceptance of any religion we surveyed. Neither have I been sent scurrying back into the bosom of some childhood denominational doctrine.

So, in the matter of personal faith, I guess you could say there had been no change. This faith holds:

That God exists.

God—a power and intelligence within the universe, yet apart from it. The creative force which has ordained and set in motion the wheels of life. A dynamic omnipresence to which nothing is unknown or unimportant —which, verily, marks the sparrow's fall.

The host of superlative names used by all the religions in describing God would also apply to my concept of Him, but I am especially persuaded that He, or She, as Creator, is a loving parent deeply concerned with the welfare and happiness of all creatures—that, because man is the most highly developed organism in this presently visible sphere, he is regarded keenly—and with immeasurable affection.

I believe that God—as the very essence of love—draws men unto Him—inspires men to seek Him—form partnerships with Him—yet that He gives man freedom of choice and even a not unbearable alternative if he so chooses.

Man is a puny creature, yet he has an individuality—a tiny something of his very own which is not God—a tiny seed which like the male spermatazoa issues forth from its parent creator, unites with fertile ground and grows into a separate organism—influenced by parental traits—subject to parental influence—but uniquely individualized and self-willed.

If it is true that the spirit of man has issued from God—then, like God, that spirit is divine, with all the attributes of divinity. Like the seed, these attributes are not all discernible, for they have not yet matured. Those which can be seen must be given sustenance and nurture.

I think that God is perfection unto Himself—and yet because love, of necessity, is incomplete without a beloved, I think that God needs man. To me the very fact of creation proves that—for life is deeply serious—profoundly important.

Life is not the frivolous result of some fantastic creative impulse evolving meaningless phenomena—or the experiment of some superscientist dispassionately observing the magical results of His divine chemistry out of detached celestial curiosity.

If this were so, then the moral fiber of His creation has already far outstripped the quality of its originator—an assumption too illogical to conjure with.

The study of science makes men humble—as well it should. Years ago when I took up astronomy, I became appalled at the diminutive stature of all my species in totality. I was aghast and chagrined at the pitiable speck we formed against the unfathomable infinity of the universe.

Physical facts have thus persuaded many to underestimate man's true worth. Such persons have been intimidated by mere bulk—humiliated by sheer distance.

These misguided ones have not judged properly, for they have tried to weigh the worth of unrelated values, forgetting that if the seed of the oak be watered and nourished, it one day will stand high above and far beyond the brambles and tares at its feet.

I have said before that I do not know the end purpose of creation, but, like many others, I am strongly convinced that the life we here behold is but a page in the infinite volume of immortal man. That is part of my faith.

And if we cannot bring concrete verification of this belief—if we are yet unable to place positive empirical proof upon the upturned palm of the agnostic, it is because the high purpose of man's divine calling demands that he be given an opportunity to make volitional acceptance of the concept . . . additional testimony that the Creator is a God of love.

This is not to say there are no proofs of a purpose in life—indeed, there are many, and not simply corroboration of Biblical prophets or through mystic intuition, either. For those who would know the accredited findings and documented results of a lifetime of research by a thoroughly qualified and highly respected scientist, mathematician, one might suggest the reading of *Human Destiny* by Lecomte du Noüy. At least he proves the universe could not have been the result of chance—regardless of the already vast number of possible combinations which have presented themselves.

But proofs come in other ways too. As I've followed my urge in the matter, they've presented themselves over the years in numberless, small ways that finally dispel the doubts and dismays, the puzzles and perplexities. Though it is not always easy, for it takes much self-analysis, and earnest reflection to see things through to another step of enlightenment. Our powers of reason and concentration are yet so poor.

I suppose this is why so many slip away from faith. Or why they demand an "everything or nothing" religion which insists that every word of scripture be literally true— every prophetic promise be fulfilled—every asserted aspect of God, such as His love, be eternally, easily visible—or else they will have none of it.

There are those whose faith is so insecure they will insist that every Biblical word be considered impeccably flawless, or the whole structure must fall.

The Bible is a great book—doubtless divinely inspired—as are scriptures of the other great religions, but it seems that more than the written word is necessary to sustain faith through a lifetime of the ups and downs of our earthly existence. This is why I keep citing "scientific" proofs of a faith. This is the scientific age—and people require the same element of substantiation in their ideas of God as they demand in all the other aspects of their terrestrial lives . . . religion and science must correspond.

And to the doubtful I say they can have scientific substantiation! Substantiation which, if not an absolute, concrete, photostatic reproduction of the Universal Deity, will at least stand irrefutable before the specious logic of the atheist, the mechanist, the cynic or the agnostic. If we cannot prove to them—they cannot, believe me, disprove us!

Now as to conclusions on another aspect of the tour—back of the project has been the hope that in some way increased knowledge of other peoples throughout the far-flung stretches of the free-world nations might bring us closer together and point the way to new avenues for the establishment of permanent peace.

Of course I realize that one half of the population of the world is restricted from this consideration at the moment—the communist peoples—but I must still repeat my conviction that peace has a chance of being won if we free-enterprise nations demonstrate a unity of purpose, a growing prosperity, progressive development, and fine, friendly relations among ourselves. This alone can halt communist infiltration within the existing ranks.

Accomplishing these things means, of course, that we will have to overcome prejudices of race, color, and creed, bringing ever closer into realization the long-awaited brotherhood of man.

Before starting on the journey it occurred to me that since all religions have a similar ethical code—exhorting man to the ways of virtue and brotherly love—it might be possible to unite the great religions on that basis, for the purpose of bringing about a great co-operative program for the betterment of the nations of the free world and the cause of world peace.

Not that the religions would become one faith, but that these religions, which have always preached love and peace, might recognize the value of concerted effort and embark on a united program—each getting the best its followers had to give—for improvement of world conditions everywhere.

Idealistic? Yes, but there are practical possibilities too, for if religion ever did make a strong concerted effort of this kind, it could truly invest mankind with dynamic inspiration—a spark plug for energies of unpredictable proportions.

The over-all plan is simple. It is not a new idea. A World Congress of All Faiths—and by "All" is meant every single one.

The first such convention was attempted in Chicago about 1893. Others have been gathered since at sporadic intervals in both the United States and Europe—the last being held at Cambridge, 1938. No meeting included all faiths.

Most of the activity in the early gatherings was concerned with a description and interchange of the various doctrines—getting acquainted. Only in the later ones was a mild, exploratory effort made to tackle the urgent problems impeding man's progress. Concrete results were not realized.

Today, I sincerely think that religious leaders the world over should come together for united effort in facing the present serious threat of mass destruction by nuclear warfare. They should be seated on a permanent site at regularly scheduled intervals—like the United Nations. Their de-

ALTARS OF THE EAST

cisions should result in a positive program for utilizing the efforts of each group for the greatest possible good of all in the cause of peace. And what a powerful combination it would be!

Throughout the Orient I met many leaders who approved the idea, though movements of this sort must start at the top. And we in the West, holding unquestioned leadership in the affairs of today's world, must take the inaugural steps—the rest will listen—most will join.

One reason for inertia in the realm of material problems is the emphasis on "other-worldliness" by many faiths. Concern for conditions here and now often means taking time away from preparation for the life to come—a heavenly existence which can only be reached by today's renunciations. Some of these would be the Buddhists—particularly the southern, Hinayana, sect. Yet today the Buddhists are meeting in international, intersectarian congresses of their own and bringing closer unity among all Buddhist countries.

Another deterrent is the old bugaboo of prejudice—or profound distaste for another's doctrine. Often this is the result of emphatically stressed teachings, such as Moslem abhorrence of idolatry, making a great barrier between themselves and any who permit the use of images. Hindus and Buddhists principally fall under Islamic odium, but some Christian practices are repugnant as well.

"Have your own faith and be tolerant of the beliefs of others" is a philosophy that has resounded through the ages and today this attitude finds support as never before. Bigotry in matters of spiritual interpretation has long been dead in the hearts of true men of culture, and their well-planted seeds have spread until now the whole world awaits

only notification of the joyful ceremony which will cele-
brate final interment of this harpy of human souls.

At this point I am absolutely convinced of the futility of
attaining universal conversion to any faith or sect of a faith
—Christian, Moslem, Buddhist, or any other. I am also persuaded that it is unnecessary for doing the job which lies
before us. People everywhere in civilized countries are good
people—as good as any Christians, Moslems, or Buddhists
alive.

In other lands they need bread and medicine—and education maybe—plus a good measure of the gentle love we
preach about. Yes, those things they need—as for the souls,
I say let us look to our own by fulfilling the commands
that we concern ourselves with the care and welfare of our
neighbors.

From time to time someone says he hopes I'm going to
point out that all religion is really identical—meaning he
imagines all beliefs are alike. I wish I could—but I fear it's
not so simple. Yet, here are some of the beliefs that have
been considered common denominators for merging these
great world forces into a constructive unity:

1. Immortality of the human soul.

   This one factor alone—speaking in a sense of the
   divinity in man—should be sufficient ground for common effort. All religions consider men to be pilgrims
   whose destination is a higher plane;

2. A purpose in life beyond health and propagation of
   the species. Also that a divine plan is manifested in
   life;

3. That divine wisdom has been revealed through inspired men. Strangely enough, this last seems to be

one of the identifying marks of a religious faith—the unique phenomenon setting religion apart from science.

As to practices—out of endless diversification, we find few similarities. However, one teaching prescribed and admonished by all religions concerns:

1. The rules of ethical and moral conduct.
   Except for emphasis in minor indulgences these are alike in all major respects. Some faiths demand greater consecration to the ideal of selflessness, but there is no obstacle to unity here;
2. Prayer to an unseen force or power.
   This practice is universal. Even by Hinayana Buddhists, where prayers are directed inwardly to promote growth of understanding.

Doubtless there are more unifying elements—some probably better. But here enumerated are surely enough points of conformity to justify the meeting of the world's religious leadership for purposes of finding the way to greater prosperity for all.

And maybe we wouldn't even need those listed. It would never even be suggested, for instance, that all faiths should stand in prayer together—this might doom the plan at the outset.

Actually, the term "Brotherhood of Man" stands alone as justification for organized welfare—organizations which, in a measure, already exist, but with the dynamic force of inspired religion thrown into the breach, the magnitude of its possible accomplishments in the realm of sociology is as staggering as are the potentialities of the term thermonuclear in physics . . . a just and fitting equivalent in the realm of the spiritual for the ever-mounting tempo of the material.

For those who have envisioned a great religious revival sweeping across the face of the earth, this could be a reasonable parallel. To you I say, make this one compromise in the name of tolerance and see all your dreams come true.

This could be our answer to the fantastic developments of science today.

A unified force for moral order in a world packed with the unleashed atoms of chaos.

A means not to combat the progress of our God-given science, but to encourage it for the welfare of all—to chasten it—to guide it.

And there is yet another reason for the unity of religious energy. We have long heard political leaders of the free world speak of defending our right to faith; is it not then high time the Faiths themselves make an effort on their own behalf—an effort going further than tacit tolerance—a gigantic effort combining all the mighty God-inspired intellects of earth in mature deliberations for mutual defense?

And for this noble purpose we must see Christian Bishops sit with the Grand Mufti and the Aga Khan—the Buddhist patriarchs of Siam and Burma with the High Priest of the Parsis—Hindu Swami and Chief Rabbi of the Jews —Sikh President, Shinto Priest, Taoist Pope, Jain Saint— Coptic, Quaker, Orthodox, Mennonite—Minister, Mullah, Mormon, Lama. . . . Yes, and with them all I want to see Rome—strong, tall and clear-voiced. Without hesitancy, I say I want to see the revered red hat of a Cardinal

283

and hear him speaking for the democratic spirit of brotherhood that surges through the millions of his devout parish-
ioners. This time—and for this cause—no man of faith must
be unrepresented.

Conceivably, it is no longer a question concerning the
survival of *which* faith . . . is it not the blessed privilege
of faith, itself, hanging precipitously in the balance?